Willis Hall

THE LONG AND THE SHORT AND THE TALL

Doris Lessing

EACH HIS OWN WILDERNESS

Michael Hastings

YES, AND AFTER

PENGUIN BOOKS

Penguin Books Ltd, Harmondsworth, Middlesex, England
Penguin Books, 625 Madison Avenue, New York, New York 10022, U.S.A.
Penguin Books Australia Ltd, Ringwood, Victoria, Australia
Penguin Books Canada Ltd, 2801 John Street, Markham, Ontario, Canada L3R 1B4
Penguin Books (N.Z.) Ltd, 182–190 Wairau Road, Auckland 10, New Zealand

—

THE LONG AND THE SHORT AND THE TALL
First published by William Heinemann Ltd 1959
Reprinted in Penguin Plays 1964, 1965, 1968, 1971, 1973, 1975, 1977
Copyright © Willis Hall, 1959

EACH HIS OWN WILDERNESS
First published in Penguin Books 1959
Reprinted in Penguin Plays 1968, 1971, 1973, 1975, 1977
Copyright © Doris Lessing, 1959

YES, AND AFTER
First published in Penguin Books 1962
Reprinted in Penguin Plays 1968, 1971, 1973, 1975, 1977
Copyright © Michael Hastings, 1962

—

Made and printed in Great Britain by
Cox & Wyman Ltd, London, Reading and Fakenham
Set in Monotype Bembo

Donation

THE LONG AND THE SHORT AND THE TALL
EACH HIS OWN WILDERNESS
YES, AND AFTER

Willis Hall was born in 1929 and has written a number of plays for the theatre, among them *Kidnapped at Christmas* and, in collaboration with Keith Waterhouse, *Billy Liar*; several television plays, including *They Don't All Open Men's Boutiques*, and a series (with Keith Waterhouse) *The Upper Crust*; and some children's books, including *The Gentle Knight*.

Michael Hastings was born in 1938 and is both a dramatist and novelist. His first play, *Don't Destroy Me* was produced when he was only seventeen. He has also written *Yes, and After* and *Lee Harvey Oswald*, as well as television scripts, a biographical essay on Rupert Brooke, *The Handsomest Young Man in England*, and two novels, *The Game* and *Tussy Is Me*.

Doris Lessing was born in 1919 and is a journalist, playwright, poet and novelist. Her plays include *Play With a Tiger*. Her volume of short stories, *Five*, won the Somerset Maugham Award for 1954 and her novel, *The Golden Notebook*, received critical acclaim when it was published in 1962. Her other novels include *The Summer Before the Dark* and *Memoirs of a Survivor*.

CONTENTS

WILLIS HALL

The Long and the Short and the Tall

THE LONG AND THE SHORT
AND THE TALL

Commissioned by the Oxford Theatre Group and first performed on the 'Fringe' of the Edinburgh Festival 1958, directed by Peter Dews.

The play was first produced in London on 7 January 1959 at the Royal Court Theatre. It was presented by the English Stage Company in association with Oscar Lewenstein and Wolf Mankowitz with the following cast:

465 SGT MITCHEM, R.	Robert Shaw
839 CPL JOHNSTONE, E.	Edward Judd
594 L/CPL MACLEISH, A. J.	Ronald Fraser
632 PTE WHITAKER, S.	David Andrews
777 PTE EVANS, T. E.	Alfred Lynch
877 PTE BAMFORTH, C.	Peter O'Toole
611 PTE SMITH, P.	Bryan Pringle
A JAPANESE SOLDIER	Kenji Takaki

The play directed by LINDSAY ANDERSON
with décor by ALAN TAGG

The action of the play takes place in the Malayan jungle during the Japanese advance on Singapore early in 1942.

ACT ONE

Time: Late afternoon.

The curtain rises on the wooden-walled, palm-thatched, dingy interior of a deserted store-hut in the Malayan jungle. The hut is set back a few hundred yards from a tin mine which is now deserted. There is a door in the rear wall with windows on either side looking out on to the veranda and jungle beyond. The hut has been stripped of everything of any value by the mine-workers before they fled – all that remains are a rickety table and two chairs, centre-stage, and a form, right.

> [We hear a short burst of heavy gunfire in the distance – and then silence. A pause and then we hear the chirruping of crickets and the song of a bird in the jungle. A figure appears at the left-hand window, looks cautiously inside and ducks away. A moment later the door is kicked open and JOHNSTONE stands framed in the doorway holding a sten at his hip. When the door was kicked open the crickets and the bird ceased their song. JOHNSTONE glances around the room and, finding it to be unoccupied, makes a hand signal from the veranda. JOHNSTONE returns into the room and is joined a few seconds later by MITCHEM, who also carries a sten.]

JOHNSTONE [shifts his hat to the back of his head and places his sten on the table]: All Clear. Stinks like something's dead.

MITCHEM [placing his sten beside Johnstone's]: It'll do. To be going on with. [He crosses to the door and motions to the rest of the patrol.] Come on, then! Let's have you! . . . Move it! Move!

> [One by one the members of the patrol double into the room. With the exception of WHITAKER, who carries the radio transmitter/receiver on his back, the men are armed with rifles. SMITH carries Whitaker's rifle. They are tired and dishevelled.]

JOHNSTONE: Move yourselves! Gillo! Lacas! Lacas!

> [As the last member of the patrol enters the room MITCHEM slams the

door. The men stack their rifles in a corner of the hut and sit gratefully on the floor. WHITAKER *takes off the 'set' and sets it up on the table.* BAMFORTH *shrugs off his pack, places it as a pillow on the form, and makes himself comfortable.*]

JOHNSTONE: How long we here for?

MITCHEM [*glances at his watch*]: Half an hour or so, and then we'll push off back. Better mount a guard. Two men on stag. Fifteen minute shifts.

JOHNSTONE: Right ... [*He notices* BAMFORTH *who is now fully stretched out.*] Bamforth! ... Bamforth!

BAMFORTH [*raises himself with studied unconcern*]: You want me, Corp?

JOHNSTONE: Get on your feet, lad!

BAMFORTH: What's up?

JOHNSTONE: I said 'move'! [BAMFORTH *pulls himself slowly to his feet.*] You think you're on your holidays? Get your pack on!

BAMFORTH: You going to inspect us, Corp?

JOHNSTONE: Don't give me any of your mouth. Get your pack on! Smartish! Next time you keep it on till you hear different.

BAMFORTH [*heaves his pack on to one shoulder*]: Alright! O.K. All right.

JOHNSTONE: Right on!

[BAMFORTH *glances across at Mitchem.*]

MITCHEM: You heard what he said.

BAMFORTH [*struggles the pack on to both shoulders. He speaks under his breath*]: Nit!

[*There is a pause.* JOHNSTONE *crosses to face Bamforth.*]

JOHNSTONE: What was that?

BAMFORTH: Me. I only coughed.

MITCHEM: O.K., Bamforth, Just watch it, son.

JOHNSTONE: Too true, lad. Watch it. Watch it careful. I've had my bellyfull of you this time out. You watch your step. Put one foot wrong. Just one. I'll have you in the nick so fast your feet won't touch the ground. Just you move out of line, that's all.

BAMFORTH: You threatening me, Corp?

JOHNSTONE: I'm warning you!

BAMFORTH: I got witnesses!

JOHNSTONE: You'll have six months. The lot. I'll see to that,

Bamforth. I'll have your guts. One foot wrong, as sure as God I'll have your guts.

BAMFORTH: Try. Try it on for size.

MITCHEM [*crosses to intervene*]: Right. Pack it in. That's both of you. [BAMFORTH *turns away from Johnstone.*] I want two men for guard. First stag. Two volunteers ... Come on, come on!

SMITH [*pulls himself to his feet*]: First or second – what's the odds ...

MACLEISH [*follows suit*]: It's all the same to me.

MITCHEM: Better stay inside. Don't show yourselves. Cover the front. If anything's to come it's coming from out there. [MACLEISH *and* SMITH *take up their rifles and move across to cover the windows.*] How's the set?

WHITAKER [*looks up from tuning in the radio*]: It's dead. Still dis. U/s. Can't get a peep. I think the battery's giving up. Conking out.

BAMFORTH: Now he tells us! Signals! Flipping signallers – I've shot 'em. Talk about up the creek without a paddle.

MITCHEM: You got any suggestions, Bamforth ...

BAMFORTH: Only offering opinions.

MITCHEM: Well don't! Don't bother. If we want opinions from you we'll ask for them. From now on keep them to yourself. Now, pay attention. All of you. We're sticking here for half an hour at the most. After that we're ... heading back for camp. [*A murmur of relief from the men.*] Anybody any questions?

EVANS: Can we have a drag, Sarge?

MITCHEM: Yeh. Smoke if you want. You can get the humpy off your backs. Get what rest you can. Your best bet is to grab some kip. It's a long way back. Another thing, you'd better save your grub. I make it we'll get back before tomorrow night – but just in case we don't, go steady on the compo packs. O.K.? [*There is a murmur of agreement from the men.*] I want to have a sortie round. Outside. See how we're fixed. Check up. Fancy a trot, Johnno?

JOHNSTONE: Suits me.

[*The patrol remove their packs and place them on the floor.* MITCHEM *and* JOHNSTONE *pick up and check their stens.*]

MITCHEM: Keep at it on the set, Sammy son. Have another shot at getting through.

WHITAKER [*puts on headphones*]: Right, Sarge. Don't think it's going to do much good.

MITCHEM: Keep bashing. Mac!

MACLEISH [*turns from window*]: Aye?

MITCHEM: We're having a stroll as far as the road. You're i/c. We won't be long. As far as we know there's nothing in the area for miles – but if anything crops up – I mean, if you should see anything – don't shoot. Unless you've got to. Right?

MACLEISH: Fair enough.

MITCHEM: Ready, Johnno? [*Johnstone nods and follows Mitchem to the door.*] And keep your voices down, the lot of you.

JOHNSTONE: Bamforth! That includes you!

BAMFORTH [*who has been delving into his pack*]: I heard!

MITCHEM: Come on.

[MITCHEM *opens the door and exits, followed by* JOHNSTONE. *We see them move past window and disappear down the veranda steps.*]

BAMFORTH [*throwing down his pack in disgust*]: The creep. The stupid nit!

EVANS: Johnno's got it in for you, boyo. He'll have your guts for garters yet. He's after you. Chases you round from haircut to breakfast time.

BAMFORTH: Flipping toe-rag! He wants carving up. It's time that nit got sorted out. When this lot's over – when I get back to civvy street – I only want to meet him once. In town. That's all. Just once. Will someone see me now and hear my prayers? If I could come across him once without them tapes to come it on! I'll smash his face.

EVANS: Go on, man! He's twice the size of you! You wouldn't stand a chance, tapes or no tapes.

BAMFORTH: What do you know about scrapping? That's how you want them when you're putting in the nut. Up there. Bigger than yourself. And then you wham 'em – thump across the eyes. Straight across the eyes and then the knee and finish with the boot. All over. Send for the cleaners.

EVANS: You wouldn't fight like that, Bammo?

BAMFORTH: You want to lay me odds? I'll take fives on that. What do you know about it, you ugly foreigner? Get back to Wales, you Cardiff creep. Only good for digging coal and singing hymns, your crummy lot.

EVANS: Shows how much you know, boy. You want to see some real fighting, Bammo, you go to Cardiff on a Saturday night. Round the docks. Outside the boozers. More fights in one night than you've had hot dinners.

BAMFORTH: Country stuff, son. Country stuff. You haven't got the first idea. You ever want to see a bloke carved up? Proper. So his missis thinks he's someone else. You hand that job to London boys.

SMITH [glancing over his shoulder from the window]: Why don't you jack it in?

BAMFORTH: What's that?

SMITH: You heard. I said, give it a rest.

BAMFORTH: I never heard your name and number in this conversation.

SMITH: I'm just telling you, that's all. I've had about enough. Bloody southerners shouting the odds. Always shouting the odds. You're like the rest. One sniff of a barmaid's apron and you're on the floor.

EVANS: That's how you want a barmaid, Smudge.

BAMFORTH: Good old Taff! Show us your leek! Get him! Getting barmaids on the floor! And I always thought you were a presbyterian.

EVANS: Strict Chapel. Every Sunday.

BAMFORTH: Sunday's his day off. When he leaves the milkmaid alone. Tuesdays and Wednesdays he's going steady with a Eisteddfod.

SMITH: Come again?

BAMFORTH: One of them bints in a long black hat and bits of lace. Always singing songs. Every time you go to the pictures you see them on the news. Singing songs and playing harps and that. Hymns. Like being in church only it's outside. Dodgy move – so they can whip them up the mountainside for half an hour afterwards. Very crafty boys, these Taffs. You've got to hand it to them.

EVANS: Go on, man!

BAMFORTH: Straight up. It's straight up, son. Got any fags, have you, Taff?

EVANS: I thought you must be after something.

[EVANS *takes a packet of cigarettes from his trouser pocket and offers one to Bamforth as he crosses towards him.* BAMFORTH *takes the cigarette.*]

BAMFORTH: So what? As long as it's only your fags I'm after, you've no need to worry, have you, son? My name's not Johnno.

MACLEISH [*turning at window*]: Bamforth, why don't you pack it in? We've heard about enough from you.

BAMFORTH: Silence in court! Acting Unpaid Lance Corporal Macleish is just about to pull his rank! Don't it make you sick! Doesn't it make you want to spew, eh? Sew a bit of tape on their arms and all at once they talk like someone else. What's the matter, Mac? You chasing your second stripe already?

MACLEISH: Are you looking for trouble, Bamforth? Because if you are you can have it, and no messing.

BAMFORTH: Ah, shut up, you Scotch haggis! Dry up, boy! It's not your fault. All Corps are bastards, we all know that.

MACLEISH: Watch your mouth! As far as I'm concerned the tape's not worth it. Just remember that. As far as I'm concerned I'll jack the tape tomorrow to drop you one on. And that's a promise, Bamforth.

BAMFORTH: Go stuff your tape.

[EVANS *lights his cigarette behind dialogue.*]

MACLEISH: So just you watch your mouth.

BAMFORTH: Aw, come off it, son. Where I come from it's just a name.

MACLEISH: It so happens I don't like it.

SMITH: Drop it, Mac. He didn't mean no harm.

MACLEISH: I'm willing to accept his apology.

BAMFORTH: So what's the argument about? Here, Taffy, give us a touch, boy.

EVANS [*hands his cigarette to* BAMFORTH *who lights his own and passes it back*]: I don't see, Mac, what you got to complain about. Bammo's only having you on. Before you got that tape you moaned about Johnno just as much as the rest of us. More, perhaps.

SMITH: Just let it drop, Taff, eh?

MACLEISH: It so happens that I accepted the rank of Lance Corporal.

Having accepted the rank, and the responsibility that goes with it, I feel it's my duty to back up my fellow N.C.O.s. And that decision is regardless of any personal prejudices I might hold.

BAMFORTH: King's Regulations, Chapter Three, Verse Seventeen. The congregation will rise and sing the hymn that's hanging up behind the door of the bog.

MACLEISH: You're just a head case, Bamforth. You're a nutter. Round the bend.

BAMFORTH [*jumping up on chair*]: With the inspired help of our dear friend and member, Fanny Whitaker, who will accompany the choir on her famous five-valve organ. All together, please! The chorus girl's lament! [*Sings*]

> My husband's a corporal, a corporal, a corporal,
> A very fine corporal is he!
> All day he knocks men about, knocks men about, knocks men about,
> At night he comes home and knocks me!

[EVANS *joins Bamforth in the chorus.*]

> Singing Hey-jig-a-jig, cook a little pig, follow the band.
> Follow the band all the way!
> Singing Hey-jig-a-jig, cook a little pig, follow the band,
> Follow the band all the way!

WHITAKER [*glances up from tuning set*]: Pack it in, Bamforth.

BAMFORTH [*unheeding*]: Order if you please! Second verse. [*Sings*]

> 'Cause my little sister Lily has a stroll on Piccadilly,
> And my mother has another on the Strand,
> And my father's flogging charcoal
> Round the Elephant and Castle,
> We're the finest flipping family in the land!

[EVANS *joins Bamforth again in the chorus.*]

> Singing Hey-jig-a-jig, cook a little pig, follow the band.
> Follow the band all the way!
> Singing Hey-jig-a-jig . . .

WHITAKER [*rising, angrily*]: Will you pack it in!

BAMFORTH [*jumps to floor*]: Hello! Our little blue-eyed signaller doing his nut now. That's all we wanted – him!

WHITAKER [*putting headphones on the table*]: Why don't you keep quiet, Bamforth man! I got something on the set!

BAMFORTH: 'Course you did, my old flower of the East. What was it, Sammy son? Henry Hall? Tune it up a bit – let's have a listen. Bit of music always makes a change.

WHITAKER: I told you – I got something coming through.

MACLEISH: You think it was the camp?

BAMFORTH: We're fifteen miles from base. He's not Marconi. This boy couldn't get the Home Service in the sitting room.

WHITAKER: I don't know what it was. I got something.

BAMFORTH: Fifteen miles from base! A doolally battery and ten-thumbed Whitaker i/c! What you want? A screaming miracle?

SMITH: Try them again, Sammy. Have another go.

MACLEISH: Try it on transmit.

EVANS: Tell them I'm coming home tomorrow night, boyo. Ask them in the cookhouse what's for supper. What's tomorrow? Friday! It's fish and chips!

SMITH: Do you think of anything except your stomach?

BAMFORTH: He's a walking belly.

[WHITAKER *sits down and replaces headphones. He picks up the microphone and adjusts the set.* BAMFORTH *and* EVANS *approach table.*]

WHITAKER: Blue Patrol ... Blue Patrol calling Red Leader ... Blue Patrol calling Red Leader ... Are you receiving me ... Are you receiving me ... Blue Patrol calling Red Leader ... Are you receiving me ... Are you receiving me ... Over. [WHITAKER *flicks switch to 'receive'. There is a pause during which we hear some interference – but nothing else.* WHITAKER *flicks back to 'transmit'.*] Blue Patrol calling Red Leader ... Are you receiving me ... Are you receiving me ... Over. [WHITAKER *again flicks to 'receive'. More interference. Whitaker turns down the set and removes the headphones.*] It's dis. I think the battery's gone again.

BAMFORTH: So what's the use.

WHITAKER: I got something through, I tell you!

BAMFORTH: That's your story, boy. You stick to it.

EVANS: Perhaps you imagined it, Sammy boy.

WHITAKER: I had something coming through!

BAMFORTH: Don't give us that. Got through! You couldn't get through a hot dinner, my old son. You couldn't get through a NAAFI tart.

MACLEISH: Why don't you wrap up, Bamforth.

BAMFORTH: Eight-double-seven Private Bamforth to you, Corporal Macleish. You want to come the regimental, boy, we'll have it proper.

SMITH: That will be the day, Bamforth. When you can work it regimental. The biggest shower since the flood, that's you. Fred Karno's not in it. When you start giving us the heels together I'll be commanding the Camel Corps.

BAMFORTH: Get your bucket and spade, Smudger, and I'll lay it on. This boy can work it any way at all. If I go creeping after tapes I'll get them.

EVANS: Corporal Bamforth, NCO i/c latrines. It's you who'll want the bucket, Bammo.

BAMFORTH: That's all you know, you Welsh rabbit. You'd be the first to suffer. I'll have you running round the depot like a blue house-fly. Report to my tent at 1600 hours. Extra duties. Gas cape and running shoes.

EVANS: And can I have a week-end pass?

BAMFORTH: You what! What do you think you're on? Your father's yacht?

SMITH: You get some kip, Taff. Dream of home. It's the nearest you'll get to Welsh Wales.

[BAMFORTH *crosses to form, picks up his pack, punches it into a pillow and lies down.* WHITAKER, *who has been attempting to tune set, puts on headphones and switches to* 'transmit'.]

WHITAKER: Blue Patrol calling Red Leader ... Blue Patrol calling Red Leader ... Are you receiving me ... Are you receiving me ... Come in Red Leader ... Over.

[WHITAKER *switches to* 'receive' *and again attempts to tune in set.* EVANS *opens his pack and takes out a crumpled magazine.* BAMFORTH *glances across at Evans.*]

BAMFORTH: What you got there, Taff?

EVANS: A book.

BAMFORTH: Two's up.

EVANS: I'll let you have it when I've finished.

BAMFORTH [*sitting up*]: What is it? Sling it across.

EVANS [*crosses and sits on form*]: My mother saves me them. [*He hands the magazine to Bamforth.*]

BAMFORTH: And you've been carting this around for days!

EVANS: Why not?

BAMFORTH: Here, Smudger! Seen this?

SMITH: What's that?

BAMFORTH: Taff's library.

SMITH: Yeh?

BAMFORTH: 'Ladies' Companion and Home.'

SMITH: Get on.

EVANS: My mother sends it to me every week. I'm following the serial. What's wrong with that?

BAMFORTH: And you've been humping this since we left camp? Well, flipping stroll on! That's all. Stroll on.

EVANS: Why not? I've told you. I'm following the serial.

SMITH: Any good, Taff?

EVANS: Yes. It's all right. It's interesting. There's this bloke, see. In the army. Second Looey. He's knocking about with this girl who's a sort of nurse in a Military Hospital. Only before they have time to get to know each other proper, he gets posted overseas.

MACLEISH: Very exciting.

BAMFORTH: I'm crying my eyes out.

SMITH: So what happens then, Taff?

EVANS: Thing is, see, she doesn't know anything about it.

BAMFORTH: He should have taught her.

EVANS: I mean about this overseas posting. He's supposed to meet this bint one night round the back of the Nurses' Quarters.

BAMFORTH: The dirty old man.

EVANS: Who's telling this story, Bammo? Me or you?

SMITH: Get on with it, Taff.

EVANS: I'm just coming to the interesting bit if you'll give me a chance.

BAMFORTH: Come on then. Give. Let's have it. I can hardly wait to hear how Roger gets on in the long grass.

EVANS: That's just it. He doesn't.

BAMFORTH: I knew there'd be a catch in it.

EVANS: He never turns up, see. Been posted. Special Mission. Got to blow up an airfield in North Africa.

SMITH: What? On his tod?

EVANS: Last one I had he'd been captured by a tribe of marauding bedouins. Savage heathens.

SMITH: Get away!

EVANS: And it finished up the last time with them tying him, hand and foot, and hanging him upside down above a blazing fire. In a sort of oasis. There was him, toasting away if you like, with the sweat dripping down off the end of his nose. And these white-robed bedouins is dancing round, waving carbines, singing heathen songs, and not a care in the world. That was how it finished up in the last instalment.

SMITH: So what happens this week?

EVANS: That's just it. I can't make head or tail of it. This week starts off with him and this here nursing bint having an honeymoon in Brighton. Posh hotel, made up to captain, fourteen days' leave, smashing bit of crumpet, and the weather's glorious. Doesn't make sense to me. I think perhaps the old lady slipped up and sent me the wrong one first.

BAMFORTH: She slipped up all right. When she had you. Marauding bedouins! You'll lap up any old muck.

SMITH: After you with it, anyway, Taff.

BAMFORTH: You wait your turn. I'm two's up. [*He flicks through the pages of the magazine.*] Here – this is the bit I like. Margaret Denning Replies. All these bints writing up 'cause someone's left them in the club.

SMITH: Read us one out, Bammo.

BAMFORTH: Here's a right one. Get this. 'Dear Margaret Denning, I have been walking out for six months with a corporal in the Army who's a very nice boy.' Well, there's a lie for a kick-off.

EVANS: What's she want to know?

BAMFORTH: 'I like him very much and we plan to marry when the war is over. Lately, however, he has been making certain suggestions which I know are wrong.'

EVANS: Certain suggestions!

BAMFORTH: 'He says I ought to agree if I love him. What shall I do? Ought I to fall in with his wishes or should I stand by my principles and risk losing him? I have always wanted a white wedding. Yours, Gwynneth Rees, Aberystwyth.' It's another Taffy!

SMITH: So what's she tell her?

BAMFORTH: Dear Miss Taffy, I am sorry to hear that you have had the misfortune to fall in love with a corporal. The next time he starts making improper suggestions you should kick him in the crutch and marry a private.

EVANS: It doesn't say that, does it?

BAMFORTH [rises and slings the magazine at Evans]: What do you think, you ignorant burk?

EVANS: Oh, I don't know . . . What do you reckon she ought to do, Smudger?

SMITH: Same as Bammo says.

EVANS: I don't know, really. I suppose you've got to wait until you're married, proper. I mean, it spoils it otherwise, they say. But if this bloke she's going out with is in the army, perhaps he's up for overseas posting himself. I mean, things is different when there is a war. You never know, do you? He might get pushed off overseas for years, perhaps. Then where would he be?

BAMFORTH: Same as you. Up the creek without a paddle.

EVANS: That's what I'm getting at.

BAMFORTH: Wrap up, boy! Look. Don't be a creamer all your life. Have a day off. You've got a bint yourself, have you? Back home?

EVANS: I've got a girl friend. Well, of course I have. You know as well as I do. You've seen her picture.

BAMFORTH: So when you see her last?

EVANS: Embarkation leave, of course. Over a year ago. Eighteen months about.

BAMFORTH: Eighteen months! Stroll on! For all you know she could be weaning one by now. You know what Blighty is these days, do you? It's a carve up, son. A rotten carve up. Overrun with home postings wallahs, sitting back easy, sorting out the judies from Land's End to how's your father. They've got it all laid on, son. We're the mugs in this game. It's a den of vice, is Blighty. Unoriginal sin. Poles and Yanks and cartloads of glorious allies all colours of the rainbow. Even the nippers look like liquorice-allsorts. They're lapping it up, Taff. You think the bints are sitting knitting?

EVANS: Mine's all right, boy. Don't you worry about that.

BAMFORTH: You mean you hope she is. You're a bloody optimist. She's probably up the mountains right this minute with a big buck Yank.

EVANS: Go on, man! She's not like that.

BAMFORTH: They're all like that. So why should yours be any different?

EVANS: Well, if anything was wrong I'd hear about it.

BAMFORTH: Famous last words. What gives you that idea?

EVANS: Her mother's my auntie.

BAMFORTH: You can't marry her then. It's disgusting.

EVANS: Not my real auntie. She lives next door but one to us at home. I only call her my auntie. They've been friends, see, her mother and my mother for ever such a long time. My father's brother married her cousin, that's all. I've called her my auntie since I was a little lad.

BAMFORTH: You make it sound like rabbits.

EVANS: All the same, if anything was wrong with her, my mother would write and let me know.

BAMFORTH: You hope.

EVANS: Well, of course she would!

BAMFORTH: Look, son. Do yourself a favour, eh? Don't give me all that bull. There's only one way to keep them faithful. And that's like Smudger. Marry them sharpish and leave them with a couple of snappers running round the drum. Keep them occupied. With three or four nippers howling out for grub they don't have time to think about the other. Right, Smudge?

SMITH: That's about it.

MACLEISH: I fail to see, Bamforth, what experience you've had on the subject.

BAMFORTH: Get lost, you Scotch haggis.

EVANS: How many you got, Smudge?

SMITH: Two.

EVANS: Boys?

SMITH: One of each.

EVANS: Boy and a girl. Must be smashing.

SMITH: What? Kids?

EVANS: Not only that. You know. Having home, like. You know, something to go back to – afterwards. Home of your own, I mean. Wife and family and home and that. Got a house of your own yet, have you?

SMITH: Bit of a one. Council. Up on the new estate.

EVANS: Go on!

SMITH: It's all right. Bit of a garden, not much, but it's all right. Better than nothing.

EVANS: Did you do any gardening, Smudge, before you came in the army?

SMITH: Not a lot. Few veg. round the back – cabbages and that, brussels, couple of rows of peas, one or two blooms. Not a lot. You know – the usual.

EVANS: I know what you mean.

SMITH: Always left the front. Made a sort of a bit of a lawn of it. Sit out on Sundays on it after dinner. Me and the Missis. Saturday afternoons sometime – when there was football on the wireless. Just big enough to sit on – two of you. Nice bit of grass. At least, it was. I suppose the kids have racked it up.

EVANS: You don't know. Perhaps the missis has been looking after it.

SMITH: Perhaps.

EVANS: Must be worse for you, I suppose. Being stuck out here. Not like the rest of us. Having a family to think about, I mean.

BAMFORTH: Well, don't let that get you down, Taff. By the time you get out of this lot your Cardiff bint'll have a couple running round to call you 'dad'. I heard they've just posted in a regiment of Gurkha boys to Wales. For special training. They'll give her special training if I know them. Couple from that stud should just suit you. They'll match your battledress.

SMITH: That'd give the neighbours something to think about, Taff.

EVANS: I'd give her something to think about if she did.

BAMFORTH: Don't be like that, Taffy. Allies is allies, my old son. No good having allies if you're not willing to share what little bit you've got.

EVANS: They wouldn't be no allies of mine, then.

BAMFORTH: You're not democratic, that's your trouble. Just think! I can see you now – nipping off to Chapel Sundays with a little Sambo clinging on each hand. Right up your street, is that.

EVANS [*rises and throws magazine at Bamforth*]: I'll be up yours, Bammo, if you don't give it a rest!

BAMFORTH: You and who else?

EVANS [*crossing and playfully sparring up to Bamforth*]: Just me, boy. You're just my size.

BAMFORTH: Come on then, you Welsh Taff! Stick me one on!

EVANS: All right! You asked for it!

[EVANS *closes in on Bamforth and throws a punch.* BAMFORTH *grabs Evans's hand and twists it up and round his back.* BAMFORTH *flings Evans to the floor, grabs a foot, and twists it from the ankle.*]

EVANS: Go steady, man! You'll break my leg!

BAMFORTH: You're an ignorant Welsh Taff! What are you? An ignorant Welsh Taff!

EVANS: Get off my leg, you rotten fool!

BAMFORTH: Say you're an ignorant Welsh Taff! Say you're an ignorant Welsh Taff!

EVANS: You'll break my leg!

WHITAKER [*adjusting radio controls*]: Something coming through again!

BAMFORTH [*to Evans*]: Tell them! Come on, tell them what you are!

EVANS: Will you let go, man!

BAMFORTH: Tell them what you are.

EVANS: I'm an ignorant Welsh Taff . . . I'm an ignorant Welsh Taff!

MACLEISH: Bamforth! Evans! Knock it off, the pair of you!

BAMFORTH [*disengaging himself from Evans*]: What's the matter now?

EVANS [*climbs to his feet*]: You want to go easy, Bammo boy. You damn near crippled me.

[BAMFORTH *and* EVANS *move across to where Whitaker is seated. The radio operator is again attempting to contact base.*]

WHITAKER [*flicking transmitter switch*]: Blue Patrol ... Blue Patrol calling Red Leader ... Are you receiving me ... Are you receiving me ... Over ... [WHITAKER *flicks to 'receive' and adjusts controls. He fades up the volume and we hear the crackle of interference on the set. For a moment there is also the sound of distorted speech on the radio – though the distortion and interference are too strong to make the voice distinguishable.*] It's there again!

EVANS: He's right, Bammo! I heard it myself.

BAMFORTH: Ah, so what.

EVANS: I heard voices, Bammo!

BAMFORTH: So what does that make you? Joan of Arc? What if you did? Could have been from any of the mobs up the jungle.

EVANS: Could have been base, boyo.

[WHITAKER *takes off the headphones.*]

MACLEISH: Could you make out what it was Whitaker?

WHITAKER [*shakes his head*]: Too much interference. [*He switches the set off.*] I'd better leave it. No sense in wasting the battery. I'll leave it now till Mitch gets back.

BAMFORTH [*crosses to form, picks up his pack, and takes out a food pack*]: You do that, son. You tell old mother Mitchem all about it. What a good boy you've been. Please, Sergeant, I've been working ever so hard. Please, Sergeant, I've been fiddling about with my little wireless all the time that you were out. Please, Sergeant, can I have a stripe? You make me sick. [*He tears open the food pack.*] Stroll on! Look here. Bungy. Bloody cheese again. I'll swing for that ration corporal one of these days.

EVANS: What do you reckon it was, Smudge?

SMITH: What's that?

EVANS: On the set. You think it might have been camp?

SMITH: Don't ask me. Whitaker's the boy to ask.

WHITAKER: Must have been. It's only fifteen miles to base. The nearest mob to us are nearly thirty miles up country.

EVANS: What the hell are we supposed to be doing anyway? Stuck here in the middle?

SMITH: Playing at soldiers. What they call a routine patrol, Taff. Keeping out of mischief. Out of the NAAFI bar. It keeps you under control. Keeps the Colonel happy. It's good for morale.

EVANS: It's no good for my rotten feet. These boots, I think. The rubber soles that draw them.

BAMFORTH: It's a crumb patrol. It's just about the crummiest detail in the Far East is this, and no messing. Two days humping kit and two days back! Routine Patrol! You can stick this for a game of soldiers. Talk about the P.B.I. If ever there was an all-time crumb patrol, we're on it. [*He glances round at* WHITAKER, *who has taken a needle, ball of wool, and a pair of socks from his pack and is busily engaged in darning.*] What the hell are you supposed to be doing? [WHITAKER, *bent over his task, does not look up.*] You!

WHITAKER [*looks up*]: What's up?

BAMFORTH: What are you on like?

WHITAKER: My socks.

BAMFORTH: What for?

WHITAKER: Kit Inspection Saturday morning.

BAMFORTH: Well, that just about beats the lot, does that. Now I've seen everything. Rotten stroll on! The third day's hump we're on – three days out and bright boy's sweating on a kit inspection! What with him and his 'Ladies' Companion' and you and your knitting! If the Japs ever get down as far as this they'll have you two grafting in their regimental brothel.

MACLEISH: And where will you be, Bamforth?

BAMFORTH: Me?

MACLEISH: When the Japs arrive?

BAMFORTH: Not here, that's certain. I wasn't meant to be a hero.

MACLEISH: I gathered that.

BAMFORTH: I'll tell you where I'll be, boy. Scarpering. Using my loaf. On the trot. I've got it all worked out. The lot. Tin of Cherry Blossom Dark Tan from head to foot. Couple of banana leaves round my old whatsits. Straight through Kew Gardens outside and head for the water. Like one of the locals.

EVANS: You reckon you could make it, Bammo?

BAMFORTH: What! If the yellow hordes were waving bayonets at me I'd be off like a whippet. You'll not see my tail for dust. There's more wog rowing boats up the coast than enough. Nip off in one of them and straight to sea.

SMITH: On your own?

BAMFORTH: Tod or nothing. When the time comes, Smudge, it's going to be every man for himself.

EVANS: Go on, man. Where could you make for?

BAMFORTH: What's it matter? Anywhere but here. Desert Island. One that's loaded with bags of native bints wearing grass frocks. Settle down and turn native. Anything's better than ending up with Tojo's boys.

EVANS: You'd never do it.

BAMFORTH: That's all you know. Come down the beach and wave me off. If you've got time to wave with all them little Nippos on your trail. I'll be in the boat, Jack. Lying back and getting sunburnt with a basket of coconuts. [*Cod American.*] And so we say farewell to this lush, green, and prosperous country of Malaya. As the sun sets in the west our tiny boat bobs peacefully towards the horizon. We take one last glimpse at the beautiful tropical coastline and can see, in the distance, our old comrade in arms and hopeless radio operator, Private Whitaker, making peace with the invading Army of the Rising Sun – and the invading Army of the Rising Sun is carving pieces out of Private Whitaker.

WHITAKER [*rising*]: Pack it in, Bamforth.

BAMFORTH: What's the matter, Whitto? Getting windy?

WHITAKER: Just pack it in, that's all.

BAMFORTH: Get knotted.

MACLEISH: I haven't seen anybody handing medals to you yet, Bamforth.

BAMFORTH: No, my old haggis basher. And you're not likely to. I've told you – I don't go a bundle on this death or glory stuff.

MACLEISH: So why not keep your trap shut?

BAMFORTH: Democracy, Mac. Free Speech. Votes for women and eight-double-seven Private Bamforth for Prime Minister.

SMITH: Show us your Red Flag, Bammo.

BAMFORTH: It's what we're fighting for. Loose living and six months' holiday a year. The General told me that himself. 'Bamforth,' he says to me, taking me round the back of the lav at Catterick, 'Bammo, my old son, the British Army's in a desperate position. The yellow peril's about to descend upon us, the gatling's jammed, the Colonel's dead, and the cook corporal's stuffed the regimental mascot in the oven. On top of all that, and as if we hadn't got enough to worry about, we've got two thousand Jocks up the jungle suffering from screaming ab-dabs and going mad for women, beer, and haggis. We're posting you out there, Bammo,' he says, 'to relieve the situation.' So before I had time to relieve myself, here I was.

MACLEISH: And what have you got against the Jocks?

BAMFORTH: Stroll on! He's off again! It's a joke, you thick-skulled nit!

MACLEISH: And I'll not stand for any of your insubordinations.

BAMFORTH: Come on, boy! Come it on! Pull the tape on me again. That's all I want. I'll blanco your belt for you for twopence.

MACLEISH: When you're on duty, Bamforth, you'll take orders like the rest.

BAMFORTH: Get the ink dry in your pay-book first. You've not had the tape a month.

MACLEISH: If I'm in charge here, that's all that matters, as far as you're concerned. It makes no difference to you if I've had the tape five minutes or five years. You'll jump to it, boy, when I'm calling out the time. You'll just do as you're told, or you're for the high jump. [BAMFORTH *swears under his breath and turns away.*] Bamforth! Bamforth, I'm talking to you!

BAMFORTH [*swings round*]: Private Bamforth! I've got a rank myself, Acting Unpaid Unwanted Lance Corporal Macleish!

MACLEISH: Evans!

EVANS: Corp?

MACLEISH: Come here. [*As* EVANS *crosses towards the window* MACLEISH *tosses him the rifle.*] Here. You're on guard. Take over from me.

EVANS: Corp.

MACLEISH [*crosses down to face Bamforth*]: I'm not giving you any second warnings, Bamforth. When you speak to me you'll watch your mouth. I mean that, Bamforth, just watch out – or as sure as I'm standing here, I'll have you.

BAMFORTH: Try taking off your tape and saying that, you Scotch get.

MACLEISH: I've already told you, this has got nothing to do with the tape. I'm not warning you for c.o.'s orders, boy. I'm not interested in having you on the c.o.'s veranda with your cap and belt off. One word to me and I'll put your teeth down your throat. I mean that.

BAMFORTH: What with?

MACLEISH [*raising his fists*]: These. Just these.

BAMFORTH [*unfastening his jacket*]: If you want to play it the hard way, Jock . . .

MACLEISH: I want to play it any way that suits me. And right now it suits me to sort you out.

SMITH [*crossing from window*]: Wrap it up, Jock.

MACLEISH: You keep out of this, Smudge. This has got nothing to do with you – it's personal between Bamforth and myself – it's got nothing to do with you.

SMITH: Like hell it hasn't. You're like a couple of kids.

MACLEISH: I said keep out of it!

SMITH: Grow up! For God's sake grow up the pair of you! What do you think you're on?

BAMFORTH: I'm waiting for you, Jock.

SMITH: So go on, Mac. You take a poke at him and where's it get you? You lose your tape, you're in the nick.

MACLEISH: The tape means nothing to me.

SMITH: So all right! You get six months in the nick.

BAMFORTH: What are you waiting for? You're pretty big with the mouth, Jock; let's see you follow it up.

MACLEISH [*raising his fists and moving in on Bamforth*]: You asked for it . . .

SMITH [*restraining Macleish*]: You dim Scotch crone! It's what he wants! He's dying for you to put him one on. Use your loaf! Screw the bomb! Sling in your tape and stick him one on then – if it's going to make you feel any better. Do it then. You put a finger on him now he'll come King's Regs on you so fast your feet won't touch the ground.

MACLEISH [*shrugging Smith away*]: I'll sort him so he never comes King's Regs again. On me or anybody else!

[EVANS *has turned away from the window and all interest is centred on Macleish and Bamforth as the door opens and* MITCHEM *and* JOHNSTONE *enter.*]

MITCHEM: So what's all this in aid of?

JOHNSTONE: Do your jacket up, Bamforth!

BAMFORTH: Must have come undone.

JOHNSTONE: And get your heels together when you speak to me, lad!

BAMFORTH [*coming slowly to attention*]: Corporal.

[*There is an apprehensive pause as* MITCHEM *crosses slowly into the centre of the room.*]

MITCHEM: On your feet! [WHITAKER *rises.*] Get fell in, the lot of you! Move yourselves! [*The members of the patrol, with the exception of Johnstone, fall in in single rank.*] Ted, stand by the door.

JOHNSTONE [*half closes the door and stands on guard*]: Check.

MITCHEM [*he walks slowly along the line of men and turns, flicking open an unbutton breast pocket on Evans's jacket as he walks back.* EVANS *steps one pace out of the ranks, fastens the button, and moves back into line.* MITCHEM *looks along the line of men. There is a long pause before he speaks.*]: Shower! Useless shower! That's all you are. The lot of you. I could have been a regiment of ruddy Nips and I walked through that door. I walked straight in! . . . Squad – shun! Stand at ease. Squad – shun! Stand at ease. Corporal Macleish!

MACLEASH [*steps one pace forward smartly*]: Sarnt!

MITCHEM: I left you in charge.

MACLEISH: Sarnt!

MITCHEM: So what happened?

MACLEISH: I . . . I had occasion to reprimand . . . I'm sorry, Sergeant. I forgot myself for the moment.

MITCHEM [*pause*]: So you're sorry. You forgot yourself. I leave you in charge of the section for ten minutes and the whole organization goes to pot. Ten minutes, Corporal, and you're running a monkey house! [*Pause.* MITCHEM *walks along the line and back.*] You had occasion to reprimand who?

MACLEISH: I . . . I forget now, Sergeant. It was one of the men.

MITCHEM: I didn't think it was a chimpanzee. Who was it?

MACLEISH: It was something that happened in the heat of the moment. I forget now.

MITCHEM: Then you'd better remember. Smartish. Corporal Macleish, who was the man?

MACLEISH: If it's all the same to you, Sergeant, I'd prefer not to say.

MITCHEM: For your information, Macleish, it's not the same to me. Just what do you think this is? Just what? All girls together and no telling tales? You think I'm running a Sunday School outing? 'Please, Miss, it was Jimmie Smith who sat on the tomato sandwiches but I promised not to tell.' [EVANS *laughs.*] Shut up!

MACLEISH: It was a personal matter I'd prefer to handle in my own way.

MITCHEM: Then let me put you straight, Corporal. Right now. Before it's too late. You haven't got no personal matters. Not while you're out with me. While you were settling it in your own way – sorting out your personal matters – you could have had seven men, including yourself, with their tripes on the floor. Remember that. Seven. Including me. And as far as I'm concerned, what happens to me's important. [*Addressing the patrol.*] To look at some of you the army's not gained all that much by his incompetence. But, all the same, I brought you out and I intend to take you back. The lot of you. I'll not stand any more from any one of you who makes it awkward for the rest. I want the man who started all this argument to stand out now. . . . Come on, come on! [*There is a pause.*] All right. Fair enough. Have it how you want. You'll all be on fatigues when we get back to camp.

MACLEISH: You can't punish all the section.

MITCHEM: I can do just what I like, Corporal. I can have your guts for garters if I want.

MACLEISH: It's against all army regulations.

[BAMFORTH *takes one pace forward.*]

MITCHEM [*crossing to face Bamforth*]: Hello! What's this? I was wrong.

It was a chimpanzee.' As if I hadn't guessed. Private Bamforth, eight-double-seven.

BAMFORTH: Sarnt!

MITCHEM: Coming it on again. Coming it on. It's about time you and me had a few words.

BAMFORTH: Sarnt?

MITCHEM: Now get this, Bamforth. Get it straight. Get it in your head. Since you've been posted out to join this mob it's crossed my mind, a time or two, that you don't like the army.

BAMFORTH: Sarnt.

MITCHEM: It's a mutual feeling, Bamforth. The army's not in love with you. If I had you in my lot in Blighty, lad, you wouldn't last a week. I've met your kind before. I've seen men who'd make a breakfast out of muck like you go in the nick and do their time and come back so that butter wouldn't melt between their crutch. Don't try and come the hard-case stuff with me, son. It doesn't work. I'm up to all them tricks myself. O.K.?

BAMFORTH: Sarnt.

MITCHEM: I've watched you, lad. I've had my eye on you. Ever since you first turned up. I've seen you try and come it on with every junior N.C.O. that's been made up. The barrack-room lawyer. The hard case. You can quote King's Regs from now until the middle of next week. Up to every dodge and skive that's in the book. There's just one thing. It doesn't work with me, 'cause I don't work according to the book. You don't know anything, Bamforth. You don't know anything at all. But if you want to try and come it on with me I'll tell you, here and now, that I can be a bastard. I can be the biggest bastard of them all. And just remember this: I've got three stripes start on you. You're a non-runner, son, I start favourite halfway down the course before the off. You haven't got a chance. So now just go ahead and play it how you want. I'm easy. [Pause.] Now get back into line the pair of you. Move! [MACLEISH and BAMFORTH step back into the rank. MITCHEM crosses to speak to Bamforth.] And if you take my tip you'll stay in line. [MITCHEM steps back to address the patrol.] Stand at ease! . . . Easy . . . [The men relax.] Now, pay attention – all of you. We've had a sortie round, Corporal Johnstone and myself; I'll try and put you in the picture now before we set off back. The main track is about sixty yards from here through the trees. The way we came – and that's the way we're going back. Round the back of here the undergrowth's so thick it would take a month of Sundays to hack half a mile. There's only one way out and that's where we came in. It's over fifteen miles from here to camp and we're moving off in fifteen minutes' time. We march at five-yard intervals – I don't want any of you closing up. Corporal Johnstone's breaking trail and I'll bring up the rear. There'll be no talking. I've said there'll be a five-yard interval between each man. You'll keep it that way. What goes for closing up goes twice as much for dropping back – I don't want any of you falling out. I've told you once it's fifteen miles, or thereabouts, to base. Due south. The other way – north – and twenty miles as near as we can estimate, the line's been built to keep the Nips at bay. All positions have been consolidated. Which means that all the mobs from round these parts have moved up to the front – or most of them – a few have been withdrawn. There's not a living soul, apart from local wogs, if any, for miles from here. If any one of you gets lost he's on his own. I don't advise it. So you keep it five yards – dead. Anybody any questions?

MACLEISH: Sergeant?

MITCHEM: Yeh?

MACLEISH: Have you any idea which of the mobs have moved up country?

MITCHEM: Only what I heard when we left camp. And they were rumours in the mess. Just about the lot, they reckon. The Fusiliers, two regiments of Jocks, and some artillery. You studying Military History?

MACLEISH: No. I've got . . . It's my brother. He's with the Highland boys.

MITCHEM: I see.

MACLEISH: He's my young brother. We've applied to get his transfer to our mob. It's not come through yet. You've heard they've moved them up already?

MITCHEM: It was just a rumour in the mess . . . Anybody else got any ticks? [*There is a negative murmur from the men.*] That makes a change. Right then, Fifteen minutes and we push off back. Who did first stag?

MACLEISH: Smith and myself, Sergeant.

MITCHEM: You two had better have a break. Bamforth, Evans!

BAMFORTH:
EVANS: } Sarge?

MITCHEM: You're both on guard. All right. The rest of you fall out. [BAMFORTH *and* EVANS *pick up their rifles and cross to windows.* MACLEISH *and* SMITH *cross to form and sit down.* JOHNSTONE *closes door and crosses into room as the two reliefs reach the windows.*]

MITCHEM: Whitaker!

WHITAKER: Sergeant?

MITCHEM: Any joy on the set?

WHITAKER: I got something through about five minutes ago, Sarge. I don't know what it was, though. Too faint to pick it up.

JOHNSTONE [*crossing to join Mitchem and Whitaker*]: You got through to base, did you say, Whitaker?

WHITAKER: No, Corp. I got something through, though. I was telling the Sergeant. I picked up something but I don't know what it was.

JOHNSTONE: How much a week do they pay you for this, lad?

MITCHEM: It's not his fault. The battery's dis. O.K., Sammy. Have another go. Better give it one more try.

WHITAKER [*sitting down at set*]: Right, Sergeant. [*He tunes in the set behind following dialogue.*]

JOHNSTONE: What you reckon, Mitch?

MITCHEM: What's that?

JOHNSTONE: What he got?

MITCHEM: Dunno ... Suppose it must have been the camp. No one else in this area pushing out signals. With a wonky set he couldn't pick up any of the front-line mobs from here. They're out of range. So it figures that it must have been the camp.

JOHNSTONE: I'd like to put the boot in on the burk who dished us out with a u/s batt. S.O.B., that's all they are, the H.O. men.

MITCHEM: We'll sort that out when we get back.

JOHNSTONE: I'd like to ram his pig-muck battery down his throat, that's all. Who was on duty in the battery shop?

MITCHEM: It's no good flapping over that. We'll let him have another go and if nothing comes up we'll pack it in. Push off back. We've got a negative report. It doesn't make a lot of difference.

JOHNSTONE: It could have been something else. It could have been important.

MITCHEM: It isn't. So we can sort it out when we get back.

[JOHNSTONE *and* MITCHEM *turn and listen as* WHITAKER *attempts to make contact.*]

WHITAKER: Blue Patrol to Red Leader . . . Blue Patrol calling Red Leader . . . Are you receiving me . . . are you receiving me . . . . Come in, Red Leader, come in Red Leader . . . Over.

[WHITAKER *flicks to 'receive' and tunes in. Sound of interference held behind.* JOHNSTONE *and* MITCHEM *listen for a moment and then turn away.*]

JOHNSTONE: Damn duff equipment! The whole damn issue's duff.

MITCHEM [*takes out a packet of cigarettes and offers one to Johnstone*]: Fag?

JOHNSTONE [*taking the cigarette*]: Ta. [*He takes a box of matches from his pocket, strikes one, offers a light to Mitchem, then lights his own.*]

MITCHEM [*inhales deeply then exhales*]: Thanks.

JOHNSTONE: Time do you reckon we'll get back?

MITCHEM: Tomorrow? 'Bout 1800 hours if we keep it up. Roll on. Roll on, let's get some kip.

JOHNSTONE: If you get the chance. Kit inspection Saturday morning. What's the betting we end up on the square after that? C.O.'s parade.

MITCHEM: Not this boy. I'm going to grab a week-end off, and chuff the expense.

WHITAKER [*pushes the headphones on to the back of his head and turns in his chair*]: Sarge!

MITCHEM [*turns*]: Yeh?

WHITAKER: Coming through again!

[MITCHEM *and* JOHNSTONE *cross to table and listen intently to the set.* WHITAKER *replaces headphones and tunes in.* MACLEISH *and*

34

SMITH, *who have been talking together on the form, sit up and listen. There is an air of expectancy amongst the patrol. As Whitaker fiddles with the controls the interference increases and dies away. A faint murmur of speech can be heard from the set.*]

WHITAKER: There it is!

MITCHEM: Come on, lad! Let's be having it.

EVANS: Ask the C.O. if he loves me as much as always, Whitto boy!

BAMFORTH: Nobody loves you, you horrible Taff!

JOHNSTONE: Shut up! Pack the talking in!

WHITAKER: I've got it now!

[*The radio bursts into life. The voice of a Japanese radio operator comes through the set clearly.* WHITAKER *turns and looks in bewilderment at Mitchem. These two are the first to realize the implications. There is a slight pause, stemming from surprise, then the patrol reacts with forced humour.*]

BAMFORTH: You've got it, Whitto son, all right. You've got the ruddy Japs.

EVANS: If that's the camp they're having rice for tea and my name's Tojo.

BAMFORTH: Bring on the geisha girls!

MACLEISH: A right ruddy radio operator you've turned out to be, Whitaker. You don't know who's side you're on.

MITCHEM [*leans across and switches off the set*]: Pack the talking in, the lot of you! Right, Whitaker. [WHITAKER, *who is staring in horror at the set, makes no reply.*] Whitaker, I'm talking to you, lad! [WHITAKER *looks up for the first time.*] How strong's the battery? . . . Come on, come on!

WHITAKER: It's almost gone. The battery's nearly dead.

MITCHEM: So what's your range at present? . . . Whitaker, your range!

WHITAKER [*pulling himself together slightly*]: It must be under fifteen miles. I can't get through to camp. It could be ten. It might be less. [*With the exception of Evans the patrol begins to comprehend.*]

EVANS: Go on, Whitto boy! You're up the creek all over. The Japs are past Jalim Besar. It's twenty miles away at least.

SMITH: We're all up the creek.

BAMFORTH: Stroll on.

JOHNSTONE: Evans! Bamforth! You're supposed to be on guard! Get on your posts!

[EVANS *and* BAMFORTH, *who have turned away from the windows during the above dialogue, return to their positions.*]

WHITAKER: It was as clear as a bell! They could be sitting right on top of us!

MACLEISH: Under fifteen miles away! So what's happened to the lads up country?

MITCHEM: Shut up.

MACLEISH: What's happened to the forward boys?

MITCHEM: Shut up.

MACLEISH: I've got my brother posted up out there!

MITCHEM: Shut up! Johnno, check the stens.

JOHNSTONE [*crossing to table where he checks Mitchem's sten and his own*]: Right.

MITCHEM [*crossing to Macleish*]: Now just shut up. It makes no difference now to you, lad, if your mother's kipping with a Jap. O.K.? [MACLEISH *is about to burst into reply but changes his mind and sits on form.*] Then just remember that. Now listen. All of you. Evans, Bamforth, don't turn round. I want your eyes out there. You got that, both of you? [BAMFORTH *and* EVANS *nod.*] Then ram a round apiece up your spouts. [BAMFORTH *and* EVANS *release the safety catches on their rifles, withdraw the bolts and slam them home.*] O.K. Now put your safety catches on. [BAMFORTH *and* EVANS *hesitate a moment and then comply.*] O.K. That's fine. That's all we need. No more than that. [*He crosses centre-stage to address the patrol.*] Fred Karno's mob. That's what you are, Fred Karno's mob. There's half of you been shooting off your mouths for days on end on how you'd fix the Japs. To listen to you talk you'd win the ruddy war on bread and jam. You've heard one slimy Nippo on the set and now you're having second thoughts. You make me laugh, that's what you do to me – make me want to laugh. [JOHNSTONE *has now finished his examination of the stens.*] O.K., Johnno?

JOHNSTONE: Both O.K.

MITCHEM [*to the patrol*]: You've heard one Nippo on the set. That might mean anything at all. It might mean that they've broken through, up country, and are pouring down. If that's a fact, then chuff your luck. That's all – just chuff your luck. They might be swarming out there now – like ants. And if they are and I'm with crumbs like you, I'm up the creek myself and that's a fact. [*The patrol murmurs uneasily.*] But all you know so far is that you've heard a Nippo griping on the set. And that could mean that somewhere in this festering heat one lousy bunch of Japs have wriggled in behind our lines – that could be half a dozen men. It could be less than that. It could be half a dozen Joskins like yourselves. Six or seven – five or six – or even two or three poor helpless wet-nurse ginks who, somewhere, close to here, are running round in circles, doing their nuts, because they've heard young Whitto pushing out a signal back to base. If that's the way things are with them, the bloke who's calling out the time for 'em has got my sympathy. I wish him luck. He's up to the short hairs in it like myself and so I wish him luck. [*The confidence of the men has been largely restored – one or two are even amused.*] I'll tell you what we're going to do. We're moving off. Right now. [*Murmur of relief from the men.*] We're going back. It's odds on that they're just a buckshee bunch of Harries like yourselves. All the same, we're not waiting to find out. The orders for the movement back still stand. Evans, Bamforth, you'll stay on guard until the others have got their gear on and are ready to move off back.

[*The men begin to struggle into their webbing equipment.*]

JOHNSTONE: Come on, then! Move yourselves! We've not got time to play about!

MITCHEM: Macleish and Smith! [MACLEISH *and* SMITH *pause in assembling their kit.*] Soon as you've got into your gear, relieve the two on guard and let them get theirs on. [MACLEISH *and* SMITH *nod and return to their task.*] Quick as you can.

JOHNSTONE [*picks up the stens and hands one to Mitchem*]: You want me to lead off back?

MITCHEM [*nods*]: Crack the whip a bit. Set a steady pace. I want to try and do it in one stint.

JOHNSTONE: I'm with you.

BAMFORTH [*unnoticed by the others,* BAMFORTH *suddenly tenses himself and raises his rifle. He flicks off the safety catch and takes aim.*]: Sarge ... Sarge!

MITCHEM [*sensing Bamforth's urgency*]: Hold it, all of you!] *The men are still and silent.*] What's up?

BAMFORTH: I thought I saw a movement down the track ... It's there again!

MITCHEM [*to the patrol*]: Get down! Get out of sight! [*Apart from the two men on guard and* MITCHEM *the members of the patrol stoop below the level of the windows.*] How many of them? Can you see?

BAMFORTH [*lowers his rifle*]: No. Out of sight again. Behind the trees. Heading this way.

[MITCHEM, *his head down below window level, moves across the hut to join Bamforth at the window.* JOHNSTONE *moves across to join Evans.*]

MITCHEM: Which way they coming from?

BAMFORTH [*pointing*]: Along the track. Down there. 'Bout fifty yards.

MITCHEM: Evans?

EVANS: Can't see a ruddy thing from here, Sarge. Not as far as that.

JOHNSTONE: There's a clump of blasted bushes in the way.

MITCHEM: Were they Japs?

BAMFORTH: Might have been anything. Only had a glimpse.

MITCHEM: Are you sure, Bamforth?

BAMFORTH: Meaning what?

MITCHEM: You saw anything at all, lad?

BAMFORTH: You think I'm going round the bend!

MITCHEM: All right. We'll take your word for it. If there is anyone down there they should come into sight again just by that bit of ...

BAMFORTH [*nudges Mitchem and points again*]: A Jap!

MITCHEM: I've got him. On his own. [*Turns slightly from window*] Now keep still, all of you. This one's on his tod. Could be a scout. He hasn't spotted this place up to press. Got him, Johnno?

JOHNSTONE: Can't see anything for this ruddy bush. Whereabouts?

MITCHEM: Just less than fifty yards. Straight ahead ... Got him, have you?

JOHNSTONE: Not yet. What do you think he's on?

BAMFORTH: He's . . . He's looking round for something. In the grass. Looking for something . . . Bending down.

JOHNSTONE: Think he's found the trail, Mitch? Up to here?

MITCHEM: Looks like that. Found something by the way he's carrying on.

[BAMFORTH *bursts into laughter.*]

MITCHEM: Shut up!

BAMFORTH: Found the trail! He's found the trail all right! He's found a place to have a crafty smoke.

EVANS: He's what, Bammo?

BAMFORTH: Having a drag. He's lighting up a fag. Well, the crafty old Nip. The skiving get. Caught red-handed. Nip down and ask him for a puff, Taff.

MITCHEM: Of all the rotten luck. He would choose this place. We'll wait and see'f he pushes off . . . [BAMFORTH *slowly raises his rifle and takes careful aim.* MITCHEM *swings round and knocks the rifle out of aiming position.*] I said no noise!

BAMFORTH: I had him right between the cheeks! I couldn't miss! He's on his tod!

MITCHEM: What gives you that idea? Do you think they march off by the dozen for a sly swallow?

JOHNSTONE: What's happening?

BAMFORTH: He's up. He's standing up and nicking out the nub. He's going back. The way he came . . . Stopped . . . Turning round . . . He's coming back. He's found the track up here. He's coming up.

MITCHEM: Move it then, the rest of you. Let's have you over by the wall! And bring your gear.

[MACLEISH, WHITAKER, *and* SMITH *pick up their rifles and the kit and scurry across to the rear wall of the hut.*]

MITCHEM [*peering round window*]: Bamforth, Evans, down on deck! [BAMFORTH *and* EVANS *drop below window level.*] And stay there all of you. There's just a chance he might not come inside. In case he does – Johnno . . . [MITCHEM *indicates the door.* JOHNSTONE *nods and sidles across to stand by the door.* MITCHEM *peers round window.*] If he should come in – you grab. Without a sound. I'll cover the outside in case. Still coming up . . . Close to the wall as you can. He might not see us yet.

WHITAKER [*notices the radio which is still standing on the table*]: Sarge! The set!

MITCHEM: Oh God, lad! Get it! Quick! [WHITAKER *moves as if to cross to table, but changes his mind and hugs the wall in terror.*] Get the set! [*Whitaker is still afraid to move. Smith is about to fetch the radio when we hear the sound of feet on the wooden veranda.*] Too late!

[*The members of the patrol squeeze up against the wall as* MITCHEM *edges away from the window out of sight.* JOHNSTONE *tenses himself. The* JAPANESE SOLDIER *can be heard clattering on the veranda for several seconds before he appears at the left-hand window. He peers into the room but fails to see the patrol and is just about to turn away when he notices the radio on the table. He stares at it for a short while and then moves out of sight as he crosses along the veranda towards the door. A further short pause.* JOHNSTONE *raises his hands in readiness. The door opens and the* JAPANESE SOLDIER *enters. As he steps into the room* JOHNSTONE *lunges forward and grabs the Japanese, putting an arm round his throat and his free hand over the soldier's mouth.* MITCHEM, *holding the sten at his hip, darts out of the door and covers the jungle from the veranda.* JOHNSTONE *and the* PRISONER *struggle in the room.*]

JOHNSTONE: Come on then, one of you! Get him! Quick! . . . Evans! Do for him! [EVANS *crosses and raises his rifle, releasing the safety catch.*] No, you burk! You want to do for me as well? Come on, lad! Use your bayonet! In his guts! You'll have to give it hump. [EVANS *unsheaths his bayonet and approaches the struggling figures.*] Sharp then, lad! Come on! Come on! You want it in between his ribs. [EVANS *raises the bayonet to stab the Prisoner, who squirms in terror.*] Not that way, lad! You'll only bust a bone. Feel for it first, then ram it in. Now, come on, quick! [*Evans places his bayonet point on the chest of the Prisoner, who has now stopped struggling and is cringing in the grip of* JOHNSTONE.] Come on! Come on! I can't hold on to him forever! Will you ram it in!

EVANS [*steps back*]: I . . . I can't do it, Corp.

JOHNSTONE: Stick it in! Don't stand there tossing up the odds! Just close your eyes and whoof it in!

EVANS: I can't! I can't! Corp, I can't.

JOHNSTONE: Macleish!

MACLEISH: Not me!

JOHNSTONE: Smith! Take the bayonet! Don't stand there gawping. Do the job!

SMITH: For God's sake do it, Taff. Put the poor bastard out of his misery.

EVANS [*proffering the bayonet to Smith*]: You!

BAMFORTH [*crossing and snatching the bayonet from Evans*]: Here. Give me hold. It's only the same as carving up a pig. Hold him still.

[BAMFORTH *raises the bayonet and is about to thrust it into the chest of the Prisoner as* MITCHEM *enters, closing the door behind him.*]

MITCHEM: Bamforth! Hold it!

BAMFORTH [*hesitates, then moves away*]: I'm only doing what I'm told.

MITCHEM: Just hold it, that's all. I want this one alive. You'll have your chance before we've done. You can count on that. So pack in all this greyhound with a bunny lark. He's not the only one; you'll have your chance. How is he, Johnno? Is he going to do his nut?

JOHNSTONE: Scared stiff. He's going up the wall. I've had enough of him – he stinks of garlic and wog grub. He won't try anything – I wouldn't trust his mouth.

MITCHEM: Hold him for a sec. [MITCHEM *crosses close up to the Prisoner.*] You speakee English? Understand? Compronney? Eh? Eh? You speakee English talk? Trust me to cop a raving lunatic. You! I want no noise, see? Understand? No noise! Quiet. [MITCHEM *points to his mouth and shakes his head.*] No speakee! Keep your trap shut, eh? Now get this, Tojo. Understand. You make so much as a mutter and I'll let Jack the Ripper have a go at you. [MITCHEM *indicates Bamforth, who is still holding the bayonet. The* PRISONER *cringes in Johnstone's grip.*] O.K.? [MITCHEM *points again to his mouth and the* PRISONER *nods vigorously.*] Good. One murmur, Jap, and Laughing Boy will slit your guts up to your ears. Universal talk. I think I'm getting through to him at last, Bamforth!

BAMFORTH [*crossing to Mitchem*]: Sarge?

41

MITCHEM: Put the carving knife away before he dies on us of fright.

BAMFORTH [*turns the bayonet over in his hand and makes a quick, playful gesture with the weapon towards the Prisoner's throat. The* PRISONER *struggles again in Johnstone's arms*]: Boo!

MITCHEM: Bamforth! Jack it in! I said put the cutlery away.

BAMFORTH: All right! [*He crosses and returns the bayonet to* EVANS *who replaces it in the sheath. The* PRISONER *calms down.*] Thanks, Taff.

MITCHEM: Right, Johnno. He'll behave himself. He'll be a good lad. Put him down.

[JOHNSTONE *pushes the Prisoner away.* MITCHEM *gestures with the sten and the* PRISONER'S *arms fly up above his head. The Prisoner is a small, round, pathetic, and almost comic character, armed to the teeth in a Gilbertian fashion; a revolver in a leather holster is slung round his chest and a string of hand grenades swings from his waist. A long two-edged bayonet hangs from his belt. He wears a drab, ill-fitting uniform, peaked cap, and a white silk muffler is tied round his throat. As the Prisoner stands alone and afraid in the centre of the hut the patrol cluster round to examine him.*]

EVANS: He looks as if he's going to fight the war himself.

MACLEISH: He's not exactly what you'd call a handsome bloke.

MITCHEM: All right, get back. What do you want, Jock? A blonde? I'll fix it so it's Rita Hayworth walks in next. Move it! Back!

[*The members of the patrol cross over to the left as* MITCHEM *ushers the Prisoner towards the right-hand wall.*]

JOHNSTONE: Come on then! Move yourselves! He doesn't put the wind up you lot now? You're round him like a lot of lambs that's had their first taste of milk. Two minutes since you wouldn't touch him with a barge pole. None of you!

MITCHEM: Bamforth! Take the armoury away.

BAMFORTH [*crosses to the Prisoner, who cringes away as he approaches*]: Stand still, you nig! Unless you want the boot! [BAMFORTH *proceeds to remove the weapons from the Prisoner, also checking him for any further arms.*]

JOHNSTONE: A right lot I've got landed with! Not one of you had the guts to give me a hand.

MACLEISH: You weren't in need of help. You cannot order men to put a bayonet in an unarmed prisoner.

JOHNSTONE: What do you think they dish you out with bayonets for? Just opening tins of soup?

MACLEISH: They're not to put in prisoners of war!

JOHNSTONE: You know what you can do with yours. You wouldn't know which end is which!

MACLEISH: If the need should arise I'll use a bayonet with the next. But I've no intention of using one on any man who can't defend himself.

JOHNSTONE: You burk!

MACLEISH: He was a prisoner of war!

JOHNSTONE: Prisoner my crutch!

MACLEISH: There such a thing as the Geneva Convention!

JOHNSTONE: He's carting more cannon than the Woolwich Arsenal! If he'd have pulled the pin on one of them grenades we'd all of us been up the shoot! You think that he'd have second thoughts before he put the mockers on the lot of us?

BAMFORTH [places the Prisoner's arms on the table]: That's about the lot.

MITCHEM: Which of you men's supposed to be on guard? The war's not won because you've copped a Nip!

EVANS: I was, Sarge.

MITCHEM: Get on your post and stay there, lad. Who else?

BAMFORTH: Me.

MITCHEM: I've got another job for you. Anybody else that's not done stag so far?

WHITAKER: I haven't been on guard yet, Sarge. I was on the set.

MITCHEM: Then get on now. Take Bamforth's number. [EVANS and WHITAKER pick up their rifles and cross to the windows.] Bamforth!

BAMFORTH: Sarge?

MITCHEM [offering his sten to Bamforth]: Here. Cop on for this. You're looking after Tojo here. I think he fancies you. If he tries to come it on he gets it through the head. No messing. He's in your charge. Look after him.

BAMFORTH [shakes his head, refusing the sten]: Like he was my only chick. [BAMFORTH picks up the Prisoner's bayonet from the table.] I'll

settle for this. [*He crosses towards the Prisoner.*] Down, Shorthouse.
[*He motions the Prisoner to sit on the form.*] Put your hands up on your
head. [*The* PRISONER *looks at Bamforth in bewilderment.*] I said, get
your hands up on your head! Like this! See! Flingers on the blonce!
All-light? [BAMFORTH *demonstrates and the Prisoner complies.* BAM-
FORTH *is delighted.*] Hey, Taff! See that, did you? He did it like I
said! Flingers up on blonce. I only talk the lingo natural!

EVANS [*turning at window*]: I always knew you were an Oriental creep
at heart, man!

BAMFORTH: You've not seen nothing yet – get this. [*To the Prisoner.*]
Allee-lightee. Flingers up to touch the loof. Come on, come on!
Touch the loof, you Asiatic glet! [BAMFORTH *raises the bayonet and
the* PRISONER *cringes away.*] He's a rotten ignoramus.

MITCHEM: All right, that'll do. Pack it in. Now listen, all of you.
We're taking this boy back to camp with us. I want to get him
there in one piece.

JOHNSTONE: It's a bit dodgy, isn't it, Mitch?

MITCHEM: Happen.

JOHNSTONE: It's going to be a dodgy number as it is. You don't
know how many more of them there are out there.

MITCHEM: Not yet.

JOHNSTONE: They could be coming down in strength.

MITCHEM: They might.

JOHNSTONE: And if they are we're up the creek all right. We've got
enough on getting this lot back. They've no experience. We'll have
to belt it like the clappers out of hell. We can't afford to hang
about.

MITCHEM: We'll shift.

JOHNSTONE: But if we're going to cart a prisoner along as well ...

MITCHEM: He'll go the pace. I'll see to that.

JOHNSTONE: You're in charge.

MITCHEM: That's right. Corporal Macleish! Smith!

MACLEISH: Sergeant?

SMITH: Sarge?

MITCHEM: I've got a job for you two. Outside. [MACLEISH *and*
SMITH *exchange glances.*] I want the pair of you to nip down as

far as the main track. Look for any signs of any more of them. O.K.?

MACLEISH: You want us to go down now, Sarge?

MITCHEM: Straight away. If the coast's clear we want to belt off back. Smartish.

MACLEISH: Right.

MITCHEM: Take it steady – careful – but don't make a meal out of it. The sooner we can make a start from here the better.

[MACLEISH and SMITH strap on their ammunition pouches.]

MACLEISH: Supposing we should . . . make contact?

MITCHEM: Don't. Not if you can help it. If you see anything that moves – turn back. Mac, you'd better take a sten. Take mine. [MACLEISH crosses and takes sten and a couple of clips of ammunition from Mitchem, SMITH unsheaths his bayonet and clips it on his rifle.] Come on. [MITCHEM, MACLEISH, and SMITH cross to the door.] What's it like out, Evans?

EVANS: Quiet. Quiet as a grave.

WHITAKER: Nothing this side, Sarge.

MITCHEM: Cover them as far as you can down the track. [EVANS and WHITAKER nod. MITCHEM opens door slowly and ushers SMITH and MACLEISH on to the veranda.] Off you go.

EVANS: So long, Smudger, Jock.

MITCHEM [closes door and crosses to where Bamforth is guarding the Prisoner]: How's he behaving himself?

BAMFORTH [fingering the bayonet]: All right. He hasn't got much choice.

MITCHEM [to the Prisoner]: You listen to me. Understand? You come with us. We take you back. We take you back with us. Oh, blimey . . . Look . . . Bamforth.

BAMFORTH: Yeh?

MITCHEM: Tell him he can drop his hands. He isn't going to run away.

BAMFORTH: Hey, Tojo! Flingers off blonce. Flingers off blonce! [The PRISONER raises his hands in the air.] Not that, you nit! Here, that's not bad though, is it? He's coming on. He knows his flingers already. Good old Tojo! [The PRISONER smiles.] Now let them

45

dlop. Dlop, see! Down! [BAMFORTH *demonstrates and the* PRISONER *slowly drops his hands.*] He picks up quick. He's a glutton for knowledge.

MITCHEM [*speaks slowly and carefully*]: You – come – with – us! Back! We – take – you – back! [*The Prisoner is mystified.*] Back to camp! [MITCHEM *turns away.*] What's the use . . . [MITCHEM *crosses to table.*]

BAMFORTH: I'll work on him. I'll chat him up a bit.

JOHNSTONE: We should have done him first time off.

MITCHEM: I'm giving the orders!

BAMFORTH: Flingers on blonce. [*The* PRISONER *complies happily.*] Dlop flingers. [*Again the* PRISONER *obeys.*] Get that! He dlops them like a two-year-old!

JOHNSTONE: Just keep him quiet, Bamforth, that's all. We don't want any of the funny patter!

BAMFORTH: I'm teaching him to talk!

JOHNSTONE: Well don't! Mitch, we've got fifteen miles to slog it back. We've got no set. We know the Japs are coming through – so someone's waiting for a report – and quick. We can't drag him along – suppose he tries to come it on? One shout from him with any of his boys around we're in the cart. The lot of us.

MITCHEM: So what do you suggest?

JOHNSTONE: Get rid of him. Right now. You going soft?

MITCHEM: And if we do? You want to make out the report when we get back?

JOHNSTONE: Report! You want to make out a report! Because we do a Jap? We whip him out and knock him off, that's all. We can't take prisoners. We're out to do a job.

MITCHEM: Reports on him don't bother me. And if I've got to do for him – I will. I'll knock him off myself. You think I'm stuffing my nut worrying about a Jap? One Jap? I've got six men. They're my responsibility. But more than that, and like you say, I've got a job to do. So all right. So I'll do it. Now you tell me what's going on out there? [MITCHEM *indicates the window.*] Just tell me how many Nips have broken through and where they are right now. You want to wait and count them for yourself?

JOHNSTONE: I want to slog it back!

MITCHEM: All right. That's what we're going to do. With him. [*Points to the Prisoner.*] With Tojo there. Because if anybody knows the strength of Nips behind our lines it's him. So far on this outing out it's been the biggest muck-up in the history of the British Army, and that's saying a lot. We've wandered round, the set's packed in, we've no idea what's going on and if there ever was an organized shambles – my God, this is it. Now things have changed. We've copped on to a lad who's going to make this detail worth its while. If I can get him back to camp what they'll get out of him could do more good than you if you should serve a score and one. So he's important for what he knows. And I'll leave any man on this patrol behind – including you – before I'll say good-bye to him. Going soft? Do you think I give a twopenny damn about his life? It's what he knows.

JOHNSTONE: Suppose he comes the ab-dabs on the way?

MITCHEM: He won't.

JOHNSTONE: But if he does? He only needs to start playing it up at the wrong time. He only wants to start coming it on when we're close to his muckers.

MITCHEM: I've said he won't.

JOHNSTONE: What if he does?

[MITCHEM *and* JOHNSTONE *glance across at the Prisoner.*]

MITCHEM: I'll put the bayonet in his guts myself. [*Pause*] You'd better check these Jap grenades. Might come in handy.

[MITCHEM *and* JOHNSTONE *turn to table to check the grenades. The Prisoner's hand goes up to his breast pocket.* BAMFORTH *raises the bayonet threateningly.*]

BAMFORTH: Watch it, Tojo boy! Just watch your step! I'll have it in as soon as look at you!

MITCHEM [*glancing round*]: What's up with him?

BAMFORTH: Going for his pocket.

[*The* PRISONER *gestures towards his pocket.*]

MITCHEM: All right. See what he wants.

BAMFORTH [*still threatening with the bayonet, he opens the Prisoner's breast pocket and takes out a cheap leather wallet*]: It's his wallet.

JOHNSTONE: Sling it out the window.

MITCHEM: Let him have it. Check it first.

[BAMFORTH *briefly inspects the interior of the wallet.*]

JOHNSTONE: You're going to let him have it?

MITCHEM: It costs us nothing. No point in getting him niggly before we start.

BAMFORTH: Looks all right, Sarge.

MITCHEM: Give it him.

[BAMFORTH *hands the wallet to the Prisoner, who opens it, extracts a couple of photographs, and hands one to Bamforth.*]

BAMFORTH: It's a photo! It's a picture of a Nippo bint! [*The* PRISONER *points proudly to himself.*] Who's this, then, eh? You got wife? Your missis? [*The* PRISONER *points again to himself.*] It's his old woman! Very good. Plenty of humpy. Japanese girl very good, eh? Good old Tojo! She's a bit short in the pins, that's all. But very nice. I wouldn't mind a crack at her myself. [*The* PRISONER *passes another photograph to Bamforth.*] Here! Get this! Nippo snappers, Sarge. Two Jap kids. Couple of chicos. You got two chicos, eh? [*The* PRISONER *does not understand. Bamforth points to photograph and holds up two fingers.*] Two! See? You got two kids. [*The* PRISONER *shakes his head and holds up three fingers.*] Three? No, you stupid raving imbecile! Two! [BAMFORTH *points again to the photograph.*] One and one's two! Dinky-doo-number two! [*The* PRISONER *holds up his hands to indicate a baby.*] What another? Another one as well! Well, you crafty old devil! You're a bit fond of it, aren't you? You're a rotten old sex maniac, you are. You're as bad as Smudge. [BAMFORTH *returns the photographs to the* PRISONER, *who replaces them carefully in his wallet and returns it to his pocket.*] Let's see if you still know your lessons. Flingers up on blonce! [*The* PRISONER *complies.*] Dlop flingers! [*Again the* PRISONER *is happy to obey.*] Stroll on! See that? He got it right both times! He's almost human this one is!

MITCHEM: All right, Bamforth, jack it in!

JOHNSTONE: We should have done him when he first turned up.

MITCHEM [*crossing to Evans*]: Where have them two got to?

EVANS: No sign yet, Sarge.

[MITCHEM *peers out of window.* BAMFORTH *takes out a packet of cigarettes and puts one in his mouth. He replaces the packet in his pocket and feels for a box of matches as his glance falls on the Prisoner, who is looking up at him.* BAMFORTH *hesitates, then transfers the cigarette from his own mouth to the Prisoner's. He takes out another cigarette for himself.* JOHNSTONE *rises and crosses to Bamforth.* BAMFORTH *is still looking for a match as* JOHNSTONE *takes out a box, strikes one, and offers Bamforth a light.*]

BAMFORTH: Ta. [JOHNSTONE *holds out the match for the Prisoner. As the* PRISONER *leans across to get a light,* JOHNSTONE *knocks the cigarette from his mouth with the back of his hand.*] What's that in aid of?

JOHNSTONE: He gets permission first!

BAMFORTH: I gave him it!

JOHNSTONE: Since when have you been calling out the time!

BAMFORTH: I don't ask you before I give a bloke a fag?

JOHNSTONE: This one you do!

BAMFORTH: Who says?

JOHNSTONE: I do, lad! [*Making a sudden grab for the Prisoner and attempting to tear open his breast pocket.*] I'll fix his photos for the Herb as well!

MITCHEM [*turns*]: Corporal Johnstone!

BAMFORTH [*drops the bayonet and clutches Johnstone by his jacket lapels. He brings his knee up in Johnstone's groin and, as* JOHNSTONE *doubles forward,* BAMFORTH *cracks his forehead across the bridge of Johnstone's nose.*]: Have that!

MITCHEM [*crossing towards the fight*]: Bamforth!

[BAMFORTH, *unheeding, strikes Johnstone in the stomach and pushes him to the floor.*]

JOHNSTONE [*pulling himself to his feet*]: All right. You've done it this time, Bamforth! You've shot your load. As sure as God you'll get three years for that.

BAMFORTH [*picks up bayonet*]: You try and make it stick.

MITCHEM: You're on a charge, Bamforth. You're under open arrest.

BAMFORTH: He started it!

MITCHEM: Tell that to the C.O.

EVANS [*raising his rifle*]: Sarge! There's someone coming up the track!

MITCHEM [*crosses to window*]: Whereabouts?

EVANS: Just coming through the trees.

[JOHNSTONE *picks up his sten and crosses to join Whitaker.*]

MITCHEM: It's all right. It's Macleish and Smith. Cover them up the track.

JOHNSTONE [*aiming the sten*]: I've got them.

EVANS: Looks as if they're in a hurry over something.

[*A pause before we hear* MACLEISH *and* SMITH *clatter up on to the veranda.* MITCHEM *opens the door and they enter the room. They lean against the wall exhausted.*]

MITCHEM: Anybody after you? [MACLEISH *shakes his head.*] What's up then?

EVANS: What's the hurry, Smudger boy? You look as if you've had the whole of the Japanese army on your tail.

SMITH [*out of breath*]: We have . . . Near enough.

MITCHEM: Sit down a tick. [SMITH *and* MACLEISH *cross the table and sit down.* MITCHEM *crosses to join them.*] Now, come on – give. Let's be having it.

MACLEISH [*regaining his breath*]: They've broken through. In strength. There's hundreds of them moving down the main trail back.

MITCHEM: Go on.

SMITH: They must have come through our defence lines like a dose of salts. They're pouring down. Happy as a lot of sand boys. Not a mark on any one of them. Up front the whole damn shoot's collapsed.

MITCHEM: You weren't spotted?

MACLEISH [*shakes his head*]: They're not even looking for anybody. They seem to know they've got this area to themselves. Smudge and myself got down in the long grass. They've got no scouts out. Nothing. Just strolling down the trail as if they owned the jungle . . .

MITCHEM: Do you think they'll find this place?

MACLEISH: Not yet awhile. We watched about a company march past. There was a break then in the file. We managed to cover up the entrance of the trail up here.

SMITH: We stuffed it up with bits of branch and stuff.

MITCHEM: Good.

MACLEISH: The next batch came along as we were finishing. We patched up what we could and scooted back.

JOHNSTONE: So what happens now?

MITCHEM: It's put the kybosh on the journey back. We can't move out of here just yet, and that's a certainty.

MACLEISH: You never saw so many Japs. There must be at least a thousand of them now between ourselves and base. We're right behind their forward lines.

MITCHEM [*crosses down-stage and turns*]: Let's say, for now, they march without a stop. That brings them close up on the camp before tomorrow night. If they've got stuff up in the air to back them up – and if they don't know back at base they've broken through – the base mob gets wiped up.

MACLEISH: But they'll know by now the Japs are through.

MITCHEM: We can't count on that.

JOHNSTONE: If the main road's free, they'll have heavy transport loads of Nips chugging down before tomorrow.

MITCHEM: Let's hope the Engineers have sewn that up. They'll have it mined at least. No, this is the back way in. Cross-country – and it's hard graft cutting trail – they'll have to do the lot on foot.

JOHNSTONE: So?

MITCHEM: So that means we can put the blocks on them. We get there first.

JOHNSTONE: You think the Japs are going to open ranks and let us pass?

MITCHEM: What's the time now? [*He glances at his watch.*] It'll be dark in just over an hour. We might make it then.

JOHNSTONE: And so you think we stand a chance at creeping through a regiment of ruddy Nips!

MITCHEM: What's your suggestion?

JOHNSTONE: We haven't got a chance.

MITCHEM: We've got no choice. We might make it in the dark and in that shrub. They'll be blundering about themselves. At least we know the way – we've done it coming up. It's all new ground to them. We might creep through.

JOHNSTONE [*indicating the Prisoner*]: What? With him in tow?

MITCHEM [*glancing across at the Prisoner*]: No ... We're ditching him. Whitaker!

WHITAKER [*turning at window*]: Sarge?

MITCHEM [*indicating set*]: Come on. You'd better give it one more try.

WHITAKER: I don't think it'll do any good, Sarge. The battery's nigh on stone dead.

MITCHEM: Try it, lad! Don't argue. Relieve him, Smith.

[SMITH *crosses to take Whitaker's place at the window as* WHITAKER *crosses to table and sits at set. He switches on to 'transmit' and pauses.*]

MITCHEM: Come on, lad! Get on with it! We haven't time to mess about.

WHITAKER [*turning in his chair to speak to Mitchem*]: If there are any Japs near here switched to receive they'll get a fix on us.

MITCHEM: That can't be helped. Come on, come on!

WHITAKER [*putting on headphones and tuning in*]: Blue Patrol to Red Leader ... Blue Patrol to Red Leader ... Are you receiving me ... Are you receiving me ... Come in Red Leader ... Come in Red Leader ... Over ... [WHITAKER *switches to 'receive' and tunes in. We hear the crackle of interference.*] Nothing yet ...

MITCHEM: Come in, Sammy son, come in ...

WHITAKER [*adjusting tuning dial*]: There's something here ... [*The interference dies away and we hear the voice of the Japanese* RADIO OPERATOR *as before.*] It's the Jap transmitting. Same as before.

MITCHEM: Get off the ruddy line, you Nip!

[*The voice continues in Japanese for a few seconds and then stops. It continues in taunting broken English.*]

OPERATOR: Johnee! ... Johnee! ... British Johnee! We – you – come – to – get ... We – you – come – to – get.

[WHITAKER *starts up in fear and* MITCHEM *pushes him back into his chair. The patrol turn and look at the Prisoner. The* PRISONER, *noting that all attention is centred on himself, and feeling that he is expected to entertain the patrol, raises his hands in the air and slowly places them on his head. He smiles round blandly in search of approbation.*]

CURTAIN

ACT TWO

Time : Thirty minutes later.

[As the curtain rises we discover BAMFORTH, EVANS, *and* JOHN-
STONE *asleep on the ground by the wall, left.* MACLEISH *is guarding the Prisoner, who is still sitting on the form where we left
him.* SMITH *and* WHITAKER *are standing at the rear windows.*
MITCHEM *is seated at the table cleaning his sten. A bird sings out in
the jungle and* WHITAKER *starts and raises his rifle. He realizes the
cause of his fears and glances round the room in embarrassment. The
other occupants, however, have not noticed this lapse on the part of
Whitaker.* MITCHEM *places his sten on the table and crosses to
Smith.]*

MITCHEM: All O.K., Smudge?

SMITH: All O.K.

MITCHEM: Sammy?

WHITAKER: Nothing to report here, Sarnt. What time is it now?

MITCHEM *[glances at his watch]* : 'Bout quarter past. *[He returns to his
task at the table.]*

SMITH: Why don't you buy a watch?

WHITAKER: I had one, Smudger. Bought one down the town once.
When I had a week-end off one time. Twenty-eight bucks it was.
A good one.

SMITH: Twenty-eight! For a watch? They saw you coming, and no
mistake.

WHITAKER: No, man, it was a good one, I tell you. Smasher. Told
you the date and what day it was and all that. Little red jewels for
numbers and a sort of little moon came up to tell you when it's
night.

SMITH: You can see when it's night. It gets dark.

WHITAKER: Aye, but it was a smashing watch, Smudge. You can't
get watches like that one was in Blighty. There was a bloke in the

53

NAAFI offered me forty bucks for it once. Forty bucks and a sort of Siamese ring he was wearing.

SMITH: You took it?

WHITAKER: I turned it down.

SMITH: What for?

WHITAKER: I'm not a fool altogether. You wouldn't get another watch like that. I was going to give it to the old man as a present when we get back home. I wouldn't have minded the ring though. That was a beauty. Peruvian gold.

SMITH: I thought you said it was Siamese?

WHITAKER: It was. It had a kind of Siamese bint on the front. Doing a sort of dance with her knees bent in front of a temple – her hands sticking up in the air.

SMITH: So where is it?

WHITAKER: It wouldn't come off his finger.

SMITH: I mean the watch.

WHITAKER: I wasn't going to swop the watch for that, boy. I've got more sense than that. I could have flogged it for a fortune back in Blighty – if I hadn't have been going to give it to the old man for his present.

SMITH: So where is it then?

WHITAKER: I lost it. Well, it got knocked off. It was half-inched back in camp. I left it in the ablutions one morning while I went off to the latrine. I wasn't gone above two minutes – it was about the time they were giving us fruit salad twice a day and dehydrated spuds. When I came back it was gone. Two minutes at the most. My tooth-paste was gone as well. That was the most expensive trot to the lav that I ever had, I know that. Boy, there's some thieving rascals round that camp.

SMITH: You should have reported it to the RSM. Had a personal kit inspection.

WHITAKER: Ah, what would have been the use? I wouldn't have got it back. If anybody pinched a watch like that he wouldn't leave it lying around in his locker, man. He'd want his head looking at. I've never bought another one since then. I haven't had the heart for it. What time did you say it was, Sarnt?

MITCHEM: I've just told you.

WHITAKER: I forgot.

MITCHEM: Quarter past.

WHITAKER: Roll on. Roll on my relief and let me get my head down. Sergeant Mitchem?

MITCHEM: What is it? What's up now?

WHITAKER: What time we setting off?

MITCHEM: I'll tell you. When it's time to move. We won't leave you behind. Don't worry. No need to flap.

[WHITAKER, *who has been talking to take his mind off other things, relapses into silence.*]

MITCHEM [*takes out his water bottle and has a drink. He glances across at the Prisoner and hands the water bottle to Macleish*]: Here, Jock. See'f Noisy Harry wants a gob.

MACLEISH: Right, Sarge. [MACLEISH *offers the water bottle to the Prisoner who accepts it gratefully. The* PRISONER *takes two pulls at the bottle, wipes the mouth, recorks it, and hands it back to Macleish who, in turn, returns it to Mitchem.*] Your bottle.

MITCHEM [*glances up from cleaning the sten as* MACLEISH *places the water bottle on the table*]: Right. Thanks.

MACLEISH [*anxious to start a conversation*]: He doesn't seem a bad sort of bloke.

MITCHEM: Who? Him?

MACLEISH: I suppose there's good and bad wherever you look. I mean, he's quiet enough.

MITCHEM: What did you expect?

MACLEISH: Oh I don't know . . . You hear these tales. I suppose it is all over? Up country, I mean?

MITCHEM: You saw them coming through, lad.

MACLEISH: Aye. Only I was wondering if they'd taken many prisoners themselves. The Japs, I mean.

MITCHEM: Search me.

MACLEISH: It seems to me . . . I've been thinking it over, like, in my mind. And I was thinking, at the little time it's taken them to get down here – as far as this – they couldn't have had a lot of resistance.

I mean, do you think it's possible there's been a sort of general jacking in from our lads?

MITCHEM: Happen. I don't know.

MACLEISH: I mean, if there'd been anything like a scrap at all they'd still be at it now, if you see what I mean.

MITCHEM: It follows. They might be still at it, for all we know. Mopping up. We don't know how much of the front still stands – if any. It could be just a section of the line packed in.

MACLEISH: I was wondering about Donald – that's my brother.

MITCHEM: Yeh?

MACLEISH: Well, if you work on the assumption that it's all over – that they've come straight through . . .

MITCHEM: It doesn't do to count on 'ifs' in this lark.

MACLEISH: No. But if they have it's likely that they've copped a lot of prisoners, the Japs. That stands to reason.

MITCHEM: That's fair enough.

MACLEISH: So it's possible my brother is a P.O.W. already.

MITCHEM: There's a chance of that.

MACLEISH: You hear so many stories – you know, on how the Japs treat P.O.W.s.

MITCHEM: Pretty rough, they reckon.

MACLEISH: I'm not so sure. You hear all kinds of things. As if they're almost . . . animals. But this bloke seems a decent sort of bloke.

MITCHEM: It's hard to tell.

MACLEISH: I mean, he's a family man himself.

MITCHEM: So what? Is that supposed to make a difference?

MACLEISH: He's human at least.

MITCHEM: What do you want for your money? Dracula? Look, son, forget the home and family bull. You put a bloke in uniform and push him overseas and he's a different bloke to what he was before. I've watched it happen scores of times.

MACLEISH: But if a bloke's got a wife and family himself . . .

MITCHEM: You get a bloke between your sights and stop to wonder if he's got a family, Jock, your family's not got you. There's half of them got families and most of them are nigs like us who don't know why we're here or what it's all in aid of. It's not your worry that. You're not paid to think.

MACLEISH: I used to wonder ... Worried me a lot ... I've often wondered, if it came to the push, was it inside me to kill a man.

MITCHEM: It's inside all of us. That's the trouble. Just needs fetching out, and some need more to bring it out than others.

MACLEISH: You know – when we got this one – when he first came in – I couldn't do it. I just couldn't move. I don't know now whether I'm sorry or I'm glad.

MITCHEM: You'll do it if it's necessary.

MACLEISH: I'm not worried, mind. I mean, I'm not afraid or anything like that. At least, I don't think I'm afraid no more than anybody else. I think if it was outside it would be different. The way you look at things, I mean. If it was him or me. Something moving about in the trees – something you can put a bullet in and not have to ... have to look into its eyes.

MITCHEM: I've told you once – you think too much. Outside or else in here – what's the difference?

MACLEISH: Outside he's got a fighting chance.

MITCHEM: Don't come that. It's not a game of darts. You can't wipe the board clean and start all over again. Mugs away. The mugs have had it. There are far too many mugs about. We're all mugs, and I'll tell you why. I'll tell you what's the trouble with this world, Jock – bints.

MACLEISH [amused]: Go on!

MITCHEM: It's right. Straight up. They cause more upset than enough. Half the scrapping in this world is over judies. There's half the blokes out here now who'd be sitting back in Blighty still with wangled home postings if it wasn't for a bint. It's bints who go a bundle over uniforms. You take a bloke – an ordinary bloke who gets called up. He doesn't want to go. He doesn't want to come out here, or if he does he's round the bend. Then, one day, this poor Charlie winds up with a bird – it happens to us all in the end. A blonde bird, happen, with small brains and big breasts. She whips him up the dancers once and that's the end of that. She likes the colour of his uniform and that makes him feel big. Six months before he was sitting behind a desk, copping on a weekly, picking his nose, and chatting up the pigeons on the window-sill. Now – all at once – he feels like he's a man. Before he knows where he is he's standing on the boat deck and the bint's waving him off from the docks with a bitsy hanky and tears clogging up her powder. My hero stuff. The captain blows the whistle on the bridge. The gang-plank's up. There's a military band on the quay-side, best boots and battledress, playing 'Where was the Engine Driver?' 'Goodbye Dolly I must leave you'. So there stands Charlie Harry, five foot four in his socks, and feeling like he's Clive of India, Alexander the Great, and Henry Five rolled into one.

MACLEISH: You're a real one for handing out the patter.

MITCHEM: Few weeks after that he's on his back with his feet in the air and a hole as big as your fist in his belly. And he's nothing.

MACLEISH [uneasily]: I reckon that it's you who thinks too much.

MITCHEM: I'm not a thinking kind of man. I look at facts. It happens to us all. Do you think that bint is going to float off to a nunnery? [Indicating the Prisoner] Just take a look at him. For all you know, his missis back in Tokyo thinks he's a sort of Rudolph Valentino.

MACLEISH: If she does she wants glasses.

MITCHEM: Happen so. But that's the way it is. So just you drop the home and bint and family bull. You might end up like him.

MACLEISH: How's that?

MITCHEM: What do you mean?

MACLEISH: So how does he end up when we head back?

MITCHEM: We're stacking him.

MACLEISH: That's what I understood. You mean we're leaving him behind.

MITCHEM: It's a sticky number as it is. We've got to go right through the lot of them. We'd never make it with a prisoner as well. It's odds against us now. With him as well we wouldn't stand a chance.

MACLEISH: I was beginning to get quite fond of him.

MITCHEM: He's no use now. He couldn't tell us any more than we know already. He's no cop to us. He's lost his value.

MACLEISH: Are we going to leave him here?

MITCHEM: Yeh.

MACLEISH: In the hut?

MITCHEM: That's right.

MACLEISH: That's a bit risky, isn't it?

MITCHEM: How do you mean?

MACLEISH: Suppose they find the track up here? Suppose the Japs come up and cut him loose? He lets them know what time we left. How many there are of us.

MITCHEM: He won't.

MACLEISH: Aye, but if he did? If they knew how much start we had on them they'd catch us up in no time. If he could tell them that . . .

MITCHEM: He won't.

MACLEISH: There's nothing to stop him.

MITCHEM: I've told you twice, he won't!

MACLEISH: I mean, it seems to me the risk's as big as if we tried to take him back with us. They know we're somewhere in this area. It's only a matter of time before they find this place.

MITCHEM: They don't know anything.

MACLEISH: They know we're round about here somewhere. Why else would they be bashing out the patter on the set?

MITCHEM: It's regular procedure with the Nips. Routine stuff. They push out muck in English on the off-chance. To put the wind up anyone who might be hanging round. It doesn't mean a thing.

MACLEISH: We won't have time to cover up the entrance of the track again. We'll have to go straight through. I mean, the path up here is going to be wide open. It's going to be like putting up a sign. The minute we move out of here it's ten to one they'll find the track straight off.

MITCHEM: They'll find him, that's all.

MACLEISH: Aye. But he can tell them. About us.

MITCHEM: He won't tell anybody. Anything.

MACLEISH: What's to stop him?

MITCHEM: I'll see to that.

MACLEISH: I fail to see what you can do about it.

MITCHEM: You don't have to.

MACLEISH: You're not . . . you're not going to knock him off?

MITCHEM: Just you do your job, Mac, that's all.

MACLEISH: You're not going to knock him off!

MITCHEM: Do you want to do it?

MACLEISH: He's a p.o.w.!

MITCHEM: Shut up.

MACLEISH: You can't kill him!

MITCHEM: That's my worry.

MACLEISH: The man's a prisoner-of-war!

MITCHEM: There's thousands more like him between this mob and base. It's him that's playing at home today, not you and me. If anybody's p.o.w.s it's us – not him.

MACLEISH: He gave himself up.

MITCHEM: He should have had more sense.

MACLEISH: You can't just walk him outside and put a bullet into him.

MITCHEM: No. I know that. It'd make too much noise.

MACLEISH [glancing down at the bayonet he holds in his hand]: Oh, God . . . Not that.

MITCHEM: Do you think I'm looking forward to it?

MACLEISH: Not that . . . Not like that.

MITCHEM: I've got six men and one report to come out of this lot. If I hang on to him it could work out I lose the whole patrol. I could lose more than that. For all we know, the unit's sitting back on its backside with thousands of these little Harries streaming down in that direction. You reckon I should lose my sleep over him?

MACLEISH: There must be something else.

MITCHEM: There isn't.

MACLEISH: There's another way.

MITCHEM: It's no good.

MACLEISH: Suppose we tied him up and ditched him in the bushes. Round the back, say. Out of sight. So it took a while for them to find him.

MITCHEM: It's no good!

MACLEISH: It's a damn sight better than doing him in.

MITCHEM: Is that what you think? Use your head. Do you think I haven't thought of that already? We hide him up out here he starves to death. That could take days. Do you think that's doing him a favour?

MACLEISH: What do you think you're doing?

MITCHEM: Me? My job. What they pay me to do.

MACLEISH: To knock off P.O.W.s!

MITCHEM: To put first things first.

MACLEISH: It's bloody murder, man!

MITCHEM [*crossing to Macleish*]: 'Course it is. That is my job. That's why I'm here. And you. [*He indicates his stripes.*] That's why I'm wearing these. And I'm wearing these 'cause I'm the one that makes decisions. Like this. If you want to do that, Jock, you can have my job right now. Here and now. It stinks. To me, it stinks. It stinks to me to do for him. But, come to that, the whole lot stinks to me. So what am I supposed to do? Turn conshi? Jack it in? Leave the world to his lot?

MACLEISH: I've got a brother who could just be sitting back – right now. Like him.

MITCHEM: Jock, I can smell your kind a mile away.

MACLEISH: What's that supposed to mean?

MITCHEM: The Bamforth touch.

MACLEISH: Bammo?

MITCHEM: You're as bad as Bamforth, boy.

MACLEISH: Me! You think that I'm like Bamforth?

MITCHEM: All the bloody way.

MACLEISH: You're off your nut.

MITCHEM: It's the book. According to the book. You can't forget the book. All along the road – the book. It doesn't work. You'd make a right pair. Nothing to choose between you – except that Bammo fiddles it to suit himself. You like to come the greater glory of mankind.

MACLEISH: It seems to me you're talking out of the back of your head.

MITCHEM: Don't you believe it. And to think that it was me who put you up for that tape. You're right – I must be going round the bend.

MACLEISH: You can strip me when you want. You know what you can do with the tape.

MITCHEM: And wouldn't that be lovely, eh? Wouldn't that just suit you down to the ground?

MACLEISH: How's that?

MITCHEM: It lets you out of this. On the ground floor. You're back in the ranks. One of the boys and none of the responsibility.

MACLEISH: Perhaps I'd rather be one of the boys.

MITCHEM: You can say that again. So why did you cop on for the tape in the first place?

MACLEISH: I've never complained about doing my job – that doesn't mean I'm willing to be a party to what you're suggesting.

MITCHEM: Lad, have you got lots to learn? How did you reckon it was going to be? Like in the comics? Fearless Mac Macleish charging up a little hill with a score of grenades and highland war cries? Wiping out machine guns single-handed? The gallant lance-jack gutting half a dozen Nips with a Boy Scout penknife and a Union Jack? Walking back to Jock-land with enough medals to sink a destroyer?

MACLEISH: You're talking through your hat.

MITCHEM [crossing to Macleish]: Yeh? Reckon, do you? Happen so. Perhaps you're right. You happen haven't got the guts for that. I'll tell you this much, boy – a touch like that's the easiest thing on earth. The army's full of square-head yobs who keep their brains between their legs. Blokes who do their nuts for fifteen seconds and cop a decoration, cheer boys cheer, Rule Britannia, and death before dishonour. All right. Why not? Good luck to them. Lads like that win wars so they should have the medals. They deserve them. But a touch like this comes harder. The trouble is with war – a lot of it's like this – most of it. Too much. You've that to learn.

MACLEISH: There's nothing you can teach me.

MITCHEM: You're dead right there.

MACLEISH: I make my own decisions.

MITCHEM: It's the only way. I'll just say this much, Jock: before you get much older you'll grow up. If this war shapes the way I think it will, you'll grow up, lad, in next to no time. [He crosses towards *table.*] Before the month is out you'll do a dozen jobs like this before you have your breakfast. [*He sits at table.*] So just think on.

WHITAKER [*turning at window*]: Sergeant Mitchem.

MITCHEM: You again? What is it now?

WHITAKER: I . . . I was wondering what the time was now.

MITCHEM: Not again! What's up? Do you want changing?

WHITAKER: It was just that I was wondering what time it was.

MITCHEM [*glances at his watch*]: Half past – all but.

WHITAKER: I thought it must be getting on that way.

MITCHEM: Another minute and I'll give the lads a shout.

[*The* PRISONER *gestures towards his breast pocket.*]

MACLEISH: Sarnt . . . Sergeant Mitchem!

MITCHEM [*glancing round*]: I ought to change my name. What's your complaint?

MACLEISH: It's him. I think there's something that he wants.

MITCHEM: If it's outside he can't. Tell him to hold it.

MACLEISH: Something in his pocket.

MITCHEM: Again? Oh – all right. O.K. See what it is. You get it for him.

MACLEISH: Right. [*To the Prisoner*] Now, you behave yourself, my lad. [MACLEISH *opens the Prisoner's breast pocket and extracts the wallet.*] Is this it? [*The* PRISONER *shakes his head.* MACLEISH *replaces the wallet and takes a cigarette case from the Prisoner's pocket.*] Is this it? Is it this that you were wanting? [*The* PRISONER *nods his head.*] Is it all right for the prisoner to have a drag, Sarge?

MITCHEM: Yeh. O.K.

MACLEISH [*he hands the case to the Prisoner who takes out two cigarettes, offering one to Macleish*]: Who? Me? You're giving one to me? [*He takes the proffered cigarette. The* PRISONER *closes the case and places it on the form.*] That's . . . that's very kind of you. [MACLEISH *takes a box of matches from his pocket.*] My name's Macleish. [*Points to himself*] Macleish. Do you understand? [*Pointing again to himself*] Macleish – me. [*He points to the Prisoner.*] Who – are – you? [*The* PRISONER *places his hands on his head.*] Is that the only thing you know?

MITCHEM [*crosses towards the sleeping figures of Bamforth, Evans, and*

Johnstone]: I shouldn't get too attached to him. [*He shakes Johnstone.*] Johnno! . . . Johnno!

[MACLEISH *gives the Prisoner a light behind the following dialogue.*]

JOHNSTONE [*wakes and sits up*]: Yeh?

MITCHEM: Half past.

JOHNSTONE [*rubs his eyes*]: Right.

MITCHEM [*crosses and shakes Bamforth*]: Come on, come on! Wakey-wakey, rise and shine. Let's have you! [BAMFORTH *sits up as* MITCHEM *crosses to wake Evans.*] Evans! Evans, lad!

EVANS [*sitting up*]: I feel horrible.

MITCHEM: You look it. Get your skates on. Let's be having you. The sun's burning your eyes out. Move yourselves, then!

EVANS: What's the time, Sarnt?

MITCHEM: Don't you start that as well. It's turned half past. [*He crosses to table and sits down, then glances across at Bamforth and Evans, who have not, as yet, made any attempt to rise.*] Come on! I said, move yourselves!

BAMFORTH: I've got a mouth like the inside of a tram driver's glove.

EVANS: Had a good kip, Bammo boy?

BAMFORTH: What? Kipping next to you? Kipping with a Taff? I'd rather bed down with an Eskimo's grannie. [*He lights a cigarette.*] I was having a smashing dream, though, son.

EVANS: Who was she?

BAMFORTH: Why should I tell you – you dream about your own. You dream about the milk-maids, Taff. They're more in your line. Have a sordid nightmare. The bints in my dreams have got class. Society bints.

EVANS: I bet they are.

BAMFORTH: Straight up.

JOHNSTONE: What do you know about society bints, Bamforth?

BAMFORTH: All the lot. You have to kiss them first.

[EVANS *laughs.*]

JOHNSTONE [*now on his feet*]: Got all the answers, haven't you?

BAMFORTH: Most of them. You've got to have with bints.

MITCHEM: All right, less of the love life, Bamforth. Let's have you on your feet.

[BAMFORTH *and* EVANS *rise and adjust their uniforms as* JOHN-
STONE *crosses to the table.*]

JOHNSTONE: Anything fresh?

MITCHEM [*shakes his head*]: Not yet. We haven't tried the set again.
Nothing new outside. [*He glances up as* BAMFORTH *crosses towards
the door.*] What you on, then?

BAMFORTH [*at door*]: I want to go outside!

MITCHEM: What for?

BAMFORTH: I can't help it.

MITCHEM: I don't want anybody moving round outside.

BAMFORTH: It's not my fault!

MITCHEM: All right. Go on. And make it sharp.

BAMFORTH [*to Smith*]: So what am I supposed to do? Write out an
application?

MITCHEM: If you're going, Bamforth, you'd better get off now.

BAMFORTH [*opens door*]: All right! [*To Smith*] So long.

EVANS [*crossing to stand by Smith*]: Bring me back a coconut, boy!

BAMFORTH [*as he exits*]: Fetch your own.

MITCHEM: Whitaker!

WHITAKER [*turning at window*]: Sarge?

MITCHEM: Cover him outside.

WHITAKER: Righto.

JOHNSTONE: What time we pushing off?

MITCHEM: Another half an hour, happen. Maybe more. As soon as it
gets dark enough to give us cover.

JOHNSTONE [*inclining his head towards the Prisoner*]: And him?

MITCHEM: It's settled what we're going to do with him.

JOHNSTONE [*takes out a packet of cigarettes and offers one to Mitchem*]:
Who?

MITCHEM [*shakes his head, declining the cigarette*]: Meaning what?

JOHNSTONE [*lights his own cigarette before answering*]: Who gets to do
the job?

MITCHEM: Are you volunteering?

JOHNSTONE [*blows out a cloud of smoke*]: I don't mind.

MITCHEM: Do you know, I think you would at that.

JOHNSTONE: Somebody's got to do it.

MITCHEM: It's got to be arranged yet, has that. We could draw lots. I don't know – perhaps I ought to do the job myself.

JOHNSTONE: It wants doing quick.

MITCHEM: I know.

JOHNSTONE: And quiet.

MITCHEM: I know.

JOHNSTONE: It's a skilled job.

MITCHEM: I know all that!

JOHNSTONE: So it wants somebody who knows what they're doing. You or me. We could toss up.

MITCHEM: Look – don't try and teach me my job, eh?

JOHNSTONE: Only trying to help. Just making a suggestion. It wants a professional touch. [*He glances across at the Prisoner who is still smoking.*] Who gave him that?

MITCHEM: You what?

JOHNSTONE [*crosses and grasps the Prisoner's wrist*]: Macleish! Have you been keeping him in smokes?

MITCHEM: I gave him permission.

JOHNSTONE [*releasing the Prisoner's hand in disgust*]: All right. Carry on.

MACLEISH: I didn't give him the fag, in any case. [*He indicates his own cigarette.*] As a matter of fact, it was him who gave me this.

JOHNSTONE: Going mates already?

MACLEISH: 'Course not.

JOHNSTONE: What's up then? Do you fancy him?

MACLEISH: I can't see that there's any harm in accepting a fag from the bloke.

JOHNSTONE: You wouldn't.

MACLEISH: There's no harm in that!

JOHNSTONE: Not much. You ought to go the whole way, lad. Turn native. You'll be eating your connor from banana leaves next. I wouldn't touch his stinking wog tobacco.

MACLEISH: It's just an ordinary cigarette.

JOHNSTONE: You what? Let's have a shufti.

MACLEISH [*holding up his cigarette for Johnstone's inspection*]: It's just the same as any other cigarette. There's no difference.

JOHNSTONE [*taking the cigarette from Macleish*]: You wouldn't chuckle. It's the same all right. There's not a bit of difference. It's a Blighty fag. [*He snatches the cigarette from the Prisoner.*] They're British smokes. They're British army issue!

MITCHEM [*rising and crossing to join Johnstone*]: Give us hold. [JOHNSTONE *hands one of the cigarettes to Mitchem, who examines it closely.*] They're army issue right enough. He must have thieved them from the lads up country.

[MITCHEM, MACLEISH, *and* JOHNSTONE *turn and look at the Prisoner.*]

EVANS [*crossing to join the group*]: What's the matter, Jock? What's happened?

MACLEISH: It's him. It's bright boy there. He's carrying a load of British issue fags.

EVANS: How did he get hold of them?

JOHNSTONE: How do you think? You can have three guesses. The thieving Nip!

MITCHEM [*drops the cigarette and grinds it beneath his heel*]: If there's one thing gets my hump it's knocking off – it's looting.

JOHNSTONE [*holding out the cigarette to Macleish*]: Well, come on, Jock, you'd better finish it. You're the one he gave it to. You reckon you're his mate.

MACLEISH [*snatching the cigarette*]: I'll ram it down his rotten throat! I'll make him eat the rotten thing! [*He hesitates – for a moment we feel that he is about to carry out the threat – he hurls the cigarette across the room.*]

JOHNSTONE: You don't want to waste it, Jock. Not now you've started it. You never know how much that fag has cost. He's happen stuck his bayonet end in some poor Herb for that.

EVANS: There's some of them would kill their mothers for a drag.

MITCHEM [*to Macleish*]: And you were telling me how they treat P.O.W.s.

EVANS: He wants a lesson, Sarge. He ought to have a lesson taught to him.

MACLEISH: I'll kill him!

MITCHEM: Will you? You swop sides quick. [*There is a pause as they turn to look at the* PRISONER, *who, uncertain of their attitude towards him, picks up the case, opens it, and offers a cigarette to Mitchem.*] Stick 'em! [MITCHEM *strikes the case from the Prisoner's hand. The* PRISONER *raises his hands and places them on his head – on this occasion, however, the action is without humour.*] Thieving slob!

JOHNSTONE [*raising a fist*]: Who goes in first?

MITCHEM: Hold it.

JOHNSTONE [*advancing threateningly on the Prisoner*]: Who gets first crack?

MITCHEM: Hold it a sec.

[*Johnstone checks himself.*]

MACLEISH [*almost to himself*]: My brother's just nineteen. He's only been out here a couple of months. I haven't seen him since he docked. They whipped him straight up country. He's only just nineteen. [*A loud appeal to the patrol – as if in the hope of receiving a denial.*] For all I know he's dead!

MITCHEM: Jock – see'f he's lugging anything else he's lifted from our lads.

MACLEISH [*moving to the Prisoner*]: Get up! Get on your feet! [*The* PRISONER *cowers on the form and* MACLEISH *jerks him savagely to his feet.*] Do as you're told! [MACLEISH *goes through the Prisoner's pocket and removes the wallet.*] There's this.

JOHNSTONE [*taking the wallet*]: I'll have a look at what's in this. You carry on.

MACLEISH [*as the Prisoner reacts slightly at the loss of the wallet*]: Stand still!

[MACLEISH *goes through the Prisoner's trouser pockets and removes the usual miscellaneous assortment of articles: handkerchief, keys, loose change, etc.* MACLEISH *places these on the form.* JOHNSTONE, *slowly and carefully, tears the photographs into pieces and drops these and the wallet on the floor. The* PRISONER *starts forward and* MACLEISH *rises and strikes him across the face.* BAMFORTH, *who has just re-entered from the veranda, notices this incident.*]

MACLEISH: I said, stand still!

BAMFORTH: What's up? What's he done to ask for that?

EVANS: He's been looting, Bammo. From our lads.

BAMFORTH [*crossing to join the group around the Prisoner*]: He's been what?

MACLEISH: We caught him with a fag-case stuffed with British army smokes!

BAMFORTH: You Scotch nit! You dim Scotch nit! I gave him them!

MITCHEM: You did?

BAMFORTH: I'm telling you. I gave him half a dozen snouts!

EVANS: You gave them him?

[MACLEISH *edges away from the Prisoner and* BAMFORTH *positions himself between the Prisoner and the members of the patrol.*]

BAMFORTH: What's the matter, Taff? Are your ears bad? I slipped him half a dozen nubs!

MACLEISH: I didn't know. I thought ... I thought he'd knocked them off.

JOHNSTONE [*to Bamforth*]: And who gave you permission?

BAMFORTH: I've had this out with you before. You show where it says I have to grease up to an N.C.O. before I hand out fags. What's mine's my own. I decide what I do with it.

MACLEISH: How was I to know? I ... I've told you, boy, I thought he'd knocked them off.

BAMFORTH: You know what thought did.

MACLEISH [*searching for words*]: How was I to know? ... I mean, he gave one of them to me ... I'd lit it up ... I was having a drag ... I was halfway down the lousy thing before I realized, you know – I mean, before I knew it was a Blighty fag ... So how was I to feel? ... What would you have done? ... You tell me, Bammo ... I could have choked, you know ... I've got a brother who's up country.

BAMFORTH: If he's dropped in with a gang of Nips who think like you, God help the kiddie. God help him!

MACLEISH: I thought he'd looted them!

BAMFORTH: And so you pull the big brave hero bull. The raving highlander. Aren't you the boy? So what you waiting for? Well, come on, Jocko, finish off the job! [BAMFORTH *grabs the Prisoner, pinning his arms, and swings him round, holding him towards Macleish.*] Come on, come on! Come on, he's waiting for the hump. Let's see you slot him, Jock! Drop him one on! Let's see you do your stuff! Smash his face for him! Drop him one on!

MACLEISH: Lay off it, Bamforth.

MITCHEM: O.K., Bamforth, jack it in.

BAMFORTH: Haven't any of you got the guts to go the bundle? You were snapping at the leash when I walked in. What about you, Taff? You want to have a crack at him?

MITCHEM: I said drop it.

BAMFORTH [*loosing his hold on the Prisoner*]: I didn't start it.
   [*The* PRISONER *sits on form and returns the articles to his trouser pockets.*]

EVANS: It was a mistake, Bammo.

BAMFORTH: You bet it was.

EVANS: We thought he'd whipped them.

BAMFORTH [*stoops and picks up the wallet and a piece of the torn photographs*]: You bastards. You even had to rip his pictures up. You couldn't leave him them even!

EVANS: I'll give you a hand to pick them up.

BAMFORTH: You couldn't even leave him them!

EVANS [*bends down and collects the torn pieces of the photographs*]: Happen he can stick them together again, Bammo. Here's a bit with a head on it. He could stick them together, easy enough, with a pot of paste and a brush.

BAMFORTH: Aw ... Dry up, you Welsh burk.

EVANS [*rises and crosses to the Prisoner*]: Tojo ... Tojo, boy. [*The* PRISONER *looks up.*] I got your pieces for you. You can stick them together again. Pot of paste and a bit of fiddling and they'll be right as rain. [MITCHEM *and* MACLEISH *move away from the Prisoner.*] Good as ever they was ... Well, not quite as good happen, but if you don't mind the joins and do them careful it won't matter, will it? [EVANS *holds out the torn pieces, but the Prisoner, fearing further blows, is hesitant in accepting them.*] Go on, Tojo son, you have them back. Better than nothing, anyway. [*The* PRISONER *takes the torn fragments and examines them one by one.*] Some of them are only torn in two. All the face is there on that one. [*The* PRISONER *continues to examine the pieces.* EVANS *stoops to retrieve a scrap of a photograph which he had overlooked previously.*] A bit here I missed. Looks like a little bit of a little bit of a girlie. [*He examines the fragment closely.*] Oh no, it's a boy, is that. [*He presses the scrap into the hands of the Prisoner.*] You'll . . . you'll be needing that as well.

BAMFORTH [*handing the wallet to Evans*] : Here, Taff, stick him this.

EVANS: Right, boyo. [*He hands the wallet to the Prisoner.*] And here's your wallet, Tojo boy.

MACLEISH [*picks up the cigarette case from the floor and gives it to Bamforth*]: He's better have this back too. He'll . . . Maybe he'll be feeling in need of a smoke.

BAMFORTH: Yeh . . . Thanks, Jock. [*He crosses to return the cigarette case.*]

JOHNSTONE: Bamforth! Just a minute, lad.

BAMFORTH: Yeh?

JOHNSTONE: I'd like a look at that before you hand it on to him.

BAMFORTH: Ask him. Not me, It's his.

JOHNSTONE: He'll get it back. I only want it for a minute.

BAMFORTH [*hesitates, then crosses and hands the case to Johnstone*] : He'd better get it back.

JOHNSTONE: He will. [*He inspects the case, slowly turning it over in his hands, then tosses it to Bamforth.* BAMFORTH *crosses to return it to the Prisoner.*] Bamforth!

BAMFORTH [*turns*] : You want something else?

JOHNSTONE: No, lad. Nothing. I was just wondering, that's all.

BAMFORTH: Well?

JOHNSTONE: Are you feeling in a generous mood today?

BAMFORTH: What's that supposed to signify?

JOHNSTONE: Did you give him the case as well?

BAMFORTH: I gave him half a dozen fags, that's all. I haven't got a case myself to give away. I gave him half a dozen snouts, I've told you half a dozen times. The case belongs to him.

JOHNSTONE: Does it?

BAMFORTH: The case is his.

JOHNSTONE: That's interesting. You'd better have another shufti at it, then.

[BAMFORTH *inspects the case and is about to return it to the Prisoner.*]

MITCHEM: Pass it over, Bamforth.

BAMFORTH: What for? It's his.

MITCHEM: I'd like to once it over for myself.

BAMFORTH [*tosses the case to* MITCHEM, *who also examines it, then turns his glance upon the Prisoner*]: All right! So it's a British case!

JOHNSTONE: Made in Birmingham.

BAMFORTH: So what? What's that supposed to prove?

MITCHEM: So tell us now how he got hold of it.

BAMFORTH: I don't know. Don't ask me.

JOHNSTONE: I bloody do! The way he got the snouts.

BAMFORTH: I gave him the fags.

JOHNSTONE: So you say.

BAMFORTH: I gave him the fags!

MITCHEM: And what about the case?

BAMFORTH: Look – I don't know. I've told you – I don't know.

EVANS: So he has been on the lifting lark? Half-inching from the boys up country.

MACLEISH: It begins to look that way.

[MACLEISH *and* EVANS *move menacingly towards the Prisoner.*]

BAMFORTH [*planting himself between the Prisoner and Evans and Macleish*]: You've got it all sorted out between you.

EVANS: It stands to reason, man.

BAMFORTH: You ought to be in Scotland Yard, you lads. In Security.

MACLEISH: It's pretty obvious he's pinched the thing.

BAMFORTH: Is it?

EVANS: How else could he have got it, Bammo?

BAMFORTH: You pair of ignorant crones! Sherlock-Taffy-Bloody-Holmes and Charlie MacChan. Sexy Blake and his tartan boy assistant. How do I know where he got it from? It's you bright pair who seem to know the answers. You tell me. If I were you I'd have it cased for bloodstains and fingerprints with a magnifying glass. How does anybody cop on to a fag case? Eh? You buy them! In shops! With money! You know what money is, eh? Money, you know. The stuff they give you on a Friday night. Bits of paper and little round rings. That's the carry-on in my home town. Where you come from they still swop things for sheep.

MACLEISH: It's a British case, Bamforth.

BAMFORTH: You're a head case, Jock. I've got a little skin and blister back in Blighty. Twelve years old. She carts around a squinting Nippo doll. Know how she got it? One night, instead of being tucked up in her little bed, she was out roaming the streets with a chopper. She knocked off nine Nippo nippers in a night nursery and nicked a golliwog, two teddy-bears, and this here doll. You want to know how we found out? It's got 'Made in Japan' stamped across it's pink behind. Now, work that one out.

MITCHEM: It won't wash, Bamforth. The Nips don't import fancy swag. They churn it out themselves and flog it abroad.

BAMFORTH [*stepping aside to give Macleish and Evans access to the Prisoner*]: All right! Go on. Beat him up, then. Work him over. Enjoy yourselves for once. Have a good time. Look – listen. You want to know something? You want to know who's got the biggest hoard of loot in the Far East, bar none? Who's collected more Jap swag than any regiment? I'll introduce him. [BAMFORTH *crosses to rear of hut and raises Whitaker's hand.*] On my right and stepping in the ring at six stone six – the terror of the Newcastle Church Army Hostel: Private Winnie Whitaker!

WHITAKER [*embarrassed at being drawn into the proceedings*]: Cut it out, Bammo.

BAMFORTH: Take a bow, son. Here he is. The sole proprietor of the Samuel Whitaker War Museum. It's worth hard gelt in anybody's lingo.

[WHITAKER *manages to extricate his hand from Bamforth's grip.*]

MITCHEM: What are you getting at?

BAMFORTH: Ask the boy himself. He's the proud possessor. Come on, Whitaker, my old son, don't be bashful. Tell them all about your battle honours. What you did in the war, dad.

WHITAKER: I don't know what you're supposed to be talking about.

BAMFORTH: Don't you? Smudger knows. Smudger's seen it. He can bear me out.

SMITH: Leave the kid alone, Bammo. There's no harm in it.

BAMFORTH: It's true, isn't it?

SMITH: Look – lay off the lad.

BAMFORTH: Is it the truth?

SMITH: Yes . . . He's got a bit of swag.

BAMFORTH: A bit! That's the bloody understatement of the war, is that.

WHITAKER: It's only souvenirs, Bammo.

EVANS: What kind of souvenirs you got, Sammy?

BAMFORTH: He's got it in his locker back at camp. Smudge and me had a shufti one morning when he left it open. Well, come on Whitto, don't be shy. Tell them what you've got.

WHITAKER: Just some odds and ends, man, and a few things I've picked up, that's all.

BAMFORTH: Tell them!

WHITAKER: Some Jap buttons and a couple of rounds.

BAMFORTH: And the rest.

WHITAKER: A nippo cap badge and a belt.

BAMFORTH: Go on.

WHITAKER: That's all.

BAMFORTH: I've seen inside your locker.

WHITAKER: That's all there is.

BAMFORTH: You're lying, Whitaker!

WHITAKER: I'm not, man. I've not got anything else.

BAMFORTH: You're a lying get!

WHITAKER: Only some bits and pieces.

SMITH: Let him alone, Bamforth.

BAMFORTH: His locker's loaded with Jap loot. It's like a little Tokyo inside his locker.

WHITAKER: They're only souvenirs, Bammo.

BAMFORTH: Don't give me that. There's half the emperor's arsenal and the Imperial quartermaster's stores in there. When you get home with that lot, Whitaker, you won't half give the family the bull. Will you be able to chat them up, boy, on how you won the war. The Tyneside hero. [*To Evans and Macleish*] And you lot want to string the fives on Tojo just because he's got a Blighty fag case. If the Nips lay hands on Whitaker they'll work it out that he's a sort of military Al Capone. Him! Whitaker! Whining Whitaker! The boy who has a nervous breakdown at the thought of Madame

Butterfly. Show him a rice pudding and he gets the screaming ab-dabs. He's never even seen a Jap excepting that one there.

SMITH: Can't you leave the lad alone?

BAMFORTH: All right. I've done with him. But just for the book, Whitaker, just to put these boys here right – just tell them how you copped on to the spoils of war.

WHITAKER: I don't know. I just . . . they just came into my posses-ssion.

BAMFORTH: Tell them how!

WHITAKER: I swopped some things for them. In the NAAFI. Down the U.J. club. I swopped them for some stuff I had myself – with some blokes I met who'd come down from up country.

BAMFORTH: That's all I want to know.

WHITAKER: It's not a crime.

BAMFORTH: No. No, it's not a crime. [Crossing down-stage] It's not a crime to have a fag case either. Now, go on, Jock, beat up the Nip.

MACLEISH: You still haven't proved, to my satisfaction, that that's the way he got the case.

BAMFORTH: You try and prove it different.

MACLEISH [turning away from the Prisoner]: . . . Och, what's it matter, anyway . . .

MITCHEM: Evans!

EVANS: Sarge?

MITCHEM [tossing the cigarette case to Evans]: You'd better give him this back.

EVANS: Righto.

[EVANS gives the case to the PRISONER, who opens it, takes out a cigarette, and offers one to EVANS, who hesitates and then accepts. EVANS takes out a box of matches and gives the Prisoner a light.]

WHITAKER [desiring to change the conversation]: Sergeant Mitchem . . .

MITCHEM: What's your worry?

WHITAKER: I was wondering about the time . . .

MITCHEM: Do you ever do anything else?

WHITAKER: I mean about reliefs. For Smudger and myself. It's well turned half past now.

MITCHEM: I know! . . . All right. Who's next for stag?

MACLEISH [*collects his rifle and crosses to rear*]: Me, for one.

MITCHEM: Take over from Ticker Whitaker before he does his nut.

WHITAKER: I only mentioned it in case it might have slipped your memory, Sarge.

MITCHEM: Tick, tick, tick! You should have been a bloody clock.

WHITAKER [*having been relieved by Macleish, he crosses down-stage*]: I wasn't complaining. I thought you'd forgotten.

MITCHEM: I'm not likely to with you around. [*Points to his watch*] If ever this packs in on me I'll wrap you around my wrist. Evans!

EVANS: Sarge?

MITCHEM: Give Smudge a break. [*Indicating the Prisoner*] Bamforth, you just keep an eye on him.

BAMFORTH: He's all right.

MITCHEM: Just keep an eye on him, that's all.

EVANS [*collects his rifle and crosses towards Smith. As he approaches he shoulders his rifle and carries out a 'cod' guard mounting routine with exaggerated smartness.* SMITH *obeys the orders*]: Old guard . . . 'shun! Stand at . . . ease! 'Shun! . . . Slope . . . Arms! One – two-three, one – two-three, one! . . . Order . . . arms! One – two-three, one – two-three, one! Very good, Smudger boy. You should have joined the Guards. The sentries will now dismiss for a crafty smoke and a bit of abuse in the boiler house . . . old guard – to the guard room . . . Dis . . .

JOHNSTONE: All right, Evans. Cut out the funny stuff.

EVANS: You see how it is, Smudger? When you try to be regimental they won't have it. O.K., boyo, you scarper. I'll take over here.

SMITH: It's all yours, Taff.

[EVANS *takes up his position at the window as* SMITH *crosses down-stage.* WHITAKER *and* SMITH *prop their rifles against the wall.*]

WHITAKER: Hey, Taff!

EVANS: What is it, boy?

WHITAKER: Can I have a look at your book? That one you were reading out of earlier on?

EVANS: In my small pack, Whitto.

WHITAKER [*crossing to take magazine from Evans's pack which is on the form by the Prisoner*]: Thanks, Taffy.

BAMFORTH [*as* WHITAKER *gives the Prisoner a wide berth*]: It's all right, Whitto, he won't bite you, son. [BAMFORTH *watches* WHITAKER *as he takes the magazine from the pack and settles himself on the extreme end of the form.*] You trying to improve your mind?

WHITAKER: I just wanted to pass a few minutes on. [*He flicks through the pages.*] Where's that story that Taff was telling us about? The one with the Arabs.

SMITH: It's a serial, Sammy. No good starting that.

WHITAKER: I don't mind. It's something to read.

BAMFORTH: You screw the pictures, Whitaker. No good stuffing your head up with them long words. Have a butcher's at the corset adverts on the last page.

SMITH: He's not old enough for them.

BAMFORTH: He's got to start sometime. He can't stay ignorant for ever.

WHITAKER: Who's ignorant?

BAMFORTH: You are! Ignorant as a pig. Pig-ignorant, boy, that's you.

WHITAKER: That's all you know, Bamforth.

BAMFORTH: Hark at him! The innocent abroad. The voice of experience. They lock their daughters up in Newcastle when he's on leave. Go on, Whitaker, you've never been with a bint in your life.

WHITAKER: That just shows how much you know, boy!

SMITH: Never mind him, Sammy. He's pulling your leg.

WHITAKER: He doesn't know so much himself.

BAMFORTH: Have you ever had a woman, Whitaker?

WHITAKER: 'Course I have. I was courting when I left Blighty.

BAMFORTH: I bet.

SMITH: Newcastle girl, Sammy?

WHITAKER: No. Darlington lass. I met her at a dance once when I was stationed at Catterick.

BAMFORTH: Dancing! Get him! He'll be drinking beer and playing cards for money next.

WHITAKER: It was in a church hall – the dance, I mean. One of the lads in the billet took me. That's how I met this girl.

SMITH: Got a photograph?

WHITAKER: I've got a couple back at camp.

SMITH: What's she like? Bramah, eh?

WHITAKER: She's ... well, she's sort of pretty, you know, like. Mary. That's her name. Mary Pearson. Comes up to about my shoulder and sort of yellowish hair. Works for an insurance company. In the office. Oh, she's ... she's bloody pretty, Smudge. Nothing outstanding, like – but, boy, she's pretty. We was courting for three months very nearly. I was up there doing my basic training.

SMITH: Take her out much, did you?

WHITAKER: I used to get to meet her a couple of times a week, like. Whenever I could skive off. Get the bus from the camp centre into Darlington and meet her nights outside a shop. Some nights we'd go to the pictures – or dancing – or something – when I could afford it, like. I wasn't loaded them days. So most nights we'd just walk up through the park, you know. Along by the river. The middle of summer I was at Catterick. Was it hot then, boy! Oh, man ...! She's only seventeen just – is it a bit young, do you think?

SMITH: Doesn't seem to make much difference – these days.

WHITAKER: So we'd just walk along by the side of the river, like. Up as far as the bridge. Happen sit down and watch them playing bowls. Sit for ten minutes or so, get up and walk back. Just a steady stroll, you know. I never had much money – only my bus fare there and back sometimes – but it was ... Oh, boy! Oh, you know – we had some smashing times together, me and her. I wish I was back there now, boy.

SMITH: Write to her, do you?

WHITAKER: When I get the chance. When I'm back in camp. Every day if I've got the time.

SMITH: Roll on the duration, eh?

WHITAKER: I used to hear from her twice a week. I haven't had a letter for over a month. Almost six weeks.

SMITH: You know how it is, Sammy. Maybe she's busy.

WHITAKER: I don't know. I'm thinking happen she's got fixed up with another bloke.

SMITH: Maybe the mail's been held up.

WHITAKER: I get plenty from my mother and the old man. I think it's another bloke she's with.

SMITH: You don't want to think like that.

WHITAKER: The letters – the writing – things she said – it was different. Towards the last one, like.

SMITH: Happen be one waiting for you when you get back to-morrow.

WHITAKER: Aye. Happen so . . . I don't know. I've sort of given up, like. Hoping, you know.

[*It is early evening and the light has begun to dim. The jungle is silent and a stillness falls upon the patrol.* BAMFORTH *begins to sing – quietly and with a touch of sadness.*]

BAMFORTH: A handsome young private lay dying,
        At the edge of the jungle he lay.
        The Regiment gathered round him,
        To hear for the last words he'd say.
        'Take the trigger-guard out of my kidneys,
        Take the magazine out of my brain,
        Take the barrel from out of my back-bone,
        And assemble my rifle again . . .'

[*In an attempt to restore the previous mood,* BAMFORTH *rubs the top of the Prisoner's head playfully.*] Now then, Tojo, my old flowerpot, what did you think of that? That's better than you cop on from the Tokyo geisha fillies.

EVANS [*turning at window*]: It'll not be long before it's dark now, Sarge.

MACLEISH [*without turning from window*]: It's quiet out there. It's bloody quiet.

MITCHEM [*rising*]: Time we got ready for the push then. Got packed up. Got things – sorted out.

BAMFORTH [*having taken a swig from his water bottle, he wipes the lip and offers the bottle to the Prisoner*]: Come on, Tojo son. Get a gob of this before we go.

[*The* PRISONER *accepts the bottle gratefully.*]

JOHNSTONE: There's no more buckshees for the Nippo, Bamforth.

[*The* PRISONER, *sensing the meaning from Johnstone's tone, returns the water bottle to Bamforth without drinking.*]

BAMFORTH [*puts down the water bottle and turns to face Johnstone*]: I've warned you, Johnno. Don't overstep them tapes. I'll not take any more of the patter. Is it O.K. if I give the prisoner a drink, Sarge?

MITCHEM: You heard what Corporal Johnstone said, Bamforth.

BAMFORTH [*incredulous*]: You what?

JOHNSTONE: There's no more water for the Nippo.

BAMFORTH: Like hell there isn't. The bloke's got to drink.

MITCHEM: He's had a drink – earlier on this afternoon. I gave him one myself.

BAMFORTH: He's not a camel!

MITCHEM: I'm sorry, Bamforth. We've none to spare for him.

BAMFORTH: Sorry!

MITCHEM: We'll need every drop we've got for getting back. It's dead certain there'll be a gang of Nips around every water hole from here to base.

BAMFORTH: So we share out what we've got.

MITCHEM: No.

BAMFORTH: He gets half of mine.

MITCHEM: No! There's none for him.

BAMFORTH: He'll have to have a drink sometime. He can't go the distance without – you've got to get him back as well. [*He waits for a reply.*] We're taking him as well!

MITCHEM: I'm sorry.

JOHNSTONE: He's stopping where he is. [*He picks up the Prisoner's bayonet from the table.*] It's cobblers for him.

BAMFORTH: No.

MITCHEM: I've got no choice.

BAMFORTH: You said he was going back.

MITCHEM: He was – before. The circumstances altered. The situation's changed. I can't take him along.

BAMFORTH: What's the poor get done to us?

MITCHEM: It's a war. It's something in a uniform and it's a different shade to mine.

BAMFORTH [*positioning himself between the Prisoner and Johnstone*]: You're not doing it, Johnno.

JOHNSTONE: You laying odds on that?

BAMFORTH: For Christ's sake!

JOHNSTONE: It's a bloody Nip.

BAMFORTH: He's a man!

JOHNSTONE [*crossing a few paces towards the Prisoner*]: Shift yourself, Bamforth. Get out of the way.

BAMFORTH: You're not doing it.

MITCHEM: Bamforth, shift yourself.

BAMFORTH: You're a bastard, Mitchem.

MITCHEM: I wish to God I was.

BAMFORTH: You're a dirty bastard, Mitchem.

MITCHEM: As far as I'm concerned, it's all these lads or him.

BAMFORTH: It's him and me.

MITCHEM [*crossing to join Johnstone*]: Get to one side. That's an order.

BAMFORTH: Stick it.

MITCHEM: For the last time, Bamforth, move over.

BAMFORTH: Try moving me.

MITCHEM: I've not got time to mess about.

BAMFORTH: So come on, Whitaker! Don't sit there, lad. Who's side you on? [WHITAKER *rises slowly from the form. For a moment it would seem that he is going to stand by Bamforth but he crosses the room to stand beyond Mitchem and Johnstone.*] You've got no guts, Whitaker. You know that, boy? You've just got no guts.

WHITAKER: We've got to get back, Bammo.

BAMFORTH: You're a gutless slob!

WHITAKER: I've got to get back!

BAMFORTH: Evans. Taffy, Taff! [EVANS *turns from the window.*] Put the gun on these two, son.

EVANS: I reckon Mitch is right, you know. We couldn't get him back to camp, could we, boyo? The Nips must have a Div between the camp and us.

BAMFORTH: He's going to kill him, you nit!

EVANS: You never know about that fag case, do you, son?

BAMFORTH: What's the fag case got to do with it! ... Smudger! Smudger, now it's up to you.

SMITH: Don't ask me, Bammo. Leave me out of it.

BAMFORTH: You're in it, Smudge. You're in it up to here.

SMITH: I just take orders. I just do as I'm told. I just plod on.

BAMFORTH: The plodding on has stopped. Right here. Right here you stop and make a stand. He's got a wife and kids.

SMITH: I've got a wife and kids myself. Drop it, Bammo, it's like Mitch says – it's him or us.

BAMFORTH: Jock! . . . Jock! [MACLEISH *continues to stare out of the window.*] Macleish! . . . [MACLEISH *does not move.*] I hope they carve your brother up. Get that? I hope they carve your bloody brother up!

MITCHEM: All right, Bamforth, you've had your say. Now shift.

BAMFORTH: Shift me! Come on, heroes, shift me!

MITCHEM: Whitaker! Grab a gun and cover the Nip.

BAMFORTH: Don't do it, Whitaker. Stay out of it.

MITCHEM: Whitaker!

[WHITAKER *picks up a sten from the table and crosses to cover the Prisoner, who has realized the implications and is trembling with fear.* MITCHEM *and* JOHNSTONE *move forward to overpower Bamforth.* JOHNSTONE *drops the bayonet on the floor and, together with* MITCHEM, *grapples with* BAMFORTH. *As they fight the* PRISONER *begins to rise to his feet.*]

WHITAKER [*already in a state of fear himself*]: Get down! . . . Sit down! . . . [*The* PRISONER *continues to rise.*] Sit down, you stupid man, or I'll have to put a bullet into you . . . [*The* PRISONER *is standing upright as* WHITAKER'S *finger tightens on the trigger. A long burst from the sten shudders the hut and the bullets slam home into the body of the Prisoner like hammer blows. The* PRISONER *doubles up and falls to the floor. The fight stops. There is a pause.* WHITAKER *drops the sten and buries his face in his hands.*] God . . . God . . . God . . . [*His voice swells.*] Oh, God!

MITCHEM: Well, that should roust out every Nip from here to Tokyo. You've made a mess of that, lad. [WHITAKER, *uncomprehending, looks at his hands.* MITCHEM *seizes him by the shoulders and shakes him savagely.*] Come on, come on! Come out of it! He's just the first.

BAMFORTH: You've got the biggest souvenir of all. You've done it

this time, Whitaker. Take that and hang it on the front room
wall ...

[*Bamforth's words are cut short as* MITCHEM *strikes him across the
face.*]

MITCHEM: We've had enough from you.

[EVANS *and* MACLEISH *have left their posts and, together with*
SMITH, *are drawn in fascination towards the body of the Prisoner.*]

JOHNSTONE: All right. Get back. It's just a corpse. You'll see a whole
lot more like that before you've done.

MITCHEM: Right. All of you. We're moving out. In double time.
Get your gear together. Thirty seconds and we're off. Any longer
and this place will be rotten with Nips. Any man not ready stays
behind. Move!

[*The members of the patrol put on their packs, ammunition pouches,
etc.*]

MITCHEM: Johnno, ditch your stuff. Can you work the set? [JOHN-
STONE *nods assent and crosses to radio.*] Give it one last crack.
[JOHNSTONE *switches on the set and the crackle of interference grows
behind.*] We haven't got a snowball's chance in Hell of getting back.
So try and let them know the Japs have broken through.

JOHNSTONE [*nods and switches to 'transmit'*]: Blue Patrol calling Red
Leader ... Blue Patrol calling Red Leader ... Are you receiving
me ... Are you receiving me ... Come in Red Leader ... Over
... [JOHNSTONE *switches to 'receive' and the interference swells.*] ...
Not a rotten peep.

MITCHEM: All right. Jack it in.

JOHNSTONE [*rips off headphones, leaving the set switched on. He straps
on his ammunition pouches and picks up the sten from the floor.*]: Let's
have you then! We're pushing off!

MITCHEM [*picking up his own sten*]: Leave what you haven't got. And
move!

[*The members of the patrol collect their rifles and cross to the door.*
JOHNSTONE *glances out of the window.*]

JOHNSTONE: All clear.

MITCHEM [*opens the door*]: I'll break the trail, Johnno, you bring up
the rear. [JOHNSTONE *nods.*] All right, let's go.

[*One by one the members of the patrol follow* MITCHEM *through the door.* JOHNSTONE *is the last to leave. As the door closes behind Johnstone the interference increases on the set and suddenly it bursts into life.*]

OPERATOR [*on distort*]: ... Red Leader calling Blue Patrol ... Red Leader calling Blue Patrol ... Come in Blue Patrol ... Come in Blue Patrol ... Over ...

[*A machine gun chatters in the jungle and is joined by another. We hear the sound of one or two rifles and the screams of dying men. The noise of gunfire fades away, to leave only the whimper of one wounded man — it is Whitaker. The door is pushed open and* JOHNSTONE *enters. He has a bullet wound in his side and the blood is seeping through his shirt. Slamming the door shut, he leans upon it to regain his breath.*]

WHITAKER [*screams out from the jungle in fear*]: God! ... God! ... [*A final cry of terror louder than any we have heard previously.*] Mother ...!

[*We hear the sound of a single shot and Whitaker is dead.* JOHNSTONE *presses his hand to his side. The set splutters into life again.*]

OPERATOR [*on distort*]: ... Are you receiving me, Blue Patrol ... Are you receiving me ... Over ...

JOHNSTONE [*crosses slowly to the set, picks up hand-set, and switches to* '*transmit*']: Get knotted! All of you! You hear! The whole damn lot of you!

[JOHNSTONE *switches off the set and crosses towards the body of the Prisoner. As he passes the window there is a short burst of machine-gun fire. He ducks below window level. Squatting by the side of the body, he takes the cigarette case from the Prisoner's pocket and helps himself to a cigarette. Sticking the cigarette in his mouth, he returns the case to the Prisoner's pocket. He tugs the white silk scarf, now spattered with blood, from the Prisoner's neck and crawls across to beneath the window, where he ties the scarf round the barrel of his sten. It has all required a great effort, and he lights the cigarette and inhales deeply before continuing. Squatting below the window, he waves the white flag and, in turn, takes long pulls at the cigarette. For a moment there is complete silence and then a bird sings out in the jungle.*]

CURTAIN

DORIS LESSING

Each His Own Wilderness

EACH HIS OWN WILDERNESS

First Presented by the English Stage Society, at The Royal Court Theatre, London, on 23 March 1958, with the following cast:

TONY BOLTON	Colin Jeavons
MYRA BOLTON	Valerie Taylor
SANDY BOLES	Philip Bond
MIKE FERRIS	Vernon Smythe
PHILIP DURRANT	Ewen MacDuff
ROSEMARY	Sarah Preston
MILLY BOLES	Patricia Burke

Directed by John Dexter

SCENE

The hall of Myra Bolton's house in London

CHARACTERS OF THE PLAY

MYRA BOLTON *a middle-aged woman.*
TONY BOLTON *her son, aged 22.*
MILLY BOLES *a middle-aged woman, Myra's friend.*
SANDY BOLES *Milly's son, aged 22.*
MIKE FERRIS *an elderly Left Wing politician.*
PHILIP DURRANT *a middle-aged architect.*
ROSEMARY *a young girl engaged to Philip.*

ACT ONE

SCENE ONE

Before the curtain rises, an H-bomb explosion. CURTAIN UP *on the sound of blast. Silence. Machine-gun fire. The explosion again. These sounds come from tape-recording machine which has been left running.*

This is the hall of MYRA BOLTON'S *house in London, stairs ascending L back. Door L into living-room. Door R which is entrance from street. Window R looking into garden at front of the house.*

The essential furniture is a divan close to the foot of the stairs. A cupboard in the wall. A mirror. Odd chairs. A small radio.

Everything is extremely untidy: there are files, piles of newspapers, including the New Statesman, *posters lying about inscribed* BAN THE BOMB, WE WANT LIFE NOT DEATH, *etc. A typewriter on the floor. The radio is playing tea-room music behind the war-noises from the tape-recorder.*

[*After the second explosion* TONY BOLTON *comes in R. He is in Army uniform and has this day finished his Army service. He is a dark, lightly built, rather graceful youth, attractive and aware of it, but uneasy and on the defensive in the same way and for the same reasons as an adolescent girl who makes herself attractive as a form of self-assertion but is afraid when the attention she draws is more than gently chivalrous. His concern for his appearance is also due to the longing for the forms of order common to people who have never known order. He is at bottom deeply uneasy, tense and anxious, fluctuating between the good manners of those who use manners as a defence, the abrupt rudeness of the very young, and a plaintive, almost querulous appeal.*

He stands looking at the disorder in the room, first ironically and then with irritation. As the music reaches a climax of bathos, he rushes to radio and turns it off.]

TONY: What a mess. God, what a mess!

[*The sound of an H-bomb explosion gathering strength on the tape recorder. He turns to stare, appalled. Listens. Switches it off at explosion. There is a sudden complete silence.* TONY *breathes it in. He passes his hands over his hair, his eyes. He opens his eyes. He is staring at the window. Sunlight streams across the floor. He dives at the window, draws the curtains, making a half-dark, going to divan, lets himself fall limp across it. A moment's complete silence.*

The telephone rings.]

[*Querulously*] Oh, no, no, no. [*Leaps up, goes to telephone.*] Yes. It's me, Tony. No, I'm not on leave. I don't know where my mother is. I haven't seen her yet. Yes, Philip. I'll tell her. Who did you say? Who's Rosemary? O.K. [*Lets receiver fall back and returns to divan, where he lies as before, eyes closed.*]

[MYRA'S VOICE *upstairs, singing:* Boohoo, you've got me crying for you.]

MYRA'S VOICE: Where are you, darling? [*Continues singing.*]

[*She comes into sight at head of the stairs. A good-looking woman of about 45 or 50, and at the moment looking her age. She is wearing bagged trousers and a sweat-shirt. She peers down into the half-lit hall from the top of the stairs, and slowly comes down.*]

TONY [*languidly*]: Well, Mother, how are you?

MYRA: Tony! You might have let me know. [*She rushes at the window, pulls back the curtains, turns to look at him, the sunlight behind her.*]

TONY [*shading his eyes*]: Do we have to have that glare?

MYRA: Have you got leave?

TONY [*without moving*]: I didn't imagine it was necessary to remind you of the date my National Service finished.

MYRA: Oh, I see.

TONY: But, of course, if my coming is in any way inconvenient to you, I'll go away again.

MYRA [*stares and then laughs*]: Oh, Tony . . . [*Rushes across at him.*] Come on, get up out of that sofa.

[*He does not move. Then he languidly rises. She impulsively embraces him. He allows himself to be embraced. Then he kisses her gracefully on the cheek.*]

MYRA: Ohhh! What an iceberg! [*Laughs, holding him by the arms.*]
[*Suddenly he convulsively embraces her and at once pulls away.*]

Oh, darling, it is lovely to have you home. We must have a party to celebrate.

TONY: Oh, *no*.

MYRA: What's the matter?

TONY: A party. I knew you'd say a party.

MYRA: Oh, very well. [*Examining him, suddenly irritated*] For God's sake get out of that ghastly uniform. It makes you look like a . . .

TONY: What?

MYRA: A soldier.

TONY: I've been one for two years.

MYRA: Isn't that long enough?

TONY: I think I'm rather sorry to part with it. [*Teasing her, but half-serious*] Rather nice, the army – being told what to do, everything in its place, everything tidy . . .

MYRA: Tidy! It's lucky you weren't in Cyprus or Kenya or Suez – keeping order. [*Laughing angrily*] Keeping everything tidy.

TONY: Well?

MYRA: You don't believe in it. [*As he does not reply.*] You might have been killed for something you don't even believe in.

TONY: You're so delightfully old-fashioned. Getting killed for something you believe in is surely a bit of a luxury these days? Something your generation enjoyed. Now one just – gets killed. [*He has intended this to sound calmly cynical, but in spite of himself it comes out plaintive.*]

MYRA [*has an impulse to make a maternal protective gesture, suppresses it at the last moment. Says quietly, but between her teeth*]: All the same, get out of those clothes.

TONY [*angry, because he knows he has sounded like a child*]: All right – but what do you suppose you look like?

MYRA [*cheerfully*]: Oh, the char, I know. But I've been cleaning the stairs. If I'd known you were coming . . .

TONY: Oh, I know, you'd have changed your trousers.

MYRA: I might even have worn a dress.

TONY [*languidly charming*]: Really, Mother, when you look so charming when you try, do you have to look like that?

MYRA [*cheerfully impatient*]: Oh, don't be such a little – no one can look charming cleaning the stairs.

TONY [*unpleasantly*]: So you were cleaning the stairs. And who did you expect to find sitting here?

MYRA: Why, no one.

TONY: You came creeping down. Were you going to put your hands over my eyes and say: 'Peekaboo'? [*Gives a young, aggressive, unhappy laugh.*]

MYRA: It was dark. I couldn't see who it was. It might have been anybody.

TONY: Of course, anybody. Why don't you put your hands over my eyes now and say 'Peekaboo'? How do you know? – I might rather like it. Then you could bite my ear, or something like that. [*Gives the same laugh.*]

MYRA [*quietly*]: Tony, you've just come home.

TONY: Well, and why did you come creeping down the stairs?

MYRA: I came down because the telephone was ringing earlier. I came to see. Did you take it?

TONY: So it was. Yes. I forgot.

MYRA [*cheerfully*]: You're a bloody boor, Tony.

TONY [*wincing*]: Do you have to swear?

MYRA: Well, now you're home I suppose I'll have to stop. [*In a refined voice*] There are times, dear, when you do rather irritate me.

TONY [*stiffly*]: I've already said that I'm quite prepared to go somewhere else if it's inconvenient for you to have me at such short notice.

[MYRA *watches him: she is on the defensive.*]

Well? Who is that you've got upstairs with you? Who is it this time?

MYRA: How do you know I've got anyone upstairs with me?

TONY: Who *is* it upstairs?

MYRA [*offhand*]: Sandy.

TONY: Sandy who?

MYRA: Don't be silly. Sandy Boles.

TONY [*staring*]: But he's my age.

MYRA: What of it?

TONY: He's my age. He's 22.

MYRA: I didn't ask to see his birth certificate when I engaged him.

TONY: Engaged him?

MYRA [*briskly*]: He's at a loose end. I wanted someone to help me. He's here for a while.

TONY [*slowly*]: He's staying here?

MYRA: Why not? This empty house . . . when you're not here it's so empty.

TONY: He's in my room?

MYRA: Yes. He can move out.

TONY: Thanks. [*They stare at each other like enemies.*]

MYRA: Well, what is it?

TONY: Perhaps you'd rather I moved out.

MYRA: Tony, mind your own bloody business. I've never interfered with anything you did.

TONY: No. [*Half-bitter, half-sad*] No, you never did. You never had time.

MYRA [*hurt*]: That's unfair.

TONY: And where's dear Sandy's mamma?

MYRA: Milly is in Japan.

TONY: And what is dear Sandy's errant mamma doing in Japan?

MYRA: She's gone with a delegation of women.

TONY [*laughing*]: Oh I see. They are conveying the greetings of the British nation, with an apology because our Government uses their part of the world for H-bomb tests.

MYRA [*wistfully*]: Is it really so funny?

TONY [*not laughing*]: Hilarious. And why aren't you with them?

MYRA: Because I was expecting you.

TONY [*plaintively*]: But you'd forgotten I was coming.

MYRA [*irritated*]: I might have forgotten that you were expected home at four o'clock on Tuesday the 18th March, 1958, but I was expecting you. Otherwise, of course, I would have gone with Milly.

TONY: But Milly didn't deny herself the pleasure on Sandy's account. He could fend for himself.

MYRA: You talk as if . . . Sandy's 22. He's not a little boy who needs his mother to wipe his nose for him. He's a man.

TONY [*terribly hurt*]: That must be nice for you. I'm so glad.

MYRA [*between her teeth*]: My God, Tony. [*She moves angrily away.*]

TONY: Where are you going?

MYRA: I'm going to demonstrate about the hydrogen bomb outside Parliament with a lot of other women. [*As* TONY *laughs*] Yes, laugh, do.

TONY: Oh, I'm not laughing. I do really admire you, I suppose. But what use do you suppose it's going to be? What good is it?

MYRA [*who has responded to his tone like a little girl who has been praised*]: Oh, Tony, but of course it's some good. Surely you think so?

TONY: You've been demonstrating for good causes all your life. So many I've lost count. And I'm sure you have . . . And where are we now?

MYRA: How do you know things mightn't have been worse?

TONY: How could they possibly be worse? How could they?

[*He sounds so forlorn, almost tearful, that she impulsively comes to him where he sits on the arm of the sofa, and holds his head against her shoulder, laying her cheek against it.*]

One might almost think you were pleased to see me.

MYRA [*amazed*]: But of course I am.

[*He smiles, rather sadly.*]

Of course. [*Gaily, moving away from him*] Tony, I must tell you about what I'm doing. You know we've got that big meeting the day after tomorrow.

TONY: Actually, not.

MYRA: We've advertised it in all the papers.

TONY: I never read newspapers.

MYRA: Oh. Well, it's tomorrow. And I've worked out a simply marvellous . . . wait, I'll show you. [*She is fiddling about near the tape-machine.*]

TONY: Do you have to? I thought you said you had to go to your demonstration?

MYRA: Yes, I must rush. I'll just do the end bit. It's a sort of symposium – you know, bits of idiotic speeches by politicians – like this . . . [*Switches on machine.*]

POMPOUS VOICE: People who object to the hydrogen bomb are simply neurotic!

MYRA: And this –

PULPIT VOICE: The hydrogen bomb must be regarded by true Christians as part of God's plan for humanity.

MYRA: And then war effects, you know.

TONY: War effects?

MYRA: Listen. [*Puts on machine.*]

[*Medley of war noises. Then machine-gun fire. Then the beginning of a scream – a conventional bomb falling.*]

TONY: For God's sake stop it.

MYRA [*stopping machine*]: What's the matter? You see, the thing is, people have no imagination. You've got to rub their noses in it. [*Starts machine again.*]

[*The scream begins and gathers strength.* TONY *stands rigid, trembling. At the explosion he flings himself down on the divan, his arms over his ears.*]

[*Taking needle off*] There. Not bad, is it? [*Turning*] Where are you? Oh, there you are. Don't you think it's a good idea?

[TONY *sits limp on the divan, hand dangling, staring in front of him. He wipes sweat off his forehead slowly.*]

I'm really very pleased with it. [*She stands, looking out of the window, starts to hum.*] I must go and get dressed and go out. I do wish you young people would join in these demonstrations. Why don't you? – we're such a middle-aged lot. Why do you leave it all to us? [*Hums.*] Well, I'll finish the work on the tape tonight.

TONY: I forgot to tell you, there *was* a telephone message. From Philip. He says he wants you to put up Rosemary. Tonight.

MYRA: Who's Rosemary?

TONY: Didn't you know? He's getting married. To Rosemary.

[MYRA *slowly turns from the window. She looks as if she has been hit.*]

MYRA: Philip is getting married?

TONY: So he said.

MYRA: And he wants *me* to put her up?

TONY [*looking at her curiously*]: Why not? You're old friends, aren't you?

MYRA: Old friends?

TONY: Well, aren't you?

MYRA [*laughing bitterly*]: Of course. Old friends. As you know.

TONY [*examining her, surprised*]: But you surely don't mind. It's been years since . . .

MYRA: Since he threw me over – quite.

TONY: Threw you over? You're getting very emotional all of a sudden, aren't you – all these old-fashioned attitudes at the drop of a hat – I was under the impression that you parted because your fundamental psychological drives were not complementary! [*With another look at her stricken face*] Threw you over! I've never seen you like this.

MYRA [*dry and bitter*]: If you've lain in a man's arms every night for five years and he's thrown you over as if you were a tart he'd picked up in Brighton for the week-end, then the word friend has to be used with – a certain amount of irony, let's say. [*Briskly*] We've been good friends ever since, yes.

[TONY *slowly rises, stands facing her.*]

TONY: Why do you talk like that to *me*?

MYRA [*noticing him*]: What's the matter now? Oh, I see. [*Contemptuous*] You're not five years old. Why do you expect me to treat you as if you were five years old?

TONY: Perhaps I am five years old. But this is after all an extraordinary outburst of emotion. Dear Uncle Philip has been in and out of this house for years. Whenever he's in London he might just as well be living here. I can't remember a time when you and Uncle Philip in animated conversation wasn't a permanent feature of the landscape.

MYRA [*dryly*]: I am the woman Philip *talks* to, yes.

TONY: Why all this emotion, suddenly?

MYRA: He has not before asked me to put up his prospective wife.

TONY: For God's sake, why should you care? You've lain in men's arms since, haven't you? Well, isn't that how you want me to talk, like a big boy?

MYRA: I suppose you will grow up some day. [*Goes to the foot of the stairs.*] When's she coming?

TONY: Some time later this evening, he said. And he's coming, too. We're going to have a jolly family evening.

MYRA: You'll have to look after her until I get back. We must be perfectly charming to her.

TONY: I don't see why you should be if you don't feel like it.

MYRA: You don't see why?

TONY: No. I'm really interested. Why?

MYRA: Pride.

TONY [*laughing*]: Pride! You! [*He collapses on the divan laughing.*]

MYRA [*hurt*]: Oh, go to hell, you *bloody* little . . .

[*Her tone cuts his laughter. He sits stiffly in the corner of the divan. She makes an angry gesture and runs up the stairs. Before she is out of sight she is humming: 'Boohoo, you've got me crying for you.'* TONY *strips off his uniform and puts on black trousers and a black sweater. He rolls up the uniform like dirty washing and stuffs it into the knapsack. He throws the knapsack into a cupboard. He stands unhappily smoothing back his hair with both hands. Then he goes to the looking-glass and stands smoothing his hair back and looking at his face. While he does this,* SANDY *very quietly comes down the stairs behind him. He is an amiable young man at ease in his world.*]

SANDY [*quietly*]: Hullo, Tony.

TONY [*still standing before the looking-glass. He stiffens, letting his hands drop. He slowly turns, with a cold smile*]: Hullo, Sandy.

SANDY [*at ease*]: I see you've disposed of the war paint already.

TONY: Yes.

SANDY: That's a very elegant sweater.

TONY [*responding*]: Yes, it's rather nice, isn't it . . . [*Disliking himself because he has responded, he stiffens up. He roughly rumples up his hair and hitches his shoulders uncomfortably in the sweater.*] Don't care what I wear.

SANDY: I'll move my things out of your room. Sorry, but we didn't expect you today.

TONY: Next time we will give you good warning.

SANDY: Cigarette?

TONY: That's a very smart cigarette case. No thanks.

SANDY: Mother brought it back from China last year. You remember she went?

TONY: Yes, I remember. Mother went, too. I suppose one does have to go to China for one's cigarette cases.

SANDY: I'm rather fond of it myself. [*Pause.*] Did you know I was helping Myra with her work?

TONY: As a matter of interest, what work are you doing?

SANDY: Formally, secretarial. But in practice – your mother has every talent in the world but one.

TONY: A sense of timing?

SANDY: You wouldn't exactly call her tidy.

TONY: Perhaps that's the same thing.

SANDY: She does need someone to sort things out for her.

TONY: Luckily she realizes it. In fact she makes a point of having someone around for that purpose.

[*As* SANDY *does not take this up* –]

Do you remember James?

SANDY: James? The boy with the golden gloves? Of course. Actually your mother told me she had him here for a time last year when he was out of a job.

TONY: He wasn't actually living here.

[SANDY *keeps his temper with an over-obvious effort.*]

James is working for Shepherds now and doing very nicely, thank you. You know, the new publishers.

SANDY [*lightly*]: Your mother has been pulling strings for me, too. I'm starting in with Mike Ferris next week.

TONY: *What?* I didn't know your politics were Left Wing.

SANDY: As much Left as anything, I suppose. But these labels are all rather *vieux jeu*, aren't they?

TONY: Oh, quite so – that's just the phrase I was looking for. Well, perhaps she can fix me up in Mike Ferris's office, too. After all, I don't find the political labels just a little *vieux jeu*.

SANDY: I was under the impression you were going to finish studying for your degree.

TONY: You were? Why?

SANDY: I imagined . . . well, I suppose I got the idea from Myra. I think she expects you to.

TONY: Really? I'm quite in the dark. Why should she?

SANDY: It was rather odd, your throwing it all up three weeks before the final exam. Training to be an architect is an expensive business, and then you threw it all up.

TONY: Mother said all that? She said all that to you? She's discussed it with *you*?

SANDY: No. But surely one is bound to think it? It's not everyone who can afford to spend four years studying and then throw it all up with three weeks to go.

TONY: Mother certainly couldn't afford it. And she quite rightly told me I would have to stand on my own feet from then on. Of course she didn't reproach me. One can scarcely imagine mother reproaching one for that sort of thing. Freedom of choice is everything. My mum is a great one for freedom. Odd, isn't it? [*He hums a bar or two of the* Internationale.] No, she merely said, in her inimitable way: 'Well, if you're determined to be illiterate, you'd better learn something useful. Like mending the electric lights.' So I took her at her word. I'm now a qualified electrician. Join the army and learn a trade.

SANDY [*whimsical again*]: I don't think she expects you to settle for being an electrician.

TONY: No? Why not? It was her suggestion. [*Suspiciously*] What has she been saying to you?

SANDY: Nothing.

TONY: I expect she'll drop information about her plans for my future in her own good time. When she has a moment to spare from the H-bomb, perhaps.

[MYRA *appears at the head of the stairs. She looks beautiful, and one would hardly recognize her for the same woman. Her dress is elaborately smart.* TONY *looks at* SANDY, *winces as he sees his admiring face.* MYRA *descends, smiling with frank pleasure at the impression she is making.*]

TONY [*still looking at* SANDY]: We are repressing a desire to applaud.

MYRA: Oh, don't repress it. Please don't. [*Reaching the foot of the stairs*] Where's my hat? [*Rummaging about*] Where did I leave my hat?

TONY: What's your hat doing down here, anyway?

MYRA: Obviously I left it here when I took it off.

TONY: Why do you have to leave it in the hall?

SANDY: Darling, it's in the cupboard.

MYRA: Of course I did. [*She opens cupboard, seizes hat, throws out* TONY's *army things.*] You can't leave your battle-gear in here. It's my china cupboard.

TONY: Why do you have to keep your hat and your china in a junk cupboard in the hall? Oh, Lord, Mother!

[MYRA *puts on her hat in front of the looking-glass. It is a very smart hat.*]

SANDY: Darling, you look beautiful.

TONY: For God's sake, you aren't going to wear that for a demonstration outside the House of Commons? Why don't you chain yourself to the railings and be done with it?

MYRA: Why not? I've been telling the committee that it is gravely underrated as a political weapon. It is time it was revived.

TONY [*furious*]: Christ, and you would, too.

MYRA [*furious*]: Yes, and it would be so unladylike, wouldn't it? How the hell did I come to have such a tenth-rate little snob for a son . . . ? Oh, I'm sorry. Come on, give me a kiss.

[*She kisses him on the cheek. He suffers it.*]

I suppose you'll grow out of it. But if you only weren't so *glossy*.

TONY: Me, glossy!

MYRA [*in a fever of irritation*]: You're such a beautiful boy. [*To* Sandy, *half-laughing*] Isn't he a beautiful boy? [*Almost growling*] Ohhh! Such a beautiful, glossy, well-groomed boy, and so neat in his habits.

TONY [*half-flattered, half-puzzled*]: Why are you so cross? You know quite well you look devastating and I'm bowled over. Do you want me to pay you compliments?

MYRA: Why not?

TONY: I thought that was what Sandy was here for.

[MYRA *and* TONY *glare at each other*, SANDY *turns away*.]

And now kiss Sandy too. On the cheek.

MYRA [*angrily*]: I was going to. Dear Sandy. [*She kisses Sandy soundly on both cheeks.*] And now I must run like the wind.

[*She makes a slow and impressive exit R, watched with affectionate admiration by* SANDY, *sardonically by* TONY.]

SANDY [*chuckling*]: Dear Myra. I've never known any woman with such a sense of gesture.

TONY [*coldly*]: Really? Gesture? She's sincere about this. She's sincere about war. It's no gesture.

SANDY [*chuckling*]: Of course she is. She's absolutely splendid. She's going to be at least an hour late. And she'll be ticked off by the committee again. Really so unjust, the work she puts into it. She was up till four this morning working out this tape-recording thing with me.

TONY: She was up till four? Really? [*Gratefully*] You were both up till four.

SANDY: It's a magnificent job, it really is. Bits of speeches – she smuggled a tape-recorder into the House. That took a bit of doing.

TONY: Illegal, of course.

SANDY: Oh, she's wonderful. Really wonderful propaganda. Asinine remarks from politicians, and war effects. She's worked in a terrific bit from Japan – you know, people dying as a result of the first atom bomb. And then children. That sort of thing.

TONY: Children.

SANDY: Children crying during a bombardment. Then machine-guns and bomb noises. You really must hear it. [*Going towards machine*] I'll put it on for you.

TONY [*violently*]: No.

SANDY: I think you'd be impressed. It's a splendid job.

TONY [*bitterly*]: I've no doubt it is. Splendid. [*Goes to window.*] But I rather doubt whether she's going to get near enough to the House of Commons even to get ticked off for being late. Because she's in animated conversation with Uncle Mike in the middle of the street – she's just missed being run over. Dear Mother.

SANDY: And who's Uncle Mike?

TONY: Why, Mike Ferris – your prospective sponsor for your life as a fighter for the people.

SANDY: Why Uncle?

TONY: I've had so many uncles. Well, Uncle Sandy? Oh, don't bother to get out your boxing gloves so as to defend Mum's honour. You don't want Mike to find us brawling, do you? Besides, in these matters at least, I am a pacifist. [*Looks out of window*.] Dear Mike. The very image of a politician. The old type of politician – the platform rather than the committee man. [*Back at Sandy*.] And which are you settling for, Uncle Sandy? Of course, you're the committee man. One must keep up with the times, mustn't one? Sandy Boles, M.P., backroom boy; Sandy Boles, centre of centre of the Labour Party. Yes, you're right, Sandy, it's the Labour Party for you – the road to ministerial position with the Tories is long and arduous and you haven't got the connexions. Oh yes, I can see you. Mr Sandy Boles, M.P. for Little Puddleditch, centre of centre. A sound man. Getting sounder and sounder as maturity sets in and you become certain that there are ever so many sides to every question . . .

SANDY [*extremely polite*]: Have a cigarette, Tony.

TONY: No thanks. He's coming in. [*He almost twists up with self-dislike.*] Why am I on to old Mike? I like him. I always have. He's the salt of the earth and all that. And I'm sure he's never said one thing and meant another in the whole of his life. Well, hardly ever. He'll never be Minister for anything. Not even an Under Secretary. Without people like him the whole show really would be a bloody circus. But he's so – bloody *innocent*. When he starts talking it makes me feel a thousand years old. Sometimes I think he's parodying the ordinary kind of political pomposity, and then, God help me, I see that he means every word. Every sweet silly word of it. Well . . . suppose after all the simple-minded do-gooders do turn up trumps. We'd look silly then, wouldn't we – Mr Sandy Boles, M.P.? Well, why shouldn't they? There's nothing left but simple-minded honesty – and faith.

SANDY [*blandly interested*]: Faith in what?

TONY [*after a long pause, allowing himself to straighten up*]: I don't know. Well? You can't possibly be prepared to go through all the slot-machines? You can't be.

SANDY: What's the alternative?

TONY: Oh, *Christ*! Seven years or so of establishing oneself as a *sound* young man. Marriage – for love, of course. Then divorce. Perhaps several divorces. Who are we to think ourselves better than our parents? Oh well. You'll be all right, Uncle Sandy. The glorious battle for socialism inside the Labour Party will save you from all that, won't it? Oh, *Christ*! Look at Mother's lot – fire-eating Socialists, every one of them, and here they are, all sorted out into neat little boxes.

SANDY: As a matter of interest, what label would you stick on the box Myra is in? Or my mother?

TONY [*after a pause, laughing*]: The dilettante daughters of the revolution?

SANDY: Come, come. Dilettantes don't work.

TONY [*impatiently*]: Oh, they're women who haven't succeeded in getting or staying married.

SANDY [*ironically*]: Well, well. Have a drink, Tony, do.

TONY: The only people I think I really admire are tramps. Something like that. I hitch-hiked from camp. There were two of us. The other chap was a man who threw up his job ten years ago and he hasn't worked since. Earns enough to keep eating. And drinking – he's a soak.

SANDY: *Sounds* all right.

TONY: We need a new form of – inner emigration. Drugs. Drink. Anything. I want to opt out. I don't want any part of it. [*At Sandy's raised eyebrows.*] Well, what are you suggesting? That I'll settle down?

SANDY: Of course.

TONY: I'm in a bad mood! You sound like Mother. I'll get over it, I suppose. Well, I suppose I will. All the same, what I think now is the truth, not the lies I'll be telling myself in five years' time when I've put down the first deposit on my future. If there is a future.

SANDY: My dear chap, you really had better get drunk.

TONY: Drinking bores me. [*He throws away his cigarette.*] And smoking. [*And now he is a querulous child again.*] And women.

SANDY [*blandly*]: Women too?

TONY: What on earth do you talk to them about? All they're interested in is – Oh, hell! You can't possibly sit there and tell me you really like women.

SANDY: But I adore women.

TONY: That's what I mean. [*Irritated*] Oh, hell! – the truth is I don't care for anything in the world except this house.

SANDY: Are you going to take it on your back with you when you go tramping?

TONY: Look out, here's Mike.

[MIKE FERRIS *enters from R. He is a man between 55 and 60, portly, kindly, with the dignity that comes from sincerity and a sound conscience. There is no conflict between his public face and his private face: there never has been. He went into politics thirty years ago out of a simple and earnest conviction, and he has never lost his simplicity and his earnestness.*]

[*Languidly good-mannered*] My dear Mike, how nice to see you.

MIKE: Well, Tony, old chap. How nice to see you back in civilized clothes.

TONY [*still like a Society hostess*]: Do sit down, Mike. Can I get you a drink?

MIKE [*smiling, a little amused*]: No thanks. I just popped in to say hullo. Your mother said you were back, and I said I'd pop in to have a look at you. It really is so good to have you home again.

TONY [*deflating suddenly into awkward sincerity*]: Sit down, Mike. Don't rush off. You must have a drink.

MIKE: It's very kind of you. Just for a minute then. [*To Sandy.*] And we are all looking forward very much to having you in the office. You're joining us at an interesting time, you know.

SANDY [*gracefully*]: I'm looking forward to it, too.

MIKE: Though when you think of the big issue, the hydrogen bomb business, nothing else seems to matter so much, does it? [*Accepting a glass from* TONY] The more I think about it, the more I am convinced it is much more simple than we think. Simply a question of getting the Governments to agree, that's all.

TONY [*dryly*]: That's all?

MIKE: Well, it really is hard to believe that people will be prepared to do things that will affect their own children, isn't it? I really can't believe, when it comes to the point, that common sense won't prevail.

TONY: You really believe that the men in power care about other people getting hurt?

MIKE: My dear boy – well, no. After a lifetime in politics – no. But everything's so critical – obviously we can get agreement if we try.

TONY: Are you suggesting that the voice of the people will prevail? Or, to coin another phrase, that the people are on the march?

MIKE: If the voice of the people doesn't prevail, what will? I really can't believe – I *can't* believe that after all we've done, all the glorious achievements of humanity, we are going to consent to blowing it all up.

TONY [*puzzled, more than derisive*]: You can't?

SANDY [*very smoothly, as it were testing a public voice*]: Quite obviously, the first step is to stop tests everywhere, and then we can proceed to a general discussion on disarmament.

TONY [*staring at him with disgust*]: Oh, hear, hear!

MIKE: If the tests are stopped we still have the Lord knows how many hydrogen bombs stored here and there, waiting for some madman to set them off. But I can't believe humanity will be so stupid.

TONY [*with fierce sincerity*]: Why can't you believe it?

MIKE: But, my dear boy, we do seem to get through somehow. We get through the most appalling messes.

TONY [*fiercely*]: No, I really do want to know. Why can't you believe it? This is what interests me. Mother can't believe it either. Speaking for myself, I can believe it only too readily.

SANDY [*whimsically*]: Oh, *I* can't believe it.

MIKE: I'm so glad to hear that, Sandy. Because, generally speaking, you young people . . . well, well.

TONY: Why can't you and Mother and the rest of you believe it? [*At Sandy derisively*] And *you*, of course, Sandy. [*To Mike*] You seem to be constitutionally incapable of believing in the ultimate horrors. Why? You've lived through enough, haven't you? It gives me the creeps to listen to any of you when you're in one of your reminiscing moods – a record of murder and misery. Yet on you go, all jolly and optimistic that right will prevail.

MIKE [*with great sincerity*]: It's a question of getting agreement between men of goodwill everywhere.

TONY [*laughing incredulously*]: Good. Let's drink to that: the glorious achievements of humanity.

MIKE [*seriously*]: Yes. [*He lift his glass to drink. Seeing* TONY'S *face, lowers it again.*] You're not looking too well, young Tony. And your mother's not looking too well either.

TONY: Mother's not looking well?

SANDY: Why, Myra's on top of her form.

MIKE: I thought she wasn't looking too well. [*Wistfully*] She really does need someone to look after her.

TONY: I'm sorry you think I'm so inadequate.

MIKE: Yes. Well. But if you're going to start studying again –

TONY: But I'm not.

MIKE: You're not? What? But . . . I see. [*He is very disturbed.*] But, Tony, your mother . . . You do seem to have such a lot of problems, you young people. Of course one is rather bound to feel insecure with that Government we've got.

TONY: We can always look forward to the blissful security we'll have under the next Labour Government. [*As* MIKE *looks hurt.*] There are also the American Government and the Russian Government. And how stand the Russians these days, Mike? In the right of it as usual?

MIKE: Tony, I do hope you're not getting at your mother over this business – she's feeling very bad about it, you know. A lot of people are. I am myself. It would be easy to say we were wrong. But when it's a question of knowing you were both right and wrong, and having to decide where you were wrong – I wish you wouldn't get at Myra just now.

TONY [*irritated*]: Mike, I can't remember a time when the whole lot of you weren't tortured by something happening thousands of miles away. I don't see that anything's changed much.

MIKE: She's really so worried about everything.

TONY: Oh, I know she doesn't spare herself. But then she never has.

MIKE: No, she never has. And she has had rather a tough time of it. It's odd how some people's lives – well, well. I often think of how your mother used to be when your father was alive. They were so happy. I loved being with them. They were such a happy couple. And then he was killed that night.

TONY: It is the night Mother refers to in her inimitable way as the Night the Bomb Fell.

MIKE: Yes. And your father was killed and you and your mother were buried alive for hours. [TONY *winces, turns away to hide how much he is affected.*] Yes. Perhaps you could persuade your mother to go away with you for a holiday somewhere.

TONY [*wistfully*]: With me? Mother? [*Laughs.*] With me?

MIKE: There's that cottage of mine in Essex. It's empty.

TONY: I shouldn't imagine that a cottage in Essex with me is Mother's idea of fun at all. [*At Sandy*] Do you fancy the idea of a holiday in Essex, Uncle Sandy?

MIKE: Knowing that money is a bit short at the moment.

TONY: Yes, so I gather, but why?

MIKE [*evasively*]: Oh, one thing and another. For one thing she gave up her job to do this hydrogen bomb work and of course it's not paid. And . . . various things. I got the impression money was a bit short. And there's the cottage, empty.

TONY: It's very good of you. Thanks, Mike.

MIKE: The flat can wait. There's no problem about that.

TONY: The flat?

MIKE: I meant to tell Myra that it was all fixed up when I saw her in the street, but it slipped my mind.

TONY: What flat?

MIKE: As it happened, when Myra asked me if I could help, I could. It's an ill wind that blows nobody any good. Joan – my daughter, you know – is leaving her husband. I don't know why. I thought it was a rather good marriage. But it's broken up. Very sad. Well, well. And there's the flat. Just right for *you*.

TONY: For me? A flat?

MIKE: Didn't you know? Myra seemed to think you'd be wanting a place of your own when you came out of the Army.

TONY: I see. [*Looks at Sandy*] I see.

[*He walks out of the room, R, slamming the door.*]

MIKE: What's wrong?

SANDY: He'll get over it.

MIKE: Myra thought he'd prefer to be by himself. She's always been very anxious about being the possessive mother, you know. She said *she* had to fight to leave home, and she doesn't want Tony to feel he should stay at home just because she's lonely.

SANDY [*chuckling*]: Myra's lonely? But she's never alone.

MIKE: Yes, well. [*With deliberate pleasantness*] It must be nice to have you here.

SANDY [*whimsically*]: And nice for me.

MIKE: Yes, believe me, I'm glad. It's so nice to meet a young man who ... there's my elder son. As far as I can make out he's a homo-sexual. Or if he's not, he might just as well be.

SANDY: I assure you, if it relieves your mind, that I'm not.

MIKE: Oh it does. And I'm pleased for both Myra and yourself that ... not that I'm not jealous, I am.

SANDY: Mike, you really are wonderful.

MIKE: When I was young I had such a good time. I do believe that young people should have a good time. But they don't seem to. At least, none of my children seem to. They talk in the most sophisticated way, but when it comes to the point ... And there's young Tony. Oh dear, he is in a mood. Well, that's one of the reasons Myra would like him to have his own flat. So he'd feel free. I think it would be better not to mention it again. So there's a perfectly good flat going begging.

SANDY: But he loves this house – or so he says. God knows why. It's such a mess. Besides, he *says* he wants to be a tramp.

MIKE [*seriously*]: He does, does he? Well, well. That's interesting.

SANDY: In order to escape the corruptions of modern life.

MIKE: Oh. I must tell Myra. She'll be delighted. Well, so I suppose you don't want a flat?

SANDY: I live at home with my mamma quite happily, thank you. I have the bottom half and she has the top half.

MIKE: That sounds reasonable. But you've never had the urge to leave home? To cast its dust off your feet?

SANDY: Good Lord, why should I? Besides, Mother's such a good cook. Almost as good as Myra.

MIKE: Don't you want to revolt against us? It was my first idea. And

Myra's too. And she has been so looking forward to the moment when Tony would revolt against her.

SANDY: But how could one revolt against my mother or against Myra? They are both perfectly delightful. And besides, you've done all the revolting, haven't you? There's nothing left for us.

MIKE: Sure there must be something . . . a tramp. Good for him.

[TONY *comes in fast from R.*]

TONY: Mother and Philip are coming. Philip, but no Rosemary. [*To Mike*] Do you know who Rosemary is?

MIKE: Rosemary? The only Rosemary I know is Rosemary Paine.

TONY: Who is Rosemary Paine?

MIKE: She used to be married to old Paddy – Secretary for – I forget now. She's interested in Housing. Yes. Nice woman. Very efficient.

TONY: Well, Philip is marrying her.

MIKE: Philip's marrying again, is he? Good for him.

TONY: We're in for such a jolly time. Mother, battling day and night – or at least, part of the night, with the Bomb. And Rosemary battling with Housing. And your mother, Sandy. Sandy, when's Milly coming back?

SANDY: Very soon now, I believe.

TONY: Milly will help Mother to battle with the Bomb when she's not attending to racial prejudice and the Chinese peasantry. Oh, my God, they really are utterly intolerable. [*Flinging himself down*] I simply cannot endure them. It's their utterly appalling vitality. They exhaust me.

SANDY: Perhaps it's time you took to the roads.

TONY: You don't seem to see the horrors of the situation. We're going to have this house full of Amazons. Three of them. My mother. Your mother, popping in and out with her hands full of pamphlets and files, as is her wont. And Rosemary.

[MYRA *and* PHILIP *come in R. They are laughing together, very gay and animated.* MYRA *is carrying her hat in her hand. As she enters she throws it on to a chair.* TONY *leaps up and bundles it into the cupboard. Philip is an attractive man of about 45.*]

MYRA: Did you say Rosemary? Has she come?

SANDY: No, she hasn't come yet; why aren't you outside the House of Commons, Myra?

TONY: Yes, why aren't you?

MYRA: Philip dropped in, we got talking, and I came back with him.

TONY: What do you mean, dropped in. You talk about the House of Commons as if it were the local.

PHILIP: I was driving past, and I saw Myra with the others, and I stopped to say hullo. Where's Rosemary? She said she'd get here under her own steam.

TONY: We are all sitting here waiting for Rosemary.

PHILIP: I do hope it's all right, her coming here.

MYRA [*gaily*]: Of course, where else should she come?

PHILIP [*a bit embarrassed*]: Well, I did try to fix her up somewhere else. Somewhere more central for shopping, I mean. [MYRA *smiles ironically at* PHILIP. *He responds unwillingly.*] Well, she says she can't get married without new clothes. [*Turning away from Myra's irony*] Well, Mike – nice to see you again.

MIKE: Haven't seen you for some time, Philip. Haven't you time for politics any longer?

PHILIP: I'm up to my eyes with this new community centre we're building.

MIKE: Yes, I heard. So your firm got the contract? It's a big thing, isn't it?

MYRA [*delighted*]: Philip, darling, why didn't you tell me. I'm so glad.

PHILIP [*turning to her – they instantly make a close, absorbed pair*]: Do you remember those plans I was playing with that summer – when we were in Venice?

MYRA: But of course. They were beautiful. And you were in despair because you said you'd never see it built. [MYRA *and* PHILIP *are close together under the window.* MIKE, SANDY, TONY *stand separate, watching them.*]

MIKE [*trying to detach* PHILIP *from Myra*]: We've been missing you on the committee, Philip.

PHILIP [*who has not heard Mike*]: Myra, do you remember how I wanted that façade – remember, you said it wouldn't work?

MYRA [*laughing*]: Then I was wrong. Remember how we quarrelled about it? We quarrelled for three days?

PHILIP [*laughing*]: What, we only quarrelled for three days that time?

SANDY [*jealous and loud, with a step forward*]: I do so hope Rosemary is interested in architecture.

MYRA [*who has not heard*]: And what about the roof gardens – did you get your way about those too?

PHILIP: Yes, everything. Look, I'll show you the photographs.

[PHILIP *and* MYRA *stand side by side by the window, looking at the photographs. The door R slowly opens;* ROSEMARY *stands there. She is a girl of 19 or 20, a slight creature with a sad little face. She wears black trousers and a black sweater. In general style and type she is so similar to Tony she might very well be his sister.*

SANDY, MIKE, *and* TONY *are watching the couple by the window. No one notices her.*]

MYRA: This is going to take up a lot of your time, Philip. I do hope you aren't going to drop out of politics altogether.

PHILIP: Myra darling, can't you see everyone's fed up with politics. It's not the time.

MYRA: What do you mean, not the time . . .?

PHILIP: Not the old kind of politics. Surely you can see that? [ROSE-MARY *takes a couple of steps forward.* TONY *sees her.*]

TONY [*to Rosemary*]: Can I do anything for you?

ROSEMARY: Well, yes.

TONY: My God, you aren't Rosemary?

ROSEMARY: Yes, I am. Who did you think I was?

TONY [*dramatically, to the others*]: Rosemary is here. [SANDY *and* MIKE *turn, are stunned into silence. Simultaneously* PHILIP *and* MYRA *raise their voices. They do not hear Tony nor see Rosemary.*]

MYRA: Oh, Philip, for God's sake, you're not going to change, are you?

PHILIP: Well, why not?

MYRA: Philip, half the people I know, people who've spent all their lives fighting and trying to change things, they've gone inside their homes and shut their front doors and gone domestic and comfortable – and safe.

PHILIP: Well, what's wrong with that?

TONY [*shouting*]: Myra. Philip. Rosemary's here.

MYRA [*as she and* PHILIP *slowly turn*]: What's wrong with it? I never believed I'd hear you say that – who's that?

[PHILIP *sees Rosemary, drops his arm from Myra, moves away from her.*]

ROSEMARY [*pathetically*]: Hullo, Philip.

CURTAIN

SCENE TWO

It is next morning. The place is in total disorder. The divan has been slept in and is tangled all over with clothes, sheets, newspapers, pillows.

[TONY *is lying flat on the floor. He is wearing his black trousers and a pyjama jacket.*

ROSEMARY, *dressed as she was yesterday, in black trousers and sweater, comes half-way down the stairs.* TONY *does not move.*]

ROSEMARY: What are you doing here?

TONY: This house has eight rooms in it and this is the only corner I can find to fit myself into – together with Mother's hat, the china and the rest of the . . . [*Indicates the files, papers, etc.*]

ROSEMARY: What's in the other rooms?

TONY: People. And Things. More Things than People. Extraordinary how much space the humanitarian conscience takes up. [*He again indicates the paraphernalia in the hall.*]

ROSEMARY: I'm sorry we've taken your room.

TONY [*eagerly*]: It's a pretty room, isn't it?

ROSEMARY: Yes. The sun has been in it since six this morning. Have you seen Philip?

TONY: I've slept in it for fifteen years.

ROSEMARY: Do you know where Philip is?

TONY: I expect he's talking to mother.

ROSEMARY: Oh. Well, they're very old friends, aren't they?

TONY: Inseparable. They started quarrelling this morning at seven o'clock.

ROSEMARY: What about? I thought Philip had gone for a walk?

TONY: They both went for a walk. Around and around the garden. Quarrelling.

ROSEMARY: But what about?

TONY: Politics.

ROSEMARY: Oh.

TONY: These people talk about politics with all the passionate intensity other people reserve for sex. Extraordinary.

ROSEMARY: I didn't know Philip was interested in politics.

TONY: Are you?

ROSEMARY: I've never thought about it. And you?

TONY [*after a pause*]: No.

ROSEMARY: I really must talk to Philip. [*Turning back upstairs*]

TONY: Don't go. Stay and talk to me.

ROSEMARY: What about?

TONY: Just talk.

ROSEMARY [*going back out of sight*]: Perhaps he's gone back to our room.

TONY [*looking round*]: Oh God what a mess! [*He leaps up, makes an ineffectual attempt to clear papers, etc. His eyes fall on the looking-glass; he goes over, is about to take it off the wall when MYRA comes into sight at the top of the stairs. She is wearing her old trousers and sweat-shirt, is unmade-up, and has a cigarette between her lips.*]

MYRA: What are you doing?

TONY [*into the mirror*]: Peekaboo.

MYRA: What are you doing?

TONY: What's this looking-glass doing here?

MYRA: Well, why not?

TONY [*pointing at place over divan*]: It's always hung there.

MYRA: Has it? Oh, do leave it alone, Tony.

TONY [*leaving it, returning to the divan*]: It's always hung here.

MYRA: Oh. Yes, I remember when you came back from school you always used to go all over the house to see if everything was in the same place. [*She laughs.*]

TONY [*anxious and querulous*]: Every time I go away, when I come back it's as if a bomb's exploded in it – why is everything in such a *mess*, Mother?

MYRA [*impatiently, as she begins to strip the divan and make it*]: Oh, I haven't time. I get bored with all these *things*. They just accumulate and pile up ... When I think I once swore I would never own *things*, I'd never accumulate possessions – and now I've lived in one house for fifteen years and I feel it's sitting all over me like a – toad!

TONY [*anxious, following her around*]: Mother, how can you say that – we've always lived here.

MYRA: Always! I would never have believed once that I'd live in one place for fifteen years – it's disgusting. I'll be so pleased to be rid of it.

TONY: Rid of it? You don't mean that?

MYRA: I do.

TONY: Mother, but what's disgusting is that it's such a *mess*. Lord, everything's in a mess. Even the front door lock is broken.

MYRA: Oh, what does it matter!

TONY: Oh, I'm sure *that* appeals to you: Walk right in, walk right in, ladies and gentlemen, the humanitarian conscience is always at home and waiting.

MYRA [*pushing him out of her way*]: Oh, Tony, when I do try and clear up ... Why don't you put some clothes on? Or are you trying to get a glamorous tan?

TONY [*in disgust*]: Oh, Jesus! [*He drags his black sweater on over his pyjama coat.*] Well, how's the happy couple this morning?

MYRA: How should I know?

TONY: But you've been in animated conversation with Uncle Philip for hours.

MYRA [*grinning*]: I naturally didn't mention Rosemary – that would be in such bad taste.

TONY: You must have gathered through your antennae, so to speak, how things were going – no? Well, I'd like to know. They are sitting gazing into each other's eyes? Or perhaps they've gone back to bed. *My* bed. My well-warmed bed. First Sandy. Then Uncle Philip and Rosemary.

MYRA [*grimly amused*]: Philip asked me if I had another bed I could put into their room. So I did. Twin beds side by side like an advertisement in an American magazine. I felt so much better. [*She laughs.*]

TONY: I can't think why.

MYRA: Philip and I shared a three-foot bed for five years.

TONY: *Do you have to?*

MYRA: Yes, I do. *That he should bring her here.* God, men are the end. They really are the end.

TONY: Uncle Philip is probably not aware of your enduring passion for him.

MYRA: He's very well aware of it. *Ergo.*

TONY: *Ergo* what?

MYRA: Well, let's see what happens. [*She kicks Tony's shoes out of the way.*]

[TONY, *irritated, jumps across, puts on his shoes, returns to the floor.*]

TONY: If you go on being so charming to that poor girl she might permanently lose her powers of speech.

MYRA [*genuinely upset*]: But, Tony, I was doing my best. I really was.

TONY: Last night at dinner you were like Beatrice Lillie impersonating – our dear queen.

MYRA: What do you want me to do – burst into tears?

TONY: Why not, if you feel like it? Why don't you ever?

MYRA: I do my crying in private. Do you imagine, after putting up such a good show with Philip all this time, I'm going to behave like a jilted 16-year-old? Obviously not.

TONY: Oh, obviously.

MYRA: What I can't stand is the damned dishonesty of it. Men are so dishonest.

TONY: I'm sure you're right. But why in this case?

MYRA [*impatiently*]: Oh, surely you can see? He doesn't want to marry her. But he hasn't got the guts to do it himself, so he brings her here. He never did have any guts. I was manoeuvred into a position where

I had to break if off or lose my self-respect. And that's what he's doing with her. Bloody man.

TONY [*languidly*]: And why do you love such a despicable person?

MYRA: Oh – love. I never use the word.

TONY: I do.

MYRA: I wish you would.

TONY: When it means nothing?

MYRA [*laughs. But she is not far off tears*]: Oh, don't be so solemn. Can't you ever laugh? You're such a boring lot. The young are so boring. I've come to the conclusion I can't stand the company of anyone under the age of 35.

TONY: You mean you can't stand the company of the uncorrupted?

MYRA [*amused*]: Wh–at?

TONY: I've spent a good part of what are known as my formative years listening to the conversation of the mature. You set my teeth on edge. You're corrupt. You're sloppy and corrupt. I'm waiting for that moment when you put your foot down about something and say you've had enough. But you never do. All you do is watch things – with interest. If Philip murdered Rosemary, seduced Sandy and stole all your money, all you'd say would be: How interesting!

MYRA: He'd murder me, not Rosemary. Obviously.

TONY: Oh, obviously, obviously, obviously. That would be interesting, wouldn't it?

MYRA [*grimly amused*]: It's so hard for a man when his wife dies and leaves him unprotected!

TONY: I thought you liked his wife.

MYRA: I did. But alas, she's dead. Some men stay married because it protects them against the – necessity of marrying somebody else. Philip married her when she was 20, and after that they hardly saw each other. He was very fond of her – as the phrase goes. And so he should have been. She lived like a nun on a mountain peak, forgiving him his sins, and from time to time he returned to the *good* woman for a nice rest. But now she's dead. So there's Rosemary. The moment I heard Philip's wife was dead, I said to myself, 'Ah-ha,' I said, 'he's going to be in trouble with Rosemary before the year's out.'

TONY: I thought you'd never heard of Rosemary.

MYRA: Rosemary, Felicity, Harriet. What does it matter? Of course he doesn't want to marry her. So he brings her here, where she's thoroughly lost and humiliated. [*Turning on him*] God, you are a cowardly hypocritical lot.

TONY [*languidly*]: Why me? You forget I haven't started using the word 'love' yet.

MYRA [*grimly*]: I've no doubt you soon will. But I'm not going to cope with the sacrifices to your vanity – I'm not. You can manage them yourself.

TONY: Well, if you understand it all . . . if you understand it . . . [*He falls back on the floor.*] *You* understand it so that's enough.

MYRA: But I'm not blaming anyone for anything. It seems to me, as far as sex is concerned, or if you prefer it, love, the only thing to do is to shrug your shoulders [*she shrugs her shoulders*] and forgive everyone.

TONY: But you haven't forgiven Philip.

MYRA: No.

TONY: Do be nice to that poor girl. It's like seeing a poor little fly being hypnotized by a horrible brown spider.

MYRA: Poor little fly.

TONY: Can't you really see that she's terrified of you?

MYRA [*really surprised*]: Of me?

TONY: You've just explained to me why she should be.

MYRA: It's humiliating for both of us. But *frightened* – of *me*? [*She goes to the looking-glass and looks at herself.*] She's 20.

TONY: Then for God's sake why don't you at least make up your face? I really can't stand it, seeing you slop around the house half the day looking like that.

MYRA: When I'm cleaning the house I expect to be loved for myself.

TONY: Why do you have to clean it? [*As she does not reply, but begins to hum to herself.*] Oh, all right, be a martyr. But I don't enjoy housework so don't expect me to slump about on my knees.

MYRA: I haven't asked you to. [*She has finished the divan and now bundles objects into the cupboard haphazard.*]

TONY: What interests me much more than the convolutions of your emotions and Uncle Philip's is Rosemary. Why does a girl of 20 want to marry a jaded old – uncle. The newspapers say it's the thing these days. One marries a man old enough to be your father. Why?

MYRA: I thought you didn't read the newspapers.

TONY: Why? Because he has *experience*? Is that it?[*In disgust*] Jesus!

MYRA: Philip has always been attractive to women.

TONY: Attractive! When I was doing my time in his office I was permanently amazed at the way all the women were ready to lie down and let him walk all over them. Why? Well, you did too, didn't you? So you can explain it to me.

MYRA: I dare say they are under the impression that older men are kinder than young ones.

TONY: *Kinder!* This morning I heard Rosemary say: 'Darling, don't you love me any more?' and he said: 'Darling, you're simply being hysterical.' [MYRA *turns away sharply*.] Well, did he tell you you were hysterical?

MYRA [*breaking down and crying for a few seconds before pulling herself together*]: Tony, have some pity on me sometimes.

TONY [*appalled*]: Pity? Me? But you're not crying, are you?

MYRA: No. [*She begins rubbing a cleaner over the boards around the carpet.*] No.

TONY: I should think not.

MYRA: If Philip's off to the office then I suppose we'll have to entertain Rosemary. Of course I can always rely on you. Thank God, there's Sandy.

TONY: Yes, thank God for Sandy. He can always be relied upon to cope with any social situation. Where is he?

MYRA: Working in my room, I suppose. We've got that big meeting tomorrow night.

TONY: So interesting how that boy's turned out. Who would have foreseen this idealism in Sandy? [MYRA *stands still, leaning on the cleaner.*] What's the matter?

MYRA: Giddy. No, leave me alone.

TONY: You're not still having the change of life, are you?

MYRA: No, dear. As you know, I've finished with it.

TONY: How should I know? [*Muttering*] Change of life, change of life. Well, you haven't changed much.

MYRA: Tony, will you do me a small favour? Keep out of my way just for a couple of days.

TONY: I could move into Uncle Mike's flat.

MYRA: Oh, do anything you like.

TONY: If your sense of timing hadn't been wrong, and I had been coming home next week, what would I have found? Sandy back with Milly and a nice empty house and you all ready to entertain me.

MYRA: You know quite well you didn't let me know – just so as to catch me out.

TONY [*pathetically*]: Couldn't you really remember the date I was to finish?

MYRA: Oh, Tony, why should I? Any normal person would have let me know. It's been two years. You've been popping back and forth from camp for two years. It's a long time.

TONY: So you'd like me to move into that flat for a week?

MYRA: But you know I wouldn't. Why do you think I want to get rid of you? I thought you'd want to live by yourself.

TONY: But why?

MYRA: It's normal for a young man to want to live by himself, isn't it?

TONY: Then I'm obviously not normal.

MYRA: I was making it easy for you – that's all. I've told Mike you definitely don't want the flat.

TONY: Easy for me?

MYRA [*embarrassed*]: Well . . . in case you felt you ought to stay with me when you didn't want to.

TONY: Ought to? Why?

MYRA [*giving him a long incredulous look*]: Well, I don't know. [*Pause.*] I do wish Milly would come back.

TONY: Why?

MYRA: She's so kind.

TONY: Kind, kind! You've got Sandy, haven't you? Isn't Sandy kind?

MYRA: You're a lot of savages. The young are a lot of savages.

TONY: Then why – oh, don't tell me. Of course – he's good in bed. Is that it?

MYRA [*smoothly*]: Oh, he's very accomplished. Very. [*Irritated*] He's *so* efficient. My dear, there are times when I feel I should be clapping.

TONY: Don't tell me that's not enough. Then *why*?

MYRA [*grinning*]: *Vieillesse oblige.*

TONY: That smooth-faced well-mannered little spiv. I should have thought that Sandy was everything you hated. He'll end up as Master of the Queen's Wardrobe. Or Personnel Manager for the Federation of Imperial Industries. Something needing *tact*. Tact. Tact. Tact. Well, it's no use your trying to be tactful, Mother. Who's been alerted to talk to me? Sandy? Is it dear Uncle Sandy? Or is it Uncle Philip?

MYRA [*grinning*]: Well, actually, it's Philip.

TONY [*grinning*]: What's the plot?

MYRA: You see, it's like this . . .

   [PHILIP *and* ROSEMARY *come into view on the staircase.*]

ROSEMARY [*kissing him*]: Good-bye, darling.

PHILIP: Good-bye, darling.

ROSEMARY: Darling, you've forgotten your briefcase. [*They go back out of sight.*]

TONY [*grinning*]: He's forgotten his briefcase. Well, Mother?

MYRA: The idea was that he would handle you for me – I suggested he should take you back into his office. No, Tony, do wait a minute. It's your whole future at stake.

TONY: Yes, it's *my* future.

MYRA: It would take you six months to study for that examination.

TONY: A year, after my brain's gone to pot in the army.

MYRA: Ohhh – do stop being so sorry for yourself all the time.

PHILIP'S VOICE ABOVE: Good-bye, darling.

ROSEMARY'S VOICE: Good-bye, darling.

PHILIP'S VOICE: Good-bye.

TONY: Oh, *Christ*! It really is repulsive, you must admit. [*As* MYRA *shrugs.*] All right, it's all very beautiful and holy. Mother – when I left Philip's office before, it was because I couldn't stand it.

MYRA: Couldn't stand what?

TONY: Seeing Uncle Philip and his admiring staff, his willing harem. [PHILIP *comes into sight at top of the stairs.*]

MYRA: Oh, you impossible bloody little *prig*. [*She stands at window, back turned, furious.*]

TONY [*talking up as* PHILIP *comes down*]: Uncle Philip, Mother has left us alone for the interview.

PHILIP [*preoccupied*]: Yes. It's about this job. I expect she told you.

TONY: Thanks, I don't want it. Mother, interview over. [*Goes to divan, flings himself on it.*]

MYRA [*coming fast across to Philip*]: Oh, Philip, can't you ... [PHILIP *shakes his head gently at her, smiles, offers her a cigarette. They smile and shrug.*]

TONY: Songs without words.

PHILIP: I must be getting along to the office. It's really very good of you to have Rosemary here, Myra.

MYRA [*laughing*]: I think so, too.

PHILIP [*embarrassed*]: Yes, well. [MYRA *laughs again. He suddenly leans forward and kisses her cheek. She kisses his.*]

MYRA [*amused*]: You know you can always count on me for anything.

PHILIP: Yes.

MYRA: Dear Philip.

PHILIP: I really must hurry.

MYRA: But I want to ask you something. It's about Max. You remember Max?

PHILIP: Well, of course. You mean the Max from the International Brigade?

MYRA: He's in trouble.

PHILIP: Who isn't?

MYRA: He's been blacklisted in America and he'd like a temporary job to tide him over.

PHILIP: But I don't need script-writers in my office. Well, what are his qualifications?

MYRA: He's an awfully nice person.

PHILIP [*laughing*]: All right, send him along.

MYRA: Philip, I suppose you wouldn't like to be one of the sponsors for a new protest we're getting up?

PHILIP [*cautiously*]: A protest against what?

MYRA: I'll explain.

[*The Two of them are standing very close together by the window R, looking into each other's faces. ROSEMARY comes slowly down the stairs. She has been crying. They do not notice her.*]

PHILIP: Myra dear, I don't know how often I've told you that I don't believe in this – you can do more by quietly pulling strings than you ever can by mass protests and committees and that kind of thing.

MYRA: Since when have you told me! Yesterday. So now you believe in pulling strings. What's happened to you, Philip? What has happened? You used to be a Socialist.

PHILIP [*dryly*]: I've discovered that I was a Socialist because I believed in liberty, freedom, democracy. [*Laughs.*] Well, Myra?

[ROSEMARY, *who has been waiting for Philip to see her, looks at Tony. He pats the divan beside him. She sits by him. They sit side by side, in the same listless pose, listening.*]

[*Tenderly*] Myra dear, do you really imagine that any Government in the world cares about the protests of nice-minded humanitarians?

MYRA: They care about having pressure put on them. I've got a list as long as my two arms of people in prison, sentenced to death, deported, banned, prohibited, blacklisted . . .

PHILIP: Which side of the world this time? Ours or theirs?

MYRA: Ours.

PHILIP: And what about Dimitri?

MYRA: No. Oh, no . . . I thought he was out of prison.

PHILIP: I had a letter from Willi yesterday. He says Dimitri died in prison. Of course now he's officially rehabilitated and a hero of the people.

MYRA: Torture?

PHILIP: I suppose so. Probably. [*Putting his arm round her*] Don't cry. What's the use? [*Ironically*] Besides, he's died for socialism, hasn't he?

TONY: Don't let yourself be misled. They're talking about socialism in Russia, not Britain. It's tearing them apart, the way people are nasty to each other – in Russia.

MYRA: I can't stand your cynicism. I never could stand it.

PHILIP: You'd better stick to your Hydrogen Bomb. Stick to disarmament.

MYRA: You mean that we've got to accept the fact that in our time there's not going to be democracy, there's not going to be freedom, there's not going to be liberty?

PHILIP: Yes, of course. Who cares about liberty? The *people*? [*Laughs bitterly*]

TONY [*to Rosemary*]: One half of this lot are bogged down emotionally in the thirties with the Spanish Civil War, and the other half came to a sticky end with Hungary. If you cut them open you'd find Spain or Hungary written in letters of blood on their soft hearts – – but not Britain. Certainly not poor old Britain.

PHILIP [*with an eye on Tony, to Myra*]: Why don't you recognize the fact that we've had it? We've served our purpose.

MYRA: You mean we should leave it all to the youth? God help us, all they care about is . . .

PHILIP: I'm late. See you later, Myra. [*Goes out hastily R.*]

TONY [*to Myra*]: Yes, why don't you recognize the fact that you've had it?

MYRA [*irritably, to Tony and Rosemary*]: If we stop do-gooding and just sit back with our feet up, are you going to take over? [*Looking at their listless poses*] God, you are a petty, respectable little lot.

TONY [*facing her*]: Mother.

MYRA: Well?

TONY: I gather that at the moment your large heart is full of pity for the victims of *capitalist* witch-hunts.

MYRA: And why shouldn't it be? What are you trying to say?

TONY [*laughing*]: That's all.

MYRA: You could make out a case for the whole lot of us being so discredited, so morally discredited, that we should all take a unanimous decision to stay quiet for the rest of our lives. [*He does not reply.*] We should acknowledge our total failure and leave everything in your hands. In the hands of the glorious battling youth whose banners are unsmirched. If you had any banners, that is.

TONY [*shouting*]: You're so damned self-righteous.

MYRA: I don't feel self-righteous. Of course if we did retire gracefully from the field, you'd lose the benefit of our really rather unique experience.

TONY: Unique. All your lot have proved is that every political party lies and its members lie to themselves. Did that really need proving?

MYRA: What are you saying then? What is it that you want me to say?

TONY: I wonder how many people died in torture and misery and starvation during the years 1935 to 1939 while you stood on platforms smiling prettily and talking about democratic socialism.

MYRA: Yes, I know.

TONY: I wish I had a tape-recording of some of your speeches during that time. Well?

MYRA: What is it that you want me to say? Do you want me to give up – like Philip? Philip's going to become a nice kind-hearted business man giving money to good causes – Oh, God, *no*. [*Remembering Rosemary*] Of course, he is a wonderful architect ... Tony, I do wish you'd think about Philip's offer. You aren't really going to be an electrician, are you? [*Humorously, to Rosemary*.] Tony's going to be an electrician. He's quite determined to be. What do you think?

ROSEMARY [*fiercely*]: I think people ought to be what they want to be.

TONY: Hurray, Rosemary's on my side.

ROSEMARY: Mother wanted me to be a doctor, but I wanted to be a nurse.

TONY: Luckily Uncle Philip enjoys very good health for a man of his age. [*At Myra's angry look*] Well, he does, doesn't he?

ROSEMARY [*politely*]: Why do you want to be an electrician?

TONY: Perhaps I'll be a telephone engineer. Mother, did you know I could be a telephone engineer? Communications, that's the thing. Bringing people together. Mother, do you suppose if we talked to each other on the telephone it would be easier? We could go into different rooms and talk to each other – or play each other little items from your tape-recorder ... [*Imitates the sound of machine-gun fire*]

MYRA: Oh, damn you. What do you want? Is it that you want me to give up the H-Bomb work, is that it?

TONY: Well, of course not. Of course you should go on about the bomb. Or, as you usually refer to it – your bomb. Why, I might even help you with it.

MYRA: Then I don't know, I really don't.

TONY: The simple fight for survival – we're all in on that. But what for? Or don't you ask yourself any more? [*She shrugs impatiently.*] Why are you sitting there looking so tortured? You've got what you wanted, haven't you? Well? You've spent your life fighting for socialism. There it is, socialism. You said you wanted material progress for the masses. God knows there is *material* progress. Hundreds of millions of people progressing in leaps and bounds towards a materially-progressive heaven.

MYRA: Are you pleased about it or are you not?

TONY: Of course I'm pleased. Down with poverty. By the way, Mother, have you ever actually seen poverty? The real thing, I mean. I haven't. Well, have you? [*To Rosemary*] Have you, Rosemary?

ROSEMARY: My family aren't very well off.

TONY: Rosemary knows all about it. Hurray! In Britain people wear poverty like a medal around their necks – a sign of virtue. We aren't very well off! Mother, do you realize you've spent your whole life fighting to end something you know nothing about?

MYRA [*irritated to the point of tears*]: Would you please be kind enough to tell me what it is you want, then?

TONY: Do you know what it is you've created, you and your lot? What a vision it is! A house for every family. Just imagine – two hundred million families – or is it four hundred million families? To every family a front door. Behind every front door, a family. A house full of clean, well-fed people, and not one of them ever understands one word anyone else says. Everybody a kind of wilderness surrounded by barbed wire shouting across the defences into the other wildernesses and never getting an answer back. That's socialism. I suppose it's progress. Why not? To every man his wife and two children and a chicken in the pot on Sundays. A beautiful picture – I'd die for it. To every man his front door and his front door key. To each his own wilderness. [*He pauses for breath.*] Well?

MYRA: If you're going to put all that energy into dreaming dreams why don't you dream to some purpose?

TONY: Dreams, dreams, dreams – like your lot did? What are the words – don't say I've forgotten them, they've been stuffed down my throat all my life – liberty, democracy, brotherhood – and what's that other one? Ah, yes, comradeship, that's it. A world full of happy brothers and comrades.

MYRA: Does that really seem so silly?

TONY: Jesus, you aren't actually sitting there and telling me you still believe in – *Jesus!* [*To Rosemary*] Do you know, this lot still believe in it! What do you think?

ROSEMARY: I think I believe that people should be kind to each other.

TONY [*roaring with laughter*]: There, Mother, Rosemary's on your side – she believes people should be nice to each other.

[MYRA, *seeing* ROSEMARY *is hurt, puts out her hand to Rosemary's arm –* ROSEMARY *twitches away.*]

MYRA [*to Tony*]: So many people have died for it. Better people than you.

TONY: *Died.* [*Laughs.*]

MYRA: Just imagine, during the last fifty years hundreds of thousands of people have died in torture and in loneliness, believing they were dying for the future – for *you* Tony.

TONY [*furious*]: Well, it doesn't mean anything to me. All your damned hierarchy of Socialist martyrs – what bloody right had they to die for me? Bullying, that's what it is. I'm not going to have your holy dead hung around my neck. [*To Rosemary*] Do you realize what it is they are saying? Because hundreds of thousands of Socialist martyrs took it upon themselves to die for a world full of happy brothers and comrades, we've got to fall into line. Well, what do you say?

ROSEMARY: I don't know – my parents weren't political.

TONY: Oh, aren't you lucky!

MYRA: Tony, please tell me – what is it that you want? You must want something?

TONY: To be left alone, that's all. And I don't want any more suffering – no more fighting and suffering and dying. What for? Oh, the great company of martyrs who went singing to the stake and the thumbscrews and the firing-squads for the sake of the noble dream of ever-fuller wage packets and a chicken in every pot. To each man his own front door – to each man his own – refrigerator! [*Roars with laughter.*]

[ROSEMARY *suddenly bursts into tears.* MYRA *tries to put her arms around her.* ROSEMARY *tears herself away and runs upstairs.*]

MYRA: Oh, Tony, do you have to.

TONY [*deflated and miserable*]: But I was talking to you. What does she have to cry for?

MYRA: I dare say the poor girl was upset by your happy picture of the world.

TONY: I didn't mean to make her cry. What shall I do?

MYRA: You could go upstairs and be nice to her.

TONY: Be nice to her. Say I'm sorry.

MYRA: Oh, do I have to tell you what to do? Go upstairs and put your arms around her.

TONY: I put my arms around her and then she'll feel fine.

MYRA: Really, is it such a hard thing to do – to go upstairs to that poor child and be warm and nice to her?

TONY: Yes, it is. Oh, very well, if you want me to. [*He stands as if waiting to be ordered.*]

MYRA [*shrugging*]: If *I* want you to.

TONY: Therapy for soul-trouble, a man's arms.

[*The door bell rings, R.*]

MYRA: Oh, *no*.

TONY: Perhaps it's Philip. Well, he can go and put his arms around her. [*Goes out R.* MYRA *lets herself slump on the divan, eyes closed.* TONY *comes back.*]

MYRA: Who is it? I'm not in.

TONY: I'll give you three guesses . . . It's Milly.

MYRA [*jumping up, radiating joy*]: Milly, now?

TONY: You're surely not pleased? Now Sandy'll have to go back to his mum.

MYRA: Oh, don't be so stupid. [*Goes fast towards R.*] Where is Milly? [*To Tony.*] Oh, get upstairs to that child, be a man for once in your life, can't you?

TONY: All right, I'm going. [*Goes obediently to stairs.*]

MYRA: And could you please keep your jolly little tongue off Milly for a time? She's been traipsing back and forth across the world and she'll be tired.

TONY: Perhaps you'd like me to put my arms around her, too. Perhaps I should make love to Milly. Would it be good for her – soothing after her travels? Or good for me?

MYRA: Oh, Tony, don't take it out of Milly.

[*The door opens R and* MILLY *comes in. She is a large, firm-fleshed Yorkshire woman with a stubborn face and a practical manner. She wears her hair tight back in a firm chignon. Her voice is Yorkshire. She is beaming.*]

MILLY: Well, love, I'm back.

MYRA [*kissing her*]: Oh, Milly, I've never been so pleased to see anyone.

MILLY: Me, too. A delegation of twenty women for two weeks – not my idea of fun and games. I changed to an earlier plane and here I am.

MYRA: Milly, darling, you look marvellous. Tell me about Japan. Tell me about everything. Come and sit down and talk. We'll have a party. Yes, of course, that's what we must do. We'll have a party.

TONY [*disgusted, from the stairs*]: Oh, no, no, no, no, no.

CURTAIN

ACT TWO

SCENE ONE

The stage is semi-darkened. TONY *is lying on the divan, wearing his black cord trousers, but nothing on above the waist.*

The radio is playing an erotic tango.

[TONY *is making machine-gun noises like a small boy. His movements are all tense and anxious. Throughout the first part of the scene, that is until he leaves Milly and Myra together, he is in that state of hysteria where one is compulsively acting a part, knows it, hates one-self for it, but can't stop.*

The door R held tight by a chair wedged under the handle. There is loud knocking on this door. TONY *runs across, opens with a flourish, shows his disappointment when he sees who it is.*

MYRA *enters dressed for the party and looking beautiful. She is carrying bottles for the party.*]

MYRA: What's the matter, Tony?

[*He replaces chair under the handle.*]

Are you ill? What's wrong?

TONY: Now why should I be ill?

MYRA: Then why are you skulking in the dark, barricaded in?

TONY: This is now my bedroom.

MYRA: Oh, I see.

TONY: How many people have you got?

MYRA: About twenty, I suppose.

TONY: You blow up a party of twenty people at a couple of hours' notice?

MYRA: Some of the people who went to Japan with Milly came back this afternoon. What's that palm-court music for? What's this all about?

TONY: Milly. I'm going to seduce Milly.

MYRA [*irritated*]: Why can't you seduce Milly another time? I want her to help me cut sandwiches. [*She is on her way out L.*]

TONY [*in a Boyer voice*]: Darling, I love you.

MYRA [*irritated, but troubled*]: Tony, please stop it. I do wish you'd stop it.

TONY [*as before*]: Darling, I love you.

MYRA [*furious*]: Ohh . . . I was probably wrong not to believe in corporal punishment for children.

[*She goes out L into living-room. There is a burst of music and laughter and talk from the party as she does so. As* TONY *is returning to divan, another knock on door, R.* TONY *opens it, admits* SANDY, *showing exaggerated disappointment when he sees who it is.*]

TONY: Oh, no. [*Wedges the chair back again.*]

SANDY: What's wrong, are you ill?

TONY: Didn't you see the notice? I take it for granted that I'm invisible, that I'm simply something people walk through, but surely you saw the notice?

SANDY: What notice?

TONY: A large notice reading: No Admittance, use Tradesmen's Entrance.

SANDY: No.

TONY [*opening door to living-room, through a burst of music and talk*]: Mother, Mother!

MYRA'S VOICE: What?

TONY: Did you take down my notice?

MYRA'S VOICE: Oh, was that your notice?

TONY: I'm going to put it back.

MYRA'S VOICE: Oh, do anything you damned well like.

TONY [*shuts living-room door. Music, etc., stops*]: Everyone comes in, but simply everyone, as if my bedroom were – the hall. But not Milly, for whom I'm lying in wait.

SANDY [*blandly*]: And why are you lying in wait for my mother?

TONY [*in Boyer voice*]: I love her. The scene is set for seduction.

SANDY: Rather obviously so, perhaps. Why this cloistral gloom?

TONY [*instantly switching on more light*]: If you say so. You should know. [*In Boyer voice*] Darling, I love you. No, that doesn't sound right. [*Trying again*] Darling, I love you. How's that?

SANDY: Is it true that Philip's looking for a personnel manager?

TONY [*stares. Gives his loud laugh*]: Yes. And I turned his kind offer down. It's all yours, Sandy.

SANDY: I thought I might discuss it with him. [*He proceeds L towards living-room.*]

TONY: And Mike's looking for you to see when you can start in with the Labour Party. The people wait, Sandy, they wait.

SANDY: Yes, I must discuss the whole thing with them both.

TONY: Darling, I love you. But it's no use. She'll simply go on cutting bread and butter. My body will be carried past her on a shutter and . . . I was born out of my time. Yes, I've suddenly understood what my tragedy is. I was born out of my time.

SANDY: Why don't you offer to help her cut the sandwiches? [*Goes into living-room accompanied by a burst of music, etc.*]

TONY [*striking his forehead with his fist*]: Clown, I never thought of it. [*A knock on the door R. TONY opens it with a flourish, shows exaggerated delight as MILLY comes in. She is wearing a black sweater that leaves her shoulders bare. She drops her coat on a chair.*]

Wait, I must hang up my notice. [*Goes out R.*]

MILLY [*after him through the door*]: What notice?

TONY [*returning*]: There, we shall be undisturbed. [*Wedges the door again. Advances on her purposefully.*] But your shoulders, Milly, your shoulders, my eyes dazzle.

MILLY: What are you up to, young Tony?

TONY: I'm seducing you. [*Kisses her shoulder.*] There. Can I help you cut the sandwiches?

MILLY: What are you seducing me for?

TONY: Oh . . . to redress certain balances. [*Pulls her towards him.*] Besides, mother says I must.

MILLY [*amiably*]: Well, this is a surprise.

TONY: That's not what you should have said.

MILLY [*going calmly towards L*]: Perhaps another time. Where is my son?

TONY: You shouldn't ask that either.

MILLY: Is he coming home tonight or not? Because if not, one of the people I came back with on the plane could use his room.

TONY: You are a disgusting lot of women. [*Puts his arms around her from behind and bites her ear.*]

MILLY: Mind, I don't want to have to do my hair again . . .

TONY: You should slap my face. Then I should slap yours. Then we should fall on the bed.

MILLY: But I haven't got time. And you don't know what you're doing, inviting a punch from me. My husband hit me the once. [*Shows him a large and efficient fist.*]

TONY: Then I am afraid I am nonplussed. Doesn't that music do anything to you?

MILLY: What music? Oh – that. I've got so I never hear the radio or the telly. [*Is about to open door.*]

TONY [*in Boyer voice*]: I love you.

[*Milly does not turn.*]

I loo-ve you.

[MILLY *slowly turns, stands looking at him, hands on hips.* TONY *stares at her, derisive, rude, insulting.*]

MILLY [*quietly*]: What you're going to get from me, young Tony, is a damned good spanking.

[TONY *suddenly collapses into tired appeal, makes a helpless gesture.*]

MILLY [*in a different voice, warm and maternal*]: You take it easy, love. You just let up and take it a bit easier.

[MYRA *comes in from L. The two women stand side by side, looking at him.*]

MYRA [*irritated*]: Do put something on, Tony. You'll catch cold.

TONY [*instantly reverting to his previous aggressiveness*]: I know, and then you'll have to nurse me. [*Drags on his black sweater.*]

MILLY [*easily*]: Eh, but he's a fine figure of a boy, that Tony.

MYRA: One sees such a lot of it. [*To Tony*] For God's sake, turn off that mush.

TONY [*turning off radio*]: I have failed. I have failed utterly.

MILLY: I want a large whisky. You'd better have one too, Myra.

TONY: And me too, Oh, I see. You want me to go away. Why can't I stay? I might learn something. [MYRA *and* MILLY *are arming them-*

selves with stiff drinks.] Mother, I thought you wanted Milly to help with the sandwiches. Why don't you both go and cut the sandwiches?

MYRA: I've finished the sandwiches.

TONY [*shrill and anxious*]: You'll be tight and giggly before the thing even starts. [*To Myra*] Mother, you get giggly when you're tight. I really do hate to see women drink at all. [*To Milly, as Myra ignores him*] Do you, or do you not think I'm sexually attractive?

MILLY [*amiably but a trifle impatient*]: You're a knockout, love. [*To Myra*] You've got to put me in the picture. What's this business with your Philip?

[TONY *regards them anxiously, as they settle down for a gossip*]

MYRA: Oh, do run away, there's a good boy.

TONY: Well, I don't know, I don't really. [*Runs upstairs*]

[*The two women look at each other with raised eyebrows, sighing deeply.*]

MYRA: What am I going to do with him?

MILLY: Let me get some alcohol inside me if we are going to discuss the youth. Personally I think we should let the younger generation sink or swim without any further comment from us. [*Takes a hearty swig.*] They're only doing it to attract our attention.

MYRA: What's the good of sending one's son to a progressive school if he turns out like this? The idea was he'd be an integrated personality.

MILLY: Integrated with *what*?

MYRA: Ye-ees.

MILLY: Look what a public school did for Sandy.

MYRA: Hmmm. It did what it is supposed to do, surely.

MILLY: I walked out on Sandy's father because he was such a slick little go-getter, but one can't walk out on one's son.

MYRA: One doesn't even want to. Queer.

MILLY: Very, yes. [*There is a pause; they look at each other, eyeing each other ironically.*] He's not playing you up, is he?

MYRA: Sandy? But Sandy has such *beautiful* manners. [*She giggles.*]

MILLY [*giggling*]: I believe you. Well, give him the boot, I would. He's got what he wants, I suppose. [*At* MYRA'*s inquiring and rather hurt look*] Never in his life did my Sandy do anything that wasn't calculated.

MYRA: What, never?

MILLY: My principle with Sandy is, wait until he's worked through some situation – he's always in a better position than he was when he started. Then you know what he was after from the start. [*At sight of* MYRA'S *face*] You're not going to shed any tears over my Sandy, are you? [*Half-disgusted, half-admiring*] Wide boy . . . Oh, I'm not saying he's not in love. But my Sandy'll always fall in love where it does him most good.

MYRA: An enviable talent.

MILLY: Not yours.

MYRA: Nor yours.

[*They look at each other, grinning.*]

TOGETHER: Well, I don't know . . .

[*They roar with laughter. Pause.*]

MILLY: That Philip now.

MYRA [*dryly*]: He's brought his lady-love to stay here.

MILLY [*dryly*]: And he's going to marry her next week?

MYRA: So it would seem.

MILLY: Eh, but you're behaving nicely.

MYRA: There's such a satisfaction in behaving well. Not that one's more subtle forms of insult don't escape them entirely. [*She laughs shrilly, almost breaks down.*]

MILLY [*quiet and shrewd*]: Myra, love, you'd better take it easy.

MYRA: Yes. [*Blowing her nose*] Yes. [*Very gay*] What's happened to that man of yours? What's his name? Jack?

MILLY: Jack, yes. [*They look at each other and laugh.*]

MYRA: Well?

MILLY [*giggling*]: I walked out.

MYRA: What for this time?

MILLY: But it's always the same reason. Yes, come to think of it, it is. Well, I was at his week-end cottage. I was going to marry him on the Monday week, as I recall . . . God knows what for. What's this thing we have about getting married?

MYRA [*grimly*]: I can't think.

MILLY: Yes, well.

MYRA: Oh well. [*They laugh.*]

MILLY: My man Jack. Yes. Well, I'd cleaned the cottage up all of Friday, just for the love of the thing. Cleaned it some more on the Saturday, cooked a dinner for ten people on Saturday night, and organized the vegetable garden Sunday. On Sunday afternoon Jack went off to play golf, and the little woman hung some new curtains in the living-room.

MYRA: You don't have to tell me. He came home at seven o'clock and wanted to know why your face wasn't made up.

MILLY: No, my man Jack didn't mind me in my working dirt. It wasn't that. He came home from his golf and gave me a nice kiss. Reward for hard work, as it were. Oddly enough, it always is.

MYRA [*grimly*]: Yes.

MILLY: Quite so. Well, then there were steps outside. My God, it was Mr Stent.

MYRA: Mr Stent?

MILLY: Assistant Manager. The shoes Jack will inherit.

MYRA: All right, I know. [*She groans.*]

MILLY: Suddenly Jack went into a tizzy. [*Imitating a nervous flurried male voice*] 'Darling, that's Mr Stent. He can't see you like that. Do please change your dress.' [MYRA *giggles.*] I said to him: 'My man, your *property* is ready for display to anyone. But *I* have been cooking, cleaning, and digging for three days and I'm tired. Mr Stent will have to take me as I come.' Jack said – [*she imitates a nervous male voice*] – 'But darling, it will make such a bad impression.' [MYRA *is helpless with laughter.*] So I went up them stairs. I bathed. I changed. I made myself up like the Queen of Sheba. Then I went downstairs and cooked and served dinner for three. Then I entertained Mr Stent – oh, on his level, of course, keeping my tiny mind well in its place so as not to upset Mr Stent. Then I wished him a very good night. Then I wished Jack good-bye. Then I took my suitcase and walked out. I left the bill behind me. To charring eighteen hours at four shillings an hour. To buying and cooking and serving first-class dinner for ten, ten guineas. To planning and organizing vegetable garden, ten guineas. To making and hanging curtains, ten guineas. To acting as hostess to Mr Stent, five guineas. I didn't charge for my services in bed. Jack never did have a sense of humour. Besides, I didn't want to ruin him. And I asked him to make out the cheque for the Society for the protection of the Christian British Home.

MYRA: And did he?

MILLY: Oh yes, he did. He wrote me a letter saying why hadn't I let him know I was feeling like that. [*They both laugh.*]

MYRA: You have no discrimination.

MILLY: *I* haven't.

MYRA: Oh, all right.

MILLY: I suppose one has to make do with what there is.

MYRA: I was going to volunteer to go with those people to the testing area for the bomb. You know. Well, Tony was terribly upset. I was so happy. I was under the impression that he would mind if I got killed. Then he said: 'Mother, for God's sake have a sense of proportion.' Then I understood. It wouldn't have been respectable. That was what he minded. It wouldn't have been respectable. [*Laughs. Almost breaks down.*]

MILLY: Myra, you must let up, you really must.

MYRA: Yes.

MILLY: Your Tony's got a heart, at least.

MYRA [*surprised*]: Tony has?

MILLY: Whereas my Sandy . . . When Sandy became a gentleman as a result of his expensive education, I was expecting him to drop me – Oh! very pleasantly of course. I was surprised when he opted to stay with me. I thought it was out of love and affection. One day I heard him saying to one of his posh friends – [*imitates Sandy*] – 'You must meet my mother, she's such a character.' Light dawned on me. I played up, you can imagine. I was a woman of the people with a heart of gold. Really, I made myself sick – revolting! I'll be an asset to him in the Labour Party, won't I? Meet my mum, a working woman with a heart of gold . . . Little – wide boy.

MYRA: Milly, Sandy's very fond of you.

MILLY: Hmmm, yes.

MYRA: Milly, why did you give him that kind of education then?

MILLY [*defensively*]: I was doing the best for him.

MYRA: Were you – well? I don't think he thinks so.

MILLY: What? What's he said to you?

MYRA: Milly, are you sure there's not a good part of you that likes Sandy the way he is?

MILLY: What's he said to you?

MYRA: He once said that you've equipped him to play the racket, and he has no choice but to play it.

MILLY: No choice. Ohhh! – so it's my fault, is it?

MYRA: Aren't our children our fault?

MILLY: No choice! [*Throwing if off*] I wish you'd give him the boot before he drops you. I wish you would. It'd do him so much good.

MYRA [*with determination*]: Very well, I shall. Sandy, I shall say, Sandy, I no longer care for you.

MILLY: And do you?

MYRA [*grinning*]: It's so nice to have a man about the house.

MILLY [*grinning*]: Yeees.

MYRA: Well, it is. [*Her face changes.*] What am I going to do about Tony . . . Milly, what am I going to do? [*She almost breaks down. MILLY comes behind her, puts her arms around her.*]

MILLY: Myra, for God's sake, stop punishing yourself . . . We've lived our lives, haven't we? And we've neither of us given in to anything. We've both of us come through not too badly, considering everything. We're not going to come to a dead end in our sons?

MYRA: No.

MILLY: What's the use of living the way we have, what's the use of us never settling for any of the little cosy corners or the little cages or the second-rate men if we simply get tired now?

MYRA: Yes.

MILLY: Were you really going out with those people to the H-Bomb tests?

MYRA: Yes.

MILLY: Because you knew the Government wouldn't let anyone get near them anyway?

MYRA: No. I really wanted to – do something.

MILLY: You didn't mind getting killed?

MYRA: No.

MILLY: Myra, love, we all of us get depressed.

MYRA [*wrenching herself away from her*]: Depressed. That word annoys me. Half the time we dope ourselves up with some stimulant – men, our children, work. Then it fails and we see things straight, and it's called being depressed. You know quite well that there's only one question that everyone's asking – what are we alive for? Why? Why shouldn't that damned bomb fall? Why not? Why shouldn't the human race blow itself up? Is it such a loss? A little dirty scum on the surface of the earth – that's what we are.

MILLY [*ironically*]: Scum, scum – that's all.

MYRA [*impatiently*]: All right – laugh me out of it – it's easy enough. [*Laughs, irritably.*]

MILLY: If I remind you in a month from now of things you are saying tonight you'll laugh and say, 'Well, I was depressed then.'

MYRA: I dare say. Oh yes, I dare say. [*She is in a fever of irritation, angry, laughing, stamping about the stage, deadly serious.*] I keep dreaming, Milly. You know I keep having the same dream . . .

MILLY: Oh – dreams. So now we're going to turn into a pair of old women plotting our dreams and looking for portents.

MYRA [*almost growling*]: Ohhh! – yes. But I do. Every time I get my head on to a pillow, it's the same thing . . .

MILLY: Oh! Lord save us – get yourself tight and be done with it.

MYRA: No! Listen to me. Listen, Milly. [*She grabs Milly to make her listen. Milly is ironical, sceptical, uncomfortable.*] The whole world is full of great black machines. I am standing on the surface of the earth somewhere and everywhere about me on an enormous plain are great black machines. It is a world of cold white buildings and black motionless machines . . .

MILLY: Ho-ho – so we're against the machine now, are we; back to the Golden Age!

MYRA: . . . And I'm standing there, waiting. That's what it is, Milly, we're all waiting. No, listen . . . [*Now holds Milly fast, making her listen. Slowly* MILLY *succumbs, becomes part of the dream with Myra.*]

We are standing, waiting. We lift our eyes and see the curve of the horizon . . . it's on fire, Milly. Not a real fire – the curve of the earth crackles with the cold white crackle of electricity. Then we understand – the earth is burning. They've set the bomb off somewhere and half of the earth is already gone. Everywhere in front of us the plain is disintegrating in a cold white crackle of fire. It will reach us in a minute. And we stand there thinking, thank God. Thank God it's all over. Thank God it's all over . . .

[*For a minute* MILLY *is held fast inside Myra's persuasiveness. She pulls away.*]

MILLY [*irritably*]: Oh! Myra . . . Well, I don't have to be asleep to see all that. I can see it when I'm awake.

MYRA [*grim and humorously desperate*]: Do you realize we've only got through half of our lives? We've got to get through another thirty or forty years of being alive – if we're unlucky.

MILLY [*with her hands over her ears*]: Shut up, shut up, Myra.

MYRA: I can't face it, Milly. I can't face another forty years of being alive.

MILLY [*uncovering her ears*]: Well, we'll both have to face it. We're both as strong as mules. [*Gives Myra a drink.*] Now come clean, Myra. What's really eating you up? You've been talking around and around it . . . Philip's brought his girl here, Tony's in a bad mood, and it's all too much. That's all.

MYRA: That's all.

MILLY: Now listen to me. You had a good marriage with your husband. Then you and Philip were happy together for five years – that's more than most people get in their lives. You and Philip are good friends now. There's old Mike hanging around waiting for your first moment of weakness so you'll give in and marry him. You've got Tony. You're not doing too badly.

MYRA: Oh, don't be so complacent . . . don't be so damned sensible . . . you know quite well that nothing you say to me now makes any sense at all.

MILLY [*patiently*]: Yes, love, I know.

MYRA: I wish you'd do something for me. I wish you'd talk to Tony. I can never say anything to him. He imagines I want to get rid of him. It's like this. I've got hold of some money – enough to finish his studying. Now he says he doesn't want to be an architect. So I'd like him to take it and go off for a couple of years – doing as he likes, wherever he likes. He'll never be free again. He'll be 40 before he knows it. I wish I'd had five hundred pounds at his age to spend as I liked, to find out about the world. Well, if you could talk to him perhaps he might listen.

MILLY: You've raised five hundred pounds by doing your own housework?

MYRA: No, no, of course not.

MILLY: Myra, what've you been up to – what've you done?

MYRA: But I can't talk to him, Milly. He thinks I want to get rid of him.

MILLY [holding her and forcing her to face her]: Myra, what have you done?

MYRA: I've sold the house.

MILLY: You haven't.

MYRA: Yes, I have. To raise money for Tony.

MILLY: But, Myra, what are you going to do?

MYRA [almost airily]: I have no idea.

MILLY: You're going to marry old Mike.

MYRA: Oh, no. Why, Milly, I didn't expect you to be so – careful. What does it matter? I do hate being tied down. I always did. Surely it's more important for Tony to be free than to fuss about some bricks and a roof . . . if it comes to the worst you'll always take me in.

MILLY: But what's Tony going to say? Have you told him?

MYRA: Why should he care? He's young.

MILLY: Why haven't you told him?

MYRA: Because I can't talk to him.

[TONY comes down the stairs.]

MILLY: Look out, he's coming.

[MYRA hastily turns away to compose her face.]

TONY: Finished your girlish confidences? Though why it has to be in my bedroom . . .

MILLY: Why don't you choose some other place to park yourself?

MYRA: Obviously the hall is the place most calculated to cause the maximum inconvenience to everybody.

TONY: I do hope you're going to make up your face, Mother.

[MYRA *goes into living-room without replying.*]

What's wrong with mother?

MILLY: She's tired. [*Going towards living-room*] Come on, we've got to be gay if it kills us. Aren't you coming in at all?

TONY: No.

MILLY: You aren't interested to hear what's going on in Japan?

TONY: I'm sure the people in Japan feel like people everywhere else in the world – as if they've been handcuffed to a sleeping tiger.

MILLY: I want to talk to you sometime, young Tony.

TONY [*in Boyer voice*]: I want to talk to you, too. [MILLY *goes impatiently into living-room.*]

TONY [*collapsing on the divan*]: Thank God for the silence.

[*Almost at once he starts making machine-gun noises, pointing his arm all over the room. Stops. Imitates a bomb. More machine-gun noises.* ROSEMARY *comes in fast, from living-room. She is in a party dress and looking miserable.*]

TONY: Not in a party mood?

ROSEMARY: I can't stand listening to them talk. I can't. They talk about all kinds of horrors as if they were talking about the weather.

TONY [*laughing*]: They are.

ROSEMARY: I don't see how they can be so – matter-of-fact about everything.

TONY: Don't worry about them. They were just born thick-skinned.

[ROSEMARY *sits, listlessly.* TONY *hesitates, then after a struggle with himself, sits beside her, puts his arm around her. She immediately snuggles against him and closes her eyes. There is a look on his face of incredulous but derisive pride.*] Feeling better?

ROSEMARY: Yes. Would your mother think it rude if I left here tonight?

TONY: Don't go – unless you want to. Don't just rush away.

ROSEMARY: It was all no good. It was a mistake.

TONY: Yes, I know. Never mind. [*There is a burst of laughter and music.*]

ROSEMARY [*wistfully*]: They have a good time, don't they?

TONY: They'd have a good time if the skies were falling. If the end of the world were announced for Friday, Mother would say – 'Let's have a party'.

ROSEMARY [*fiercely*]: Yes, they're so childish.

TONY: Oh God, yes . . . Rosemary, I wish you'd tell me something.

ROSEMARY [*sitting up away from him*]: What – do you mean about politics – but I don't know about them.

TONY [*laughing*]: Yes, perhaps I do mean politics.

ROSEMARY: So *childish*. They talk as if they really believe what they do changes things. You know, 5,000 people listen to a speech and everything will be changed.

TONY [*laughing*]: Go on. Go on, Rosemary.

ROSEMARY: But it seems to me as if there are perhaps – six very important, very powerful men in the world – somewhere up there – we probably don't even know their names, and they make the decisions . . .

TONY: Go on.

ROSEMARY [*indicates living-room*]: In there they're talking about . . . I don't see how they can believe in it. If the 5,000 people killed themselves tomorrow in Trafalgar Square as a protest against – everything, the six powerful men up there wouldn't care, they wouldn't even notice. And it would be something in the news-papers for ordinary people.

TONY [*delighted, laughing*]: Go on, Rosemary, don't stop.

ROSEMARY: Just one of those important men can go mad or get drunk and – well, that's all. That's all.

TONY: Rosemary.

ROSEMARY: Yes. [*She lets herself fall back against him.* TONY *puts his arms around her, talks over her head.*]

TONY [*unconsciously rocking her*]: Rosemary, I've been thinking. What we need is something different. Something – very simple.

ROSEMARY [*eyes closed, against him*]: Yes.

TONY: Something very simple. I think I want to be a tramp. I've been thinking . . . the whole world is getting mass-produced and organized. But inside everybody's varnished and painted skin is a tramp. It's the inner emigration. Every morning in front of the bathroom mirror we polish our teeth and our hair and our skin, we set our faces to tick all day like metronomes against the image in the mirror until the lights go out at night. But inside, we've emigrated. We're tramps. Don't you see, Rosemary, we have to keep the tramp alive somehow. Would you like to be a tramp, Rosemary? [*Looks down at her face, but her eyes are closed. She is half-asleep.*] No, a tramp is solitary, a tramp is solitary ... [*Rocking her*] Shhh, Rosemary ...

ROSEMARY [*sleepily*]: Yes ...

    [*The door L bursts open, letting in a shout of music and talk.* PHILIP *comes in fast,* SANDY *after him.*]

SANDY: So if you're really looking for someone perhaps you'd try me.

PHILIP [*briefly*]: Yes, of course.

SANDY: It's really awfully good of you. May I come into your office tomorrow and talk it over with you?

PHILIP [*curtly*]: Yes, do. [*To Rosemary*] Aren't you well?

ROSEMARY: Perfectly well, thank you. [*At her leisure she disengages herself from* TONY, *but remains sitting close beside him.*]

PHILIP: It's really very rude to run away like that. It's not polite to Myra.

ROSEMARY: I'm sure Myra will bear up.

    [MYRA *comes in L, looking gay and beautiful.*]

MYRA: I can't have all the young people leaving my party. It leaves us all so dull.

SANDY [*laying his arm around her shoulders*]: Myra darling, how could any party be dull with you in it?

TONY: You should make up a Strontium-90 calypso and dance to it.

ROSEMARY: If you don't mind, Myra, I'd like to go to bed.

MYRA [*briefly*]: Of course I don't mind. [*To Tony*] I do think you might come in even if just for a few minutes.

TONY [*to Rosemary*]: Would you like to come out into the garden for a little? There's a moon tonight.

ROSEMARY [*with a defiantly guilty look at Philip*]: Yes, I'd love to ... just for a few minutes, and then I must go to bed.

[TONY *and* ROSEMARY *go out R.* PHILIP, *after a moment, walks angrily off after them.*]

SANDY [*gracefully amused*]: Lovers' quarrels.

MYRA: Oh, quite. Charming.

SANDY: How lucky we're more sensible.

MYRA [*gaily, flirting with him*]: Dear Sandy, you're always so sensible.

SANDY: Not so sensible as to be dull, I hope.

MYRA [*mocking and affectionate*]: Dull? You? Darling, never. [*Kissing him.*] Darling sensible Sandy.

SANDY: Dear Myra – so sad, isn't it?

MYRA: Sad? Sad – oh, I see. [*Bursts into laughter.*]

SANDY [*uneasily*]: I love your laugh, darling.

MYRA: Oh, I love it too. [*Regards him mockingly.*] Well, go on.

SANDY: You're in a very odd mood.

MYRA: You're quite right, darling, it's quite time for us to call it a day.

SANDY [*disconcerted*]: Yes, well, of course.

MYRA: And you've been wonderful. [*Imitating him*] Sandy, you're really so *wonderful*.

SANDY [*stiffly*]: I'm so glad we are both capable of being graceful about the end. Though of course you and I are much too close ever to part, darling.

MYRA: Oh, quite so. Exactly. [*Kissing him mockingly*] There. [*Laughing*] I've done it. Only by the skin of my teeth though. I must tell Milly. She'll be so pleased.

SANDY: Tell her what? You haven't been discussing *us* with Mother? But I'm sure she would quite agree that I did the right thing in breaking it off.

MYRA [*astounded*]: *You* did the right thing . . . [*Rocking with laughter*] Why of course, yes, you did, didn't you?

SANDY [*furious*]: Really, Myra, I do think your behaviour is in very bad taste.

[*He goes angrily out R as* PHILIP *comes in from the R.*]

PHILIP: And what's wrong with your young man?

MYRA: I might ask, what's wrong with your young woman?

[*He gives a short gruff laugh. They eye each other and both laugh.*]

PHILIP [*dryly*]: Well, Myra?

MYRA: Well, Philip?

PHILIP [*with whimsical exasperation*]: Really, women, women.

MYRA: Tell me, do you find Rosemary's behaviour in bad taste?

PHILIP [*rather sentimentally*]: I suppose it is better that she should find out what I'm like before rather than after.

MYRA [*dryly*]: It is *lucky*, isn't it? [*They eye each other, smiling, with an old and bitter emotion.*]

PHILIP [*on an impulse, dragged into saying it*]: It would be odd if we ended up with each other after all, wouldn't it?

MYRA [*tiredly*]: Rather odd, yes.

PHILIP [*with sentimental bitterness*]: You know me, Myra. I'm not much good . . . [*Turns away, frowning – the frown is a nervous spasm of irritation against himself for the role he is playing.*]

MYRA [*quickly*]: Don't do that, Philip, don't. I always did wish you wouldn't – it's so bloody insulting.

PHILIP [*gaily, but with self-dislike because he has not met her appeal*]: But, Myra, I'm proposing to you . . . I'm always proposing to you and you always turned me down.

MYRA [*ironically*]: Yes, you always were. But bigamy never did appeal to me much.

PHILIP [*half-serious, half playing at it and bitter with conflict*]: Well, old girl, what about it? Can you face all that over again?

MYRA [*against her will surrendering, smiling to him*]: What an awful prospect, all that over again . . .

[*They suddenly come together, cling together, almost kiss, passionately. But at the same moment with the same gesture of angry and bitter irritation, turn away from the embrace. They both laugh, painfully.*]

PHILIP [*the mood of surrender is gone. They are both back in their roles. He speaks with whimsical bitterness*]: No woman ever made me as unhappy as you did. I wonder why . . .

[*She says nothing but watches him ironically.*]

MYRA: I wonder why, too.

PHILIP: I wish you'd tell me the truth now, Myra . . .

MYRA [*groaning and ironical*]: Ohhh – about my infidelities?

PHILIP [*suddenly painfully and eagerly intense*]: For instance, that

American – you swore there was nothing – that he wasn't in your room that night?

MYRA [*almost groaning*]: Oh, Philip . . . do you suppose when we're both 70 you'll still be asking me . . . the one thing you can't afford to believe is that I always told you the truth.

PHILIP [*quickly*]: Oh come, come, you'll never change.

MYRA [*humorously groaning*]: Oh, Philip . . .

PHILIP [*gay, bitter, and guilty*]: After all, I can't say I don't know what I'm in for.

MYRA [*very dry*]: What you are saying is this: that you propose to marry me although you take your stand on the fact that I lied continuously to you for five years, that I was unfaithful to you for five years, and that you insist I will continue both to betray you and to lie about it.

PHILIP [*gay and guilty*]: Why, Myra dear, now that I'm older I'm more tolerant, that's all. Well, what do you say?

MYRA [*bitter, smiling*]: Obviously nothing.

PHILIP: What? [*Quickly*] There you are – that's what always happens when I propose to you – you turn me down.

[*She smiles at him. He smiles back. It is very painful. A moment of quiet.*]

[*Almost groaning*] Oh, Lord . . .

MYRA [*groaning, painful but humorous*]: Ohhh . . . [*then, suddenly furious and loud*] I wish just once I could meet a man who didn't tell himself lies and expect me to believe them.

PHILIP [*shouting*]: You know quite well I can't stand the way you're always giving yourself away to everybody and everything. *I can't stand you, Myra.*

[*A moment's quiet. They look at each other, smiling bitterly.*]

[*whimsically*] When you've given up – when you've got grey hair and wrinkles, I'll take you on then.

MYRA: Shall I dye my hair and paint on wrinkles?

PHILIP: Yes.

MYRA: No one ever loved me as you did, no one. That's what I can't forgive you for – it wouldn't have mattered if you hadn't loved me. But you did. And you turned me down.

PHILIP [*groaning, turning away*]: Oh, let's leave it, let's leave it now.

MYRA: You turned me down because I loved you. You couldn't stand being loved.

PHILIP: Oh, Lord, it is absolutely *intolerable*!

MYRA [*between her teeth*]: Absolutely hopeless! [*They shrug, stand silent.*] [MIKE *comes in from L.*]

MIKE: Why, here you are. Philip, where's your charming little Rosemary? Everybody's running away from the party. I thought I'd come and find you. [*Comes up to* MYRA.] What's wrong, dear? [*Puts his arm around her.*] Myra dear, you really do look bad, you know. You do really need someone to look after you.

MYRA [*letting her head lie on his shoulder*]: Dear Mike. You are always so sweet.

MIKE [*to Philip*]: Myra needs someone to look after her.

PHILIP [*grimly*]: Perhaps she does. [*With a short laugh*] You two look rather well together.

MYRA [*smiling painfully to Mike*]: He thinks we look well together. Philip does.

MIKE [*wistfully*]: You know what I think, dear.

MYRA [*to Philip*]: You like the sight of me and Mike together?

PHILIP [*embarrassed, hurt, and angry*]: Well, why not? If that's what you want.

MYRA [*to Mike*]: You'd like to take me on?

MIKE [*carefully*]: I don't have to tell you what I've always wanted. [*Looks doubtfully from Myra to Philip.*]

MYRA: Can you *stand* me, Mike? Can you stand me?
    [PHILIP *turns away, frowning.*]

MIKE: Stand you, dear?

MYRA: It would be awful if you couldn't stand me.

MIKE: But, Myra dear, I've loved you for years. After all, I've never made any secret of it to anybody.
    [MYRA *smiles at him. In an impulse of joy* MIKE *embraces her. But because of her reaction the embrace ends in a brotherly hug.*]

MIKE [*hopefully*]: I'm so happy, dear.

MYRA: Dear Mike.
    [*She lays her head on his shoulder and looks at Philip.* PHILIP *turns*]

away with a helpless and bitter gesture. ROSEMARY *and* TONY *come in from garden R. They have been talking animatedly but at the sight of the three they stop still.*]

ROSEMARY [*awkward because of Philip, to Tony*]: I think I'll go to bed now.

TONY [*forgetting Rosemary at the sight of* MIKE *and* MYRA *who still have their arms around each other*]: Well, Mother? Well, Mike?

MIKE: There you are, my boy.

ROSEMARY [*defiantly, to Philip*]: I must really go to bed, I'm so tired.

PHILIP [*suddenly concerned to reclaim her*]: But, Rosemary, don't go yet. Stay down here and talk a little. Have a drink.

ROSEMARY [*unwillingly reclaimed*]: Well, just for a minute – no, I won't have a drink.

[PHILIP *and* ROSEMARY *sit together on the stairs.* MYRA *and* MIKE *are standing together. His arm is still around her.*]

TONY [*looking from one couple to the other*]: Oh, no!

[MILLY *comes in from living-room.*]

MILLY: Do come and do your duty, Myra – I can't cope with all these people any longer by myself.

TONY [*fiercely to Milly*]: Ever so interesting, sex, isn't it?

MILLY [*briskly*]: I've always found it so . . . [*But she sees his face, turns to look first at Myra and Mike then at Philip and Rosemary.*]

TONY [*shrilly*]: What astounds me is the way it so obviously is everyone's favourite occupation.

MILLY [*briskly*]: Never mind, love, you'll soon get into the way of it . . . [*Looking at his face she suddenly understands he is about to crack. She lays a hand briefly on his shoulder, saying to Mike.*] Take Myra back to her guests, there's a dear.

MIKE: Of course, we're just going. [*Leads Myra across to living-room door. They go out.*]

[MILLY *locks the door, turns to Tony.*]

TONY [*pathetically*]: She's not starting something with Mike now, is she? Surely she isn't seriously going to . . .

MILLY: And why not?

TONY [*almost beside himself, he runs to foot of stairs and confronts Rose-*

mary]: Rosemary, come and have a drink with me, come and talk.

ROSEMARY [*taking Philip with her upstairs*]: No thanks, Tony, I think Philip and I'll go to bed now.

[PHILIP *and* ROSEMARY *go out of sight upstairs.* MILLY *jams door on R with chair.*]

TONY: Oh *no*. [*Whirling on Milly*] Why? Half an hour ago she was ready to kick dear Uncle Philip downstairs.

MILLY: Bless you, dear.

TONY: It's going to be such a jolly night. Imagine it – Rosemary and Uncle Philip in one bed – *my* bed, but let that pass. Then there's Mother. Will it be Sandy or Uncle Mike, do you suppose? Why not both?

MILLY [*calmly*]: You're not talking to me about your mother like that, young Tony.

TONY [*almost ecstatic with pain*]: Or they might have a little change in the middle of the night. Mother and Uncle Philip – for old time's sake. And Sandy and Rosemary might have a good deal in common – who knows? Of course they *are* pretty near the same age, probably a handicap. Then there's you and me.

MILLY: Take it easy, Tony. Take it easy.

TONY: Three happy well-assorted couples . . . [*He roars with laughter.* MILLY, *seeing what is coming, moves towards him, stands waiting.*] Three couples, each couple in a nice tidy little room with the door locked. And in the morning we'll make polite conversation at breakfast. Of course, there is an odd man out – dear Uncle Mike. Well, he can lie on the mat outside Mother's door. Why shouldn't we all ring each other up in the middle of the night and report progress. The grunts and groans of pleasurable love-making would be interrupted for the sake of a few minutes' militant conversation about the dangers of the hydrogen bomb. Then back to what everyone's really interested in. It's bloody funny, when you come to think about it . . . [*He breaks down, sobbing.* MILLY *catches him as he heels over on the divan, holds him against her, rocking him.*] I simply can't stand any of it. I can't stand it. I can't stand it.

SCENE TWO

The next morning, rather early.

The curtain rises on the room in disorder. MILLY *and* TONY *are lying on the untidy divan.* TONY *has his black trousers on, nothing above.* MILLY *is wearing a black lace petticoat. She is smoking and watching him with a calm maternal eye. The door L is wedged with the chair.*

[TONY *makes the sound of machine-gun fire with his mouth, pointing an imaginary machine-gun over the ceiling, like a small boy.* MILLY *does not move.* TONY *does it again.*]

MILLY: What's that in aid of?

TONY: I love that sound. That sound is me. I love it.

MILLY: Can't say I do.

TONY: What are you going to do when Mother comes down those stairs? For God's sake put some clothes on.

MILLY: I like myself like this. Don't you?

TONY [*examines her, drops his head on his arms*]: I don't know. I don't know.

MILLY: I know. You don't. [*She caresses the back of his neck, runs the side of her palm down his spine. He shrinks away from her.*] No? [*As he remains silent, she takes his head in her arms and cradles it.*] Is this better? [*Rocks him, half-tender, half-derisive*] Baby, baby, baby.

TONY [*shutting his eyes*]: Put on some clothes. Put some clothes on.

MILLY: You'd like me to put a veil over my face and keep my hair covered.

TONY: Yes.

MILLY: Well, I'm not going to. You'd better learn to like the female form. [*Rocking him*] You wanted to take me into bed so as to annoy your mother. Here I am. But when it comes to the point you're scared she might know.

TONY: She'll come down the stairs, see us and say: 'Milly, where's my H-Bomb file?'

MILLY [*laughing*]: Child. You're a child.

TONY: Oh, I can hear her. She said, 'Milly, I'm worried about that son of mine. He's still a virgin. Do something about it, will you?'

Then, dismissing this item on her agenda, she said: 'Where's my tape-recording of . . .' Oh, Christ . . . [*He rolls away from her.*]

MILLY [*running the side of her palm down his spine*]: Come here, young Tony.

TONY: If you're going to seduce me again then let's have some appropriate music. [*Makes machine-gun noises again.*]

MILLY [*calmly, moving away from him*]: Young Tony, I'm going to give you some good advice, and if you've got any sense you'll take it.

TONY: Action. Action is what I want. Not words.

MILLY: You'll find yourself a nice friendly tart and put in a couple of weeks learning your job. Then perhaps you'll be fit for adult society.

TONY [*grinning*]: What? You're walking out on me? You've got other fish to fry? Is that it? I thought I'd found a nice friendly tart. [*She continues to regard him amiably.*] Well, why don't you hit me?

MILLY: What for?

TONY [*shrilly*]: I've insulted you.

MILLY: *You* insult *me*?

TONY: I expected you to hit me.

MILLY: Why do you want to be hit?

TONY [*collapsing on to the divan, face down*]: Oh, I don't know, I don't know, I don't know.

[MILLY *lays a hand on his shoulder. He flings it off.*]

[*Shrilly*] I simply don't like women.

MILLY [*as she slowly puts on her black sweater*]: That's half of humanity disposed of.

TONY: All you're interested in is . . .

MILLY: I was under the impression that that night of love was your idea.

TONY: Love!

MILLY [*suddenly and for the first time hurt*]: You've made use of me, young Tony. You made use of me.

TONY [*guilty*]: Of course women are so much better than men.

MILLY [*grimly*]: Is that so?

TONY [*sentimental and shrill*]: You're so much stronger.

MILLY: That's very nice for you, isn't it?

TONY: But I mean it, you are.

MILLY: When I hear men saying that women are so much stronger than men, I feel like . . .

TONY: What?

MILLY: Reaching for my revolver.

TONY: I imagined it was a compliment.

MILLY: Did you now, love. I prefer the more obvious forms of contempt. [*She slowly puts on her black skirt.*] If you really don't like sex why don't you leave us alone? Otherwise you're going to turn into one of those spiteful little men who spend their lives punishing women in bed . . . Where's my brooch? [*She adjusts the sweater, which last night was open over her shoulders, tight to her throat with a brooch.*]

TONY: Now you look like a respectable *Hausfrau.*

MILLY: You might also put in some time asking yourself why you have to say you don't like women.

TONY [*slowly sits up on the divan, legs crossed*]: Women, women, women . . . [*He meditatively and sensuously bites his own shoulder.*]
    [MILLY *stands watching satirically, hands on hips.*]

MILLY: You might find it all more satisfactory if you took a mirror into bed with you.

TONY: I have no idea at all what you're talking about.

MILLY: Oh, I believe you. You probably don't.

TONY [*shrilly*]: You lay all last night in my arms. You were perfectly sweet. And now . . .

MILLY: What's the matter with you all, anyway? We've committed the basic and unforgivable crime of giving you birth – but we had no choice, after *all* . . . Well, God damn the lot of you. [*Going towards door R*] I'm going home. For the sake of appearances.

TONY: Oh, don't worry about my reputation, please.

MILLY [*amazed*]: Your reputation? [*Scornful*] Your reputation. Why, do you consider yourself compromised? [*Laughs*] I'm considering my Sandy.

TONY: Why? Your Sandy is such a man of the world.

MILLY: Not so far as I am concerned. I have preserved my Sandy's mental equilibrium by the practice of consummate hypocrisy. It is usually referred to as tact.

TONY: What a pity my mother thinks tact beneath her.

MILLY: It's always a mistake to treat you as if you were grown-ups. Always.

TONY [*jumping up*]: Milly, don't go. Don't go, Milly. [*He goes after her.*] You're not really going . . . I'm sorry if I hurt you.

MILLY [*coming back, she stands with her hands on her hips, looking at him*]: Young Tony, why don't you get out of here. For Christ's sake, *get out.*

TONY [*sharply*]: Mother told you to say that.

MILLY: The Lord help us. [*Goes to him, puts her hands on his shoulders from behind. He leans his head back against her and closes his eyes.*] You ought to get out, Tony. Bum around a bit. You can't stay here. Surely you can see that your mother's worried because you don't want any life of your own?

TONY: You mean, she wants a life of her own.

MILLY [*exasperated*]: Tony, you aren't ten years old.

TONY: What does she want? She wants to marry Uncle Mike? I don't believe it.

MILLY: Perhaps she thinks it would make you happy if she settled down.

TONY: With Uncle Mike? She's going to settle down with old Mike just to please me?

MILLY: But she's worried about you. You surely can see that she's bound to be worried about you?

TONY: With Aunty Mike. [*Laughs unpleasantly.*]

MILLY: And besides, she's lonely.

TONY: Lonely? My battling mum? Why on earth? She's never alone. [*Pause.*] Then if she's lonely, why does she want to get rid of me?

MILLY [*dropping her hands, shrugs, and moves away*]: I give up. I simply give up. But you should get out. You're 22. You should be banging and crashing around South America or the Middle East, getting mixed up in all kinds of things, making a fool of yourself, having women . . .

TONY [*wincing*]: Oh Christ!

MILLY: You ought to be shouting your head off about everything, revolutionizing, upsetting all the equilibriums.

TONY: Equilibrium? What equilibrium? You don't really imagine that I should want to revolutionize after watching your lot at it all my life? Upsetting the equilibrium . . . that's just it! You're so childish . . . if there was, by any miracle, an equilibrium anywhere you'd put a bomb under it just for the sake of seeing everything rock. All I want is an equilibrium – just five minutes of stability. [*Pause.*] This house is the only thing in my life that has – stayed in one place. It's the only thing I can count on. Why should I want to leave it? [MILLY *slowly comes up behind him again, cradles him against her.*] I remember after our other house was blown up, that night Mother and I were lying under the bricks waiting to be rescued, and my father was dead beside us, I remember thinking that there would never be another house. I remember thinking Mother would get killed too, and I'd have to go to an orphanage. I remember lying there under the bricks with the bombs falling . . . after that we were in one furnished room after another for months and months. Then there was this house. I remember the first few weeks we were here I used to go secretly around looking at the walls, wondering if the cracks were going to appear soon. I couldn't believe a house could be something whole, without cracks. I love this house. I don't want ever to leave it. I'd like to – pull it over my ears like a pillow and never leave it.

MILLY: Tony, love, you can't build your life around a house.

TONY: Yes I can, yes I can . . . hold me, Milly.

MILLY [*rocking him*]: Tony, suppose you had to leave?

TONY [*eyes closed, blissfully, sleepily*]: Had to? Had to? Why? No. I'll stay here always. Hold me, Milly.

MILLY: Tony, love, listen to me, I must talk to you.

TONY: No, don't talk. Just hold me.

MILLY: Tony, Tony, Tony. But I have to talk to you . . .

[MYRA *comes down the stairs, wearing her old trousers, without make-up, smoking.*]

MYRA: Good morning.

MILLY [*without letting Tony go*]: Good morning, Myra.

TONY [*from Milly's arms*]: Slept well, Mother?

MYRA: Thank you, no. [*To Milly, smiling*] You're a very early visitor.

MILLY [*grinning*]: Not too early, I hope.

[*She lets her arms fall away from Tony. TONY moves away in a drifting listless movement to the window, leans there, back turned. MYRA raises her eyebrows at Milly. MILLY gives a massive good-natured shrug.*]

TONY: More songs without words. Yes, Mother, the operation is successfully concluded.

MILLY: Do you want me to tidy up this bed again?

MYRA: I don't know, I haven't thought. I don't know what's going on, if Philip and Rosemary have made it up or not. If she's going home, then Tony can have his room back.

TONY [*turning*]: I wish someone would explain this to me – last night Rosemary was through with Uncle Philip. She hated and despised him. If she comes down those stairs announcing that the marriage is on, are you two wise women going to let her marry him? You both know quite well that she'll be miserable. [*They both shrug.*] What? You aren't going to say that you don't believe in interfering with other people's lives?

MYRA: What do you think we should do? Take her aside and warn her against Philip? How can we?

TONY: Why not?

MYRA: You should do it.

TONY: Why me?

MYRA: You're her age. She'll trust you.

TONY: Oh – hell. [*Aggressively, to his mother*] Where's Sandy? Surely he should do it? He's the boy for public and personal relations.

MILLY: Tony dear, that girl likes you.

TONY [*amazed*]: She likes *me*?

MILLY [*patting him*]: You've been kind to her.

TONY: Oh.

MILLY [*kissing him*]: Bless you, dear boy.

MYRA [*watching them, ironically*]: Oh well, I don't know. I'm feeling very old this morning. [*Goes to the mirror and looks at it.*] Oh, oh, oh.

FIRST COMEDIAN: Get hold of it by the two back legs. Keep your arms straight out in front of you and see if you can bring it up to shoulder height. And hold it there.

MR PARADOCK: Where do I get the chair from?

SECOND COMEDIAN: Imagine it.

MR PARADOCK: Shall I?

FIRST COMEDIAN: Go on.

[BRO PARADOCK *squats on his haunches, gets up and removes his jacket, squats again, and adjusts his position before going through the motions of taking a grip on the back legs of a chair. His efforts to stand up with it are successful but strenuous.* FIRST COMEDIAN *picks up a chair which he places in* BRO PARADOCK'S *outstretched hands. He holds this chair without effort.*]

MR PARADOCK: That's extraordinary! I'd never have believed it.

SECOND COMEDIAN: You were letting your imagination run away with you.

MR PARADOCK: I'd never have believed it. The one I imagined I was lifting was twice as heavy as this one.

FIRST COMEDIAN: You've just got a strong imagination. You're like me. I used it to develop my muscles.

SECOND COMEDIAN: Why don't you two have a contest of strength? We'll ask Mrs Paradock for a pair of scales when she comes in. See which of you can hang the heaviest weight on them.

FIRST COMEDIAN: What do you say, Bro?

MR PARADOCK: I'm game if you are. [*He goes to the door, opens it, and puts his head out.*] Middie! Have we still got those scales?

[MIDDIE PARADOCK *is heard off:* 'As far as I know. What do you want them for?']

MR PARADOCK: I'll go and get them now.

[BRO PARADOCK *goes out. Several seconds later* MIDDIE PARADOCK *comes in, followed by* BRO PARADOCK *with the scales.*]

MRS PARADOCK: I hear you're going to have a trial of strength between you.

SECOND COMEDIAN: Not me, Mrs Paradock. It's these two.

MRS PARADOCK: I'm surprised Bro's got a strong imagination – I'd never have said so.

MYRA [*coldly*]: Obviously not. I believe he went home.

MILLY: Oh, did he now? [MILLY *looks at Myra.* MYRA *looks at Milly, full of wild mischievous delight. She collapses in a chair, laughing.*]

MYRA: Oh, Milly, don't mind me – but this is one situation you can't walk out on.

[*As she laughs the door-bell rings,* R. TONY *looks out of window, turns to grin at Milly and Myra. Unwedges door.* SANDY *enters fast, goes straight to Milly.*]

SANDY: Mother, you might have let me know that you had plans to stay out last night.

MILLY: I might have done. If I'd had plans.

SANDY: I was worried about you.

MILLY: I never worry about you. I know you can look after yourself.

SANDY: Where were you?

MILLY: Here.

SANDY [*relieved*]: Oh, you were with Myra. Oh . . . [*Looks at Tony and stiffens.*] I see.

[MYRA *laughs.* SANDY *turns on her, furious.*]

MYRA: Sandy dear, have you been worrying about *me* all this time and I never knew it?

SANDY [*furious*]: Really, Myra, I would never have believed it possible that you could behave in such sheer bad taste, really Myra . . .

[MYRA *laughs. Her attention is caught by* ROSEMARY *and* PHILIP *at the top of the stairs.* SANDY *turns, then* MILLY *and* TONY. *They all stand and watch as* ROSEMARY *and* PHILIP *slowly descend.*]

ROSEMARY [*half-way down the stairs, in command of the situation, bravely making a necessary announcement*]: Good morning. Philip and I have talked it over and we have decided that it would be very much more sensible *not* to get married. [*No one knows what to say.*]

TONY: I'm delighted there is one sensible person in this house.

[ROSEMARY *leaves* PHILIP *at the foot of the stairs and goes to stand by Tony at the window. The stage is now like this:* TONY *and*

ROSEMARY *standing side by side, back to the window, watching.*
PHILIP *at foot of the stairs.* SANDY *and* MILLY *together near the door,*
R. MYRA *by herself at centre.*]

PHILIP: Well, Myra, I'm sorry all this has been foisted on you.

MYRA: Oh, don't mention it. [*Smiles ironically at him. Her smile brings
him across to her.*]

[THEY *are now close together, looking into each other's face.*]

SANDY [*from beside Milly*]: Philip, perhaps I could go down to the
office with you . . .

[*He is about to go over to Philip:* MILLY *grabs him by the arm and
makes him stay by her. She keeps tight hold of him.*]

PHILIP [*to Myra, in a low voice*]: So everyone's back where they
started – except you? You're going to marry old Mike?

MYRA: No.

PHILIP: Well, old girl?

MYRA [*with grim humour*]: My hair isn't grey yet . . . I wouldn't forgive you, Philip. I wouldn't be the good woman sitting on the
mountain-top forgiving you your sins.

PHILIP: Oh Lord, Myra, I'm tired . . . I really would like something –
quiet. [*Dryly, tender, bitter*] Well, Myra?

MYRA: I've told you, I wouldn't forgive you. You cast me in the
one role long enough – now you want me to be the quiet woman
waiting to welcome you home? But I wouldn't forgive you. If I
did it would be contempt. *I've* never despised you, Philip.

PHILIP [*half-groaning*]: Oh, Lord, it is utterly *intolerable*.

MYRA [*half-groaning, turning away*]: Oh God, yes . . .

SANDY: Philip, if you're going to the office, we could go together.

PHILIP [*impatiently*]: Yes.

MILLY [*holding Sandy*]: I was under the impression you came here
for me – why are you so interested in Philip all of a sudden. [TONY
suddenly laughs.] Oh, I see . . . I thought that was the job Philip had
had arranged for Tony.

SANDY: But I thought Tony had turned it down unconditionally.

TONY: He has, don't worry.

SANDY: I wouldn't have dreamed of approaching Philip unless I was
sure Tony wasn't interested.

PHILIP: I'm late. I must go.

MILLY [holding Sandy fast]: You come home. You can arrange your career with Philip another day.

PHILIP: Where's my briefcase?

SANDY [turning furiously on Milly]: Mother, if you didn't want me to get a decent job and do all the regular things why did you set me up for it?

MILLY: Oh – no one'll ever blame you for anything!

SANDY [furious]: Well, why did you? What am I doing wrong?

MILLY: Of course it's my fault. I'm your mother – that's what I'm for.

SANDY: And if Tony wants the job I'll stand down. What do you expect me to do? Be a tramp, like Tony?

MYRA [absolutely delighted]: Why, Tony darling, why didn't you tell me?

TONY: Oh, my God!

ROSEMARY [holding Tony]: Shhh, Tony.

MYRA: Why, darling Tony, that's wonderful, it would be so good for you.

PHILIP [exasperated]: Really, Myra, how can you be such a romantic.

TONY [breaking from Rosemary, standing beside Philip, accusing her]: Mother, why should it be good for me?

MYRA [at the two of them]: What have I done now? If you want to be a tramp, am I expected to lock you in the house?

TONY ⎱ [together, shouting at her]: Mother . . .
PHILIP ⎰ Myra, you're utterly intolerable!

MYRA [gaily]: What's wrong? Perhaps I'll be a tramp, too: why not?

TONY [shouting at her]: You are a tramp!

[MIKE has entered, R, carrying a bunch of flowers. PHILIP, TONY, and MYRA have not seen him.]

MILLY: Myra, you have a visitor.

[MYRA turns, PHILIP and TONY fall back.]

MIKE: Myra darling, I know it's appallingly early, but I had to come. [He holds out the flowers. She does not take them.] I've had some really lovely news, darling. Or, at least, I do hope you'll think so. I'm invited to China. For a series of lectures. And I spoke to the organizer this morning. If we're married, of course you'll come too. It would be a rather lovely honeymoon.

MYRA: I'm sorry, Mike.

MIKE: But, of course, if you feel you don't want to leave your committee work now I'll quite understand.

MYRA: Mike, I'm sorry. Last night I was just . . . [MIKE *stares at her, helpless.*] I'm so sorry. We'll just have to go on as we've always done. You must forgive me. You've forgiven me often enough, haven't you?

[MIKE *seems as if he's crumpling inwardly. He stares at her, around at the others, then blunders out, R, still holding the flowers.*]

TONY: Oh, *Mother*! [*He turns to watch out of window.*]

MYRA: Oh, that was bad, that was very bad.

MILLY: Yes, love, it was. Very bad.

PHILIP [*furious*]: Myra, you are utterly intolerable.

[MYRA *lays her head down on the back of her chair.*]

Intolerable. I'm very late. [*He is on his way out R, remembering Rosemary.*] Good-bye, Rosemary. [*At door, back to Myra*] I'll be seeing you, Myra. Look after yourself.

[ROSEMARY *has not responded to* PHILIP'S *good-bye. But she stands at the window, beside* TONY, *watching him go.*]

SANDY [*escaping from* MILLY]: I'll go with Philip. [*From door, hastily*] Good-bye, Myra. I'll be seeing you.

MYRA [*who has not lifted her head from the chair-back*]: Oh damn, damn, damn.

MILLY [*to Myra*]: Charming. All quite charming. Oh well, look after yourself, love. And don't forget that tape-recording for the meeting. We'll need it. Meet you in the pub as usual. [*Goes out R.*]

TONY [*turning from window*]: Mother, why did you do that?

MYRA: I thought you wanted me to.

TONY: Mother, he's standing in the garden, crying. He's standing there, crying. Did you have to do it like that? Oh, damn it all, Mother.

MYRA: I've broken with Mike. After twenty years.

TONY: Yes, and how did you do it? As if he were . . .

MYRA: And I've broken finally with Philip. That's all finished. And I've broken with Sandy. Well? Isn't that what you wanted?

TONY: I don't want you to do anything you don't . . . [MYRA *laughs.*] I don't want . . . All I want is to be here in this house, with you, Mother – and some sort of . . . dignity. I'm so tired of all the brave speeches and the epic battles and the gestures. Wouldn't it be enough if we were just peaceful together? This house is like a sounding-board.

MYRA: Yes, I was thinking – we should move to a flat. This house is much too big.

TONY [*appalled*]: Mother, you can't be serious.

MYRA [*evasively*]: You don't think so? Why not?

TONY: Oh no, no, no.

MYRA: But it's so big. And I've got a bit of money. We could get ourselves a nice flat.

TONY: Money, yes. Where did you get it from?

MYRA [*proudly*]: Five hundred pounds. And more later.

TONY: Five hundred pounds. But where? We've never had all that money all at once.

MYRA: Oh, money from heaven. [*She moves away to escape his questioning, notices* ROSEMARY, *still bent by the window, back turned to them. She goes to Rosemary and puts her arm around her.*] Don't cry, Rosemary. [*She turns Rosemary round and smiles at her.*]

ROSEMARY [*rather bitterly, smiling back*]: I'm not crying.

TONY [*desperately anxious, pulling Myra away from Rosemary*]: Mother, I want to know. You're not just going to get out of it like that.

MYRA: Tony, before you settle down to being an honest electrician, I wish you'd take that money and . . .

TONY: What? Sow a few wild oats?

MYRA: Oh . . . sow anything you damned well please.

TONY: Mother, I'm being serious. In about a month from now I'm going to get myself a job. As an electrician. It's what I want. Work for eight hours a day, regularly paid, three square meals a day and . . .

MYRA [*derisively*]: Security! [*To Rosemary*] All he wants is security.

ROSEMARY: But Myra, what's wrong with that?

MYRA [*shrugging contemptuously*]: Oh, I don't know . . . I suppose you'll spend jolly evenings in the local coffee bar, join a skiffle group, become a scruffy little bohemian, one of the neo-conformists, enjoying all the postures of rebellion from safe positions of utter respectability.

TONY: That's it, exactly.

MYRA: 'And thus from no heights canst thou fall.'

TONY [*derisively, to* ROSEMARY]: Heights, she wants. [*Derisively, at Myra*] Heights, heights . . . We'll leave you to skip about on the heights. Mother, why don't you leave people alone. Just leave us alone . . . do you know what I'd really enjoy doing? I'd like to paint this house. To decorate it. I really would.

MYRA: You want to decorate the house? [*To Rosemary, blankly.*] He's 22 and he wants to spend his time decorating the house.

ROSEMARY: I don't see what's wrong with it.

MYRA [*to Tony*]: Wait a bit, don't start painting the house yet.

TONY: But why should I wait? I'll go out this afternoon and choose colours. It'll be fun. [*Suspiciously*] What's up? What are you up to?

MYRA: Oh, nothing. Nothing. Look, I've got an awful lot to do this morning. Will you help me? It's that tape-recording. Sandy said he'd help me but now he's gone.

TONY: Oh, *no*.

MYRA: But I promised it for the meeting tonight.

TONY: Meetings, meetings. Who cares what's said at meetings.

MYRA: Tony, if you're trying to stop my work for the committee I'm not going to.

TONY: All these people in and out. All the noise, the speeches, the *mess*.

MYRA: I'm not going to become a sort of monument to your desire for – whatever it is.

TONY: Dignity.

MYRA: If you call dignity sitting with your hands folded waiting to be blown up – well, I'm not going to be blackmailed into inertia. Please help me. Are you an electrician or are you not? I want you to play that tape back and take out the bits that are simply dull.

TONY: Dull!

MYRA: Will you or won't you? If not I'll ring up . . .

TONY: Who? Uncle Mike?

MYRA: It seems at the moment there's no one I can ring up. At least, not with dignity. [*She suddenly bursts into tears, and turns away.*]

TONY [*appalled*]: Mother.

MYRA: Oh, leave me alone. [*Goes to window, stands with her back turned.*]

[*ROSEMARY takes his arm, shakes her head. Indicates machine.*]

TONY: Oh, all right, I'll do it.

ROSEMARY: I'll help you.

[*The two crouch by the machine. TONY starts it going. After a few seconds of war noises, shuts it off.*]

TONY: Oh Lord, *no.*

MYRA [*still with back turned, her voice almost in control*]: You see, people have no imagination. That's the trouble.

TONY [*to her back*]: Can't you see that people can't bear to think about it? It's all too big for everyone. They simply can't bear to think about it. [*As ROSEMARY shakes her head at him*] Oh, all *right.*

MYRA: There's some new tape there if you want it.

TONY [*putting on the new tape; begins to run it*]: There, that's better.

ROSEMARY: What are you doing?

TONY: Playing a record of silence.

MYRA [*still with back turned*]: Tony, you said you'd help me.

TONY: A clean sheet. A new page. Rosemary, say something very simple, very quiet, very beautiful, something I'd like to hear when I play this thing back.

ROSEMARY [*in an urgent whisper*]: Tony, your mother is *crying.*

TONY: But what can I do? . . . Say something, Rosemary, do say something.

ROSEMARY: But what?

TONY: Surely there's something you need to say.

ROSEMARY: But what about?

TONY: Anything. What you feel about – life.

ROSEMARY: But I don't know.

TONY: Then – people.

ROSEMARY: Who?

TONY: Anybody.

ROSEMARY: Why?

TONY: Oh Lord. [*He switches off machine.*] All right, let's have bombs and blasts and gunfire. Oh *Lord.* For instance, you've just decided not to marry Philip. Well *you*'re not going to cry, are you?

ROSEMARY: I've finished crying.

[MYRA *turns round from the window. She has controlled herself. Stands watching ironically.*]

TONY: Are you unhappy?

ROSEMARY: Yes.

TONY: But you wouldn't have been happy with him, would you?

ROSEMARY [*turning and seeing Myra*]: Well . . .

MYRA: Go on.

ROSEMARY: I don't think I expected to be.

TONY: Then why did you say you'd marry him?

ROSEMARY: He said . . . people should be ready to take chances. He said people shouldn't be afraid.

TONY: And so you said you'd marry him?

[ROSEMARY *turns, gives Myra another troubled but defiant look.* MYRA *nods at her to proceed.*]

ROSEMARY: Yes. Philip suddenly came into my life and made fun of everything I did. He said I wasn't alive at all. He made me read books.

TONY [*laughing*]: Books !

ROSEMARY: Yes, he said I might just as well be dead, the way I was living. He said when I came to die I wouldn't know I'd ever been alive . . .

TONY: And that's why you said you'd marry him?

ROSEMARY [*after another look at Myra, who meets it with a grave ironical nod*]: Yes. He said there was only one thing people should be afraid of – of not growing. He said happiness didn't matter. People should grow, be everything, do a lot of things, and never be afraid of being unhappy . . .

TONY [*laughing derisively*]: Philip said all that, did he? Uncle Philip did? Well, look at him now, look at him now . . .

ROSEMARY [*suddenly furious, leaping up and away from him*]: Yes, he did. And I won't have you saying things about Philip, I won't have you . . . [*She begins to cry and* MYRA *comes up and puts her arms around her from behind.*]

MYRA: There, darling. It's all right.

TONY [*shouting*]: Oh yes, that's very much your cup of tea, isn't it, Mother? You like that, don't you? Suffering – the great cult of suffering. Strength through pain . . . that's your creed.

MYRA: Oh, shut up and stop bullying people.

TONY [*shouting*]: Well, I don't want any of it – I tell you, pain doesn't exist. I refuse to feel it . . .

MYRA [*to Rosemary*]: There . . . Listen – you don't regret having known Philip, do you?

ROSEMARY: Oh *no*.

MYRA: Then that's all. [*She makes* ROSEMARY *lift her face: she smiles into it.*] There, that's better. It's all not so serious – is it?

TONY: What are you doing now? Dancing on another emotional grave.

MYRA: Oh Tony . . . [*She leaves Rosemary and comes to Tony.*] I've got to tell you something. No, listen. I've been screwing up my courage to tell you.

TONY [*already half-knows*]: No – *what*?

MYRA [*after a pause, while she screws herself up to tell him*]: Tony . . . I've sold the house.

[*There is a long silence.*]

TONY [*very quiet, almost in a whisper*]: You've sold the house. Oh, my God, you've sold the house. [*Grabbing at Rosemary, shaking her as if she were Myra*] My God, she's sold the house!

ROSEMARY: But Tony, only yesterday you were talking about being a tramp.

TONY [*after a pause, as the word tramp strikes him*]: Tramp? A tramp? . . . [*He is almost doubled up with pain.*] She's sold it. And do you know why? To raise five hundred pounds so that I can go and sow my wild oats. Oh God, God. So that I can go bumming off and having love affairs and revolutionizing . . . [*He cackles with hysterical laughter.*]

ROSEMARY: Tony, don't do that. Stop it.

MYRA: Leave him. [*She slumps down in a chair, in the pose she had before, head down against the back of it.*]

TONY: My God, my mother's done that to me. She's done that to me. She's my mother and she might just as well have taken a knife and stabbed me with it. She's my mother and she knows so little about me that she doesn't suspect that there's one thing I love in this world, and it's this house . . .

ROSEMARY: Tony, stop it, stop it, stop it.

TONY [*pulling himself away from* ROSEMARY, *shouting at Myra's head – she is sitting rocking back and forth with the pain of it*]: God, but you're destructive, destructive, destructive. There isn't anything you touch which doesn't go to pieces. You just go on from mess to mess . . . you live in a mess of love affairs and committees and . . . you live in a mess like a *pig*, Mother . . . you're all over everything like a great crawling spider . . .

ROSEMARY [*forcibly pulling him away*]: Tony, stop it at once.

TONY [*hunched up in Rosemary's grasp*]: Sometimes when I hear her come down the stairs I feel every nerve in my body shrieking. I can't stand her, I simply can't stand her . . . [*He collapses into chair, goes completely limp.* ROSEMARY *goes to Myra, is too afraid of her clenched-up pose of pain to touch her, stands helplessly looking from one to the other.*]

TONY [*limply*]: Now we'll have to leave here and live in some – damned pretty little flat somewhere. I can't bear it, I can't bear it . . . [*There is a silence.* MYRA *slowly straightens herself, stands up, walks slowly across the room.* ROSEMARY *watches her fearfully.*]

MYRA: If you hate me as much as that why do you put so much energy into getting me alone with you into this house. Well, why? For the pleasure of torturing me? Or of being tortured?

ROSEMARY: Oh Myra, he didn't mean it.

MYRA [*with a short laugh*]: Perhaps he does mean it. There's no law that says a son must like his mother, is there? [*After a pause*] And vice versa. [*She lights a cigarette. It can be seen her hand is trembling*

violently. Otherwise she is calm. Almost limp, with the same limpness as
TONY's.]

TONY [*looking at her, he begins to understand what he has done. Almost apologetically*]: I can't think why one of you doesn't say: There are millions of people in the world living in mud huts, and you make this fuss about moving from one comfortable home to another. Isn't that what I'm supposed to be feeling?

MYRA: Since you've said it, there's no need for me to.

TONY [*almost querulous*]: The other thing you could say is: Wait until you've got to my age and see if you've done any better. Well – if I haven't done any better I'd have the grace to kill myself.

MYRA: Luckily I don't take myself so seriously. Well, I'm going to leave you to it.

TONY [*desperately anxious*]: What do you mean, where are you going?

MYRA: I don't know.

TONY: You're not going?

MYRA: Why not? I don't propose to live with someone who can't *stand* me. Why should I . . . [*She makes a movement as if expanding, or about to take flight.*] It just occurs to me that for the first time in my life I'm free.

TONY: Mother, where are you going?

MYRA: It occurs to me that for the last twenty-two years my life has been governed by yours – by your needs. Oh, you may not think so – but the way I've lived, what I've done, my whole life has been governed by your needs. And what for . . . [*Contemptuously*] What for – a little monster of egotism – that's what you are. A petty, envious, spiteful little egotist, concerned with nothing but yourself.

ROSEMARY [*almost in tears*]: Oh Myra, stop, stop.

MYRA [*ignoring her, to TONY*]: Well, I'm sure it's my fault. Obviously it is. If I've spent half my life bringing you up and you turn out – as you have – then it's my life that's a failure, isn't it? Well, it's not going to be a failure in future.

TONY: Mother, what are you going to do?

MYRA: There are a lot of things I've wanted to do for a long time, and I haven't done them. [*Laughing*] Perhaps I'll take the money and go off; why not? Or perhaps I'll be a tramp. I could be, you know. I could walk out of this house with my needs in a small suitcase . . . and I shall. Or perhaps I'll go on that boat to the Pacific to the testing area – I wanted to do that and didn't, because of you.

TONY: Mother, you might get killed.

MYRA: Dear me, I might get killed. And what of it? I don't propose to keep my life clutched in my hand like small change . . .

TONY: Mother, you can't just walk off into – *nothing*.

MYRA: Nothing? I don't have to shelter under a heap of old bricks – like a frightened mouse. I'm going. I'll come back and collect what I need when I've decided what I'm going to do. [*Goes towards door, R.*]

TONY [*angry and frightened*]: Mother.

[*She turns at the door. She is quite calm, but she is crying.*]

Mother, you're crying.

MYRA [*laughing*]: Why not? I'm nearly 50 – and it's true there's nothing much to show for it. Except that I've never been afraid to take chances and make mistakes. I've never wanted security and safety and the walls of respectability – you damned little petty-bourgeois. My God, the irony of it – that *we* should have given birth to a generation of little office boys and clerks and . . . little people who count their pensions before they're out of school . . . little petty bourgeois. Yes, I am crying. I've been alive for fifty years. Isn't that good enough cause for tears . . . [*She goes out R.*]

TONY [*amazed, not believing it*]: But Rosemary, she's gone.

ROSEMARY: Yes.

TONY: But she'll come back.

ROSEMARY: No, I don't think so. [*She comes to him, puts her arm around him. They crouch down, side by side, arms around each other.*]

TONY: Rosemary, do you know that not one word of what she said made any sense to me at all . . . slogans, slogans, slogans . . .

ROSEMARY: What's the matter with being safe – and ordinary? What's wrong with being ordinary – and safe?

TONY: Rosemary, listen – never in the whole history of the world have people made a battle-cry out of being ordinary. Never. Supposing we all said to the politicians – we refuse to be heroic. We refuse to be brave. We are bored with all the noble gestures – what then, Rosemary?

ROSEMARY: Yes. Ordinary and safe.

TONY: Leave us alone, we'll say. Leave us alone to live. Just leave us alone ...

CURTAIN

MICHAEL HASTINGS

Yes, and After

YES, AND AFTER

First produced at the Royal Court Theatre, London, on
9 June 1957, with the following cast:

JEAN	Patricia Lawrence
JIM	Robert Stephens
CAIRY	Heather Sears
DR BROCK	Alan Bates
JACK	Jimmy Carroll
JERRY	Michael Wynne
MARIE	Olivia Irving
TERRY	Graham Pyle
BOB	Anthony Carrick

Directed by John Dexter

AUTHOR'S NOTE

IN Ansky's *The Dybbuk*, a boy and a girl meet for a moment without speaking and fall instantly in love. That same day the boy, Channon, a student, dies. The girl Leah is engaged to an appointed husband she has not yet met. On her wedding day she refuses to marry him, and the spirit of the dead youth Channon speaks from Leah's betrothed mouth. On her father's request the ritual of Chassidism temporarily restores her sanity. The Dybbuk, dead Channon, cannot resist the Rabbi's invocations and grudgingly relents. Leah is expected to go through with the marriage. She cries out for Channon and he appears to her. He explains that, though he has left her body, their souls can yet be joined together. Leah goes to him.

The story of Leah might help the reader to understand Cairy in *Yes, and After*; though the girls' roles are quite different both in character and in action, *the idea* of the plot in *Yes, and After* is not quite as original as it might seem.

M.G.H.

ACT ONE

SCENE ONE

The time is the present.

As the curtain rises the audience can see the ground floor interior of a small house in Stockwell. The front of the stage is taken up by the effect of two rooms, side by side, but there is no wall. On the left, facing, the more respectable furniture shows the mostly unused dining-room. Whereas next to it, on the right, you have a small sitting-room which is used every day, a settee and two arm-chairs and the usual odd things. Behind the sitting-room there is the kitchen, with sideboards and small cupboards. At the far right, at the back, there is a door leading out to the back-garden. In the centre-back of the complete stage stands an old grandfather clock. In the direct centre between the lounge and dining-room there is an automatic radiogram. On the far left again of the stage you can just see the start of the stairs: three steps, then a sharp turn. And still on the left side, facing, directly behind the dining-room, there is the main door out to the front of the house.

Now upstairs. The audience can see a small landing, farther back from the front rooms downstairs. On the left, facing, there is an alcove where the stairs end and then a door, which should lead to a bathroom. And then opposite it, although the audience cannot see it, is the door to Jimmy and Jean's room. Along the landing there could be a small airing cupboard, facing the audience, then Cairy's room. Apart from a frame door, you can see inside the whole room. By the frame door there is her bed, long-ways as the audience looks at it. Somewhere behind is a window facing into the back-garden. To the far right of her room is a small camp-bed, where Terry eventually sleeps.

Also downstairs. Behind the front door, or where the door turns back, there is another door, to a toilet. And beside the back-door, there is a small window to look out on the back-garden. There is a slight air of close-cluttered positioning.

Sunday morning, early.

[JIMMY *is making some food by the kitchen table, humming softly to himself, he is fully dressed. After a moment,* JEAN *comes out from her room upstairs, and descends slowly. She wears her dressing-gown as if it is a piece of sacking. Limp from her heavy sweating last night her hair is untidy. Her face – white from exhaustion. She is carrying her dress for the morning, squeezing and rumpling it, as if it is a rag.*]

JEAN: . . . Jim . . . Jim . . . Jim . . . are you in the . . . What are you doing? . . . What did you get up for? . . . You're cooking . . . it's too early . . .

JIM: Hungry.

JEAN: . . . What is that – breakfast? Is it breakfast or lunch? Oh, I feel dreadful . . .

JIM: Go back then – I'll bring some tea up.

JEAN [*very heavily, her face crinkling*]: Tea? . . . It's not tea-time, is it?

JIM [*non-committal*]: No –

JEAN [*slumping down on the lounge settee*]: It must be breakfast then. . . . I feel old and sick, after last night. It was a mad-house in here. What are you trying to make over there –?

JIM: Eggs.

JEAN: Doesn't smell like it.

JIM: Do you want anything else?

JEAN: What?

JIM: Take yourself back to bed.

JEAN: I don't want ever to go back to bed! And face last night again. I wish I could never sleep at any time.

JIM: Don't worry, you slept –

JEAN: I couldn't have done. I was awake the whole time. Listening. And her voice – I've never heard in all my life such – how can a girl scream like that? For hours without a break . . . then she jibbers and cries.

JIM: Sit up here, I can serve it then . . .

[*She lifts herself up by the kitchen table; she sits down.*]

JEAN: My legs . . .

JIM: All right – eggs? [*Putting them down before her*] There was some beef fat for the toast, and jam, no marmalade. You never got any – yesterday.

JEAN: Jim, how can a girl scream like that?

JIM: You asked me that once. Drink your tea. Then go back –

JEAN: I can't sleep any more. I've had enough. As long as I live.

JIM [*drinking*]: . . . I slept.

[*Pause, while they eat.*]

JEAN [*suddenly*]: I'm not untidy. I've got a slip on underneath. It's only – no stockings. I hope Dr Brock doesn't come in and see me like this. Show him I've got bad manners. I'll go up and wash again. After – after – Cairy's washed.

[*Pause again, while* JIM *is reading a paper.*]

JEAN: . . . Jim . . . .

JIM [*still reading*]: . . . Uh –

JEAN [*slightly comic, pouting*]: What are you going to do – about her?

JIM [*lost*]: What?

JEAN [*sharp*]: You must be going to do something –

JIM: How do I know?

JEAN: I don't!

JIM: Wait until Brock comes –

JEAN [*up and across to window, then turning*]: That's it. There's too much waiting. Always it's a little too late. Can't you phone them up – at the station?

JIM: It's not the end of the world.

JEAN: It is to me.

JIM [*softly*]: . . . Ooh.

JEAN: It's all so calm with you. Do you know what it's doing to me? – I'm being strangled!

JIM: You can nag louder than she screams at times.

JEAN [*more to herself*]: . . . Waiting for it to happen, and it has happened already. [*To Jim*] That noise she made. The whole of London must have heard it.

JIM: You can't act quicker than police. If you're a bag of nerves, it's your fault. I'll phone up Brock now, he'll come over and bring you something.

JEAN: I don't want anything. I want something to happen!

JIM: All I know is they'll contact me as soon as they know something. And he can't get very far, not in a few hours. He can't have much money, if he had any – and a couple of days – they'll have him.

JEAN [*over to him*]: Lend me the paper, will you? [*Crosses back.*] . . .
You read about the sort of people these things happen to . . .
[*Sitting and looking at him*] . . . Lodger rapes inspector's daughter!

JIM: I hardly knew what went on. One way or the other – between
the two.

JEAN: Well?

JIM: You tell me one or two things, when she is sick and he fusses
about, that's all I know, until, this –

JEAN: A man should at least understand his character better than I.
You've lived with him here long enough. How long has he been
here? – Nine months.

JIM: I'm not a psychologist.

JEAN: Couldn't you see it? Now and again in his actions or what he
said?

JIM: But you couldn't! [*Up*] He was here all the time during school
holidays, messing around. You even told me – he got in your way.
You had far more time than I did, girl.

JEAN: I don't know what to look for.

JIM: Yes, and the great thing about it all – he wouldn't talk with anybody else. Apart from us, here. Outside he was as dumb as a blinking rock. But you never noticed it! . . . He never drank. He never
smoked. Played chess the whole time – with himself! . . . Never
went out – what do you expect?

JEAN: I didn't ask for it to happen.

JIM: Don't get excited . . . What was he teaching – arithmetic?

JEAN: Grammar school.

JIM: Yes, that standard. He mixed with every sort of child there is. If
he wanted to be queer, he had plenty of opportunity. Long
before this. That's what stumps me. I gathered there was nobody
on more friendly terms with Cairy – than Johnson. And as quiet
and reasonable as anyone. That's the ridiculous side to it . . .
Why?

JEAN: Ask her.

JIM: I give up. [*Silence.*] . . . [*Loud.*] If there is any further nonsense
with that girl, I'll send her to a boarding school. Didn't she ask for
more than she expected?

[*Above on the landing,* CAIRY *comes out from her room, crosses the landing, slowly, then descends, off. She appears very calm and self-collected.*]

... Didn't he take her out, all over the place? Private parties, picnics, fairs, anything. It was a long – I know what he was doing. He was working up to something. You can see it now, too late.

JEAN: I can't take her everywhere ... at least he offered ... he couldn't have been in his right senses – to try.

JIM: He was clever, I'll grant him. He could have planned it so neatly, like counting a man out.

[*The telephone rings.* JIM *rises.*]

[*At phone*] ... Yes ... Yes, I am ... In fact, we both are.

JEAN: Who is it?

JIM: It's Jack. She's much better ... Yes ... And we're both very tired.

JEAN: Who is it?

JIM: It's Jack! No, you're wrong – I only rang your father last night because I felt desperate. I know you're good friends, but I'm tired.

JEAN: Well, what does he want?

JIM: He wants to help if he can ...

JEAN: What could he do!

JIM: I can't talk to you now, I'll tell you later ... No, I'm very sorry, I know you're loyal ... I know you want to help ... It's very generous of you ... [*Hangs up*] God help me if he ever becomes a copper!

JEAN: Is that why he hangs round you?

JIM: I don't know. He's kind in his way. When you find a time when you need friends, it's certainly not the time to start looking for them.

JEAN: I've never needed friends before, I wouldn't know. I don't know, not your kind.

JIM: You're full of self-pity!

JEAN: I talk and think as I think fit.

[*She stops short, as* CAIRY *comes on stage in her dressing-gown. She is slim and short, slow moving, a little concubine. They both pause to watch her come forward, tense.* JEAN *crosses, flurried, to Cairy's side.*]

... Darling ... you shouldn't have got up. We could have brought food up ... How do you feel?

[*No answer,* CAIRY *seems to look through them.*]

JIM: Come over to the table and sit down ...

JEAN [*to Jim*]: Shall I get porridge ready – I don't quite know what to do.

JIM: No ... not yet. She'll go back to bed.

JEAN [*whispers in Cairy's ear, secretively*]: Cairy, what do you want to do?

[CAIRY *crosses to the window, and stares quietly out.*]

JIM: Well?

JEAN [*appearing shrunken somehow at Cairy's nonchalance*]: Can you eat something now?

JIM [*haltingly*]: Stay in bed then.

JEAN [*weakly*]: Cairy, you can do anything you want. We won't mind. As long as you're happy. [*Smiling*] It's you. You're important. Today. Nobody – else – matters ...

CAIRY [*pausing – to herself more*]: I want to go out there ...

JIM: What for?

CAIRY: To see the garden.

JIM: And – ?

CAIRY: Yes ...

JEAN [*crossing to Cairy, she holds her shoulders away from her, as if sizing her up*]: Not now darling ... the doctor says no.

JIM: Have you left anything out there?

JEAN [*to Cairy*]: You're not serious, besides you've only got pyjamas on.

CAIRY [*softly*]: Yes.

JIM: That's your lot then, you can't.

JEAN [*leading her*]: We are your friends, Cairy. We know what is right, and we love you because we do these things. You act as if you are ignoring us completely. We are your parents – you don't want anybody any closer to you. [*Kneels.*] ... We can talk.

[JEAN *makes to fondle her a little unconsciously.*]

JIM: She's still the same. It's like concussion.

JEAN: That's what he said.

JIM: Can she understand us any of the time? It won't last long – will it?

JEAN: He said a day or two. Ask him again today. He promised to be round about twice a day.

JIM: Should be now.

JEAN: It was funny – he left no medicine. I don't think he even made out a prescription.

JIM [*getting up to light a cigarette by the book stand*]: Not that I know. I say she should be kept in bed.

JEAN [*to Cairy*]: I'll take you back upstairs. You can have a water-bottle, then breakfast. I think it's wrong you should walk about ... You understand? You are a little sick, it will blow over.

JIM: I'll see to things, you take her up.

JEAN [*putting her arm round Cairy's shoulders as if protecting her, they move left slowly*]: ... Ready? ... [*Over her shoulder*] I know what would be a good idea. To get some company for her. Why don't you ring up Marie for me. She could quite easily bring young Terry down here. To stay for a few days.

[*They are nearly off when* CAIRY *breaks loose and runs silently across the stage to the scullery door. She shakes the bolted door violently, then stops, pauses, and turns round, her eyes wide, staring into the ceiling.*]

Cairy, come back here! Jim, can't you stop her!

CAIRY: Open it, please!

JEAN [*aloud*]: What in heaven's name for – ?

JIM: Cairy, come over here ... [*To Jean*] What's out there in the garden?

JEAN [*loud*]: She seems to know more than I.

JIM: Quiet.

CAIRY [*forward*]: Let me see the tree, please ...

JEAN: You see – there's that tree out there she likes?

JIM: Why?

JEAN: Don't ask me – it's too cold. You come up with me.

JIM [*breaking any tension up, bravado*]: Oh, it's bed for you. [*He half lifts her over to Jean.*]

JEAN [*softly*]: Any time later, darling. [*She pulls her gently by the arm.*]

To Jim.] If she runs about any more in her bare feet, she will get more than a fever.

CAIRY [*loose again, her eyes tight closed, running blindly into Jim*]: Let me see it – [*Choking*]

JIM: Now – whoops! Young lady to bed. Or off with your head. And then you'll be dead. [*Bending, he sweeps her up high and then carries her off, laughing. He shouts back, off.*] If we take her too seriously we'll all end up in a mental home.

[*They re-appear on the landing.*]

CAIRY [*softly*]: Let me go out. [*He claps his hand to her mouth.*]

JIM: No more. Perhaps tomorrow. Not now. [*To Jean*] Will you phone up Marie. About Terry. It's a good idea. Now let's get you to bed, madame.

JEAN: Will they be up?

JIM [*busy*]: Yes.

CAIRY: ... I want to go down there to Henry Johnson. It's our tree ... Sssh, they're listening. Whisper. Like that ... they can't hear you. But ... it's our own language. Shall we stay out there, tonight, all night, and listen to it creaking, like an old man's back. And it is one ... You laid the leaves down on the garden, it became green for – promises. Odd isn't it? You can use it for anything. Nearly Autumn and it's like a maypole. So – May colours. And then it is black, and cold in the rain ... And a house and a throne ... can you imagine anything – it can't be? There's no other anywhere ... but you cannot buy it. They don't belong to anybody, do they?

JEAN [*picks up phone by the couch, dials*]: ... Hallo ... dear ... Jean. Yes. I haven't got you out of bed, have I? ... Good, I know what you are. You'd sleep all day if you had the chance. Yes. I know. How did you know? All right, I'll hold on ... [*To Jim*] That was Bobby. Did you tell him about Cairy?

JIM: What?

JEAN: I said that was Bob, did you tell him about Cairy?

JIM: I rang him up last night from the station.

JEAN: ... Hallo – yes – Marie? I know, dear. I've been driven crazy, here all night – listening to her. What could I do? ... We'll have to sit tight and wait ... Honestly all I know is – that he must have attacked her ... Yes. While I was out. I had to do some shopping ... Well, yesterday afternoon is the only chance I get to really look around ... and Jimmy was in the station at Streatham. You see ... I know. We had absolute trust in the man. They had the complete run of the house ... From around three to five. I got back, and she was on the floor. She was shaking to bits. I could do nothing with her. And the brute was gone ... She's completely lost touch with us.

[*Door-bell rings.* JIM *lets in* DR BROCK. *He takes his coat off quietly while* JEAN *finishes. They wait for her. Brock is a very young doctor.*]

... Darling, the Doctor has come. I'll have to be quick.

CAIRY [*soft but clear*]: Mister Johnson – Mister Johnson – Mister Johnson – Mister Johnson – [*fades*] ...

JEAN: Would you both come over here this afternoon? You and young Terry, and Bob. Really I'd like Terry to stay here, for a day or two, only to keep Cairy company. She's so nervous ... You really don't mind? ... Fine.

JIM: Come on then! We haven't got all day! Once you let these women on a phone –

JEAN: Yes, well bring some things for him, we'll manage all right ... Bless you. Two o'clock. Bye ... we will. [*Puts phone down, turns and gets up to Brock*] ... Hallo, Doctor ... [*To Jim*] They'll be here at two o'clock.

JIM: Uh. What's best? Shall I bring Cairy down here – or do you want to see her upstairs?

JEAN: Believe me, you are a welcome visitor. We are both – quite out of our minds. Worrying. I'm sorry about this. I meant to change them before you came.

JIM: I like the way she says 'we'. I'm in good control of myself.

BROCK: You should be. You're in the police, aren't you?

JIM: Don't pass the buck!

JEAN [*more to herself*]: Everything is so untidy ...

BROCK [*to her*]: I ignore what you said. It's not your clothes that worry me – it's your health.

JIM: What do you want to do? Go upstairs – ?

BROCK: Yes. I think I'll go up.

JIM: I'll show you. [*They move off.*]

JEAN: While you are up there, I can change myself –

JIM [*off*]: What into?

BROCK [*off*]: How was she last night?

JIM: I don't know. I slept like a drunk.

JEAN: Like hell you did! . . .

> [*General laughter off, then they re-appear on landing. They cross to Cairy's room.*]

BROCK: I don't think your wife believes you.

JIM: All women are cranky this time of the morning. [*He knocks lightly on Cairy's door.*] Can you guess who this is? Cairy? [*To Brock*] I can't see the point in trying to speak to her – in her present state. She doesn't even know me. [*Opens door. To Brock.*] Not her. She won't speak to her father. I'm not important enough! I'll leave you two to it. Leave the door open, if you want anything, shout. [*Crosses landing and off, then on again.*]

> [BROCK *closes door.*]

JEAN: I suppose he's staying for lunch?

JIM [*entering*]: Who?

JEAN: He said yesterday – this is the only visit he's got.

JIM: You better ask him when he comes down.

JEAN [*standing centre, putting her dress over the couch, unfastening her dressing-gown, and slipping into her dress*]: He's got nobody at his place to make him a meal. He'll be grateful for a proper one.

> [*The conversation becomes louder upstairs.*]

BROCK: Why didn't you go out with Mum and Dad yesterday, Cairy – ?

CAIRY: I've got no father. He was walking under the flower tree and – he vanished. It must have swallowed him, whole. That sounds rather splendid.

BROCK: And Mother?

CAIRY: I don't know. I can't see her. Whenever I'm in a room . . . and I hear them talking . . . and calling her . . . I look round. I see everybody else – but she's never there.

BROCK: Do you hear her?

CAIRY: When they talk to her – Mr Johnson answers back. You do – it's not her voice. I think he speaks for her, as well.

BROCK [*pausing*]: . . . Am I different from the Mr Johnson, say, of yesterday?

CAIRY: You are always the same. Like the tree out there. You can do so many things with it. But it is the same.

BROCK [*hesitant*]: . . . Cairy. Do you forgive me – for yesterday?

CAIRY: Why? What have you done? [*Chuckling*] That tragic voice. I forgive you – I don't know what for . . .

BROCK: Do you remember what happened yesterday? Do you remember what we did?

CAIRY [*slowly*]: . . . we went out –

BROCK: No.

CAIRY: Down to the park at Herne Hill –

BROCK: No.

CAIRY [*a little flurried*]: We went somewhere, there was the church choir. You knew some of the boys there. Yes, didn't we join in and –

BROCK: You don't want to, do you? Think hard.

CAIRY: Why is it that important?

BROCK: It's very important.

CAIRY: There were so many. Where did we go?

BROCK: I'm not telling.

CAIRY: You take me to such odd places. Far away – they are – so strange. I can't remember them all. Listen – can you hear water gushing away? It flows so naturally. Smooth like music. Didn't we listen to music once at the Albert Hall? I couldn't understand it. There was so much to see. The huge walls and the musicians. And people there – you had no time to listen to the music!

BROCK: Now don't say any more. Until I'm back. I won't be a moment. [*On landing*] Mrs Mount?

JEAN: Yes?

BROCK: I have her talking quite well, that is something. I don't know what to do with her now. The more she lets off steam, the more she releases herself.

JEAN: Would you like to bring her down here? If she's talking . . . perhaps she would prefer more company.

[*They talk in a semi-whispered tone.*]

BROCK: She's got a mannerism – of blacking out other people and putting Johnson there. What was his Christian name?

JEAN: Henry – Henry Johnson.

BROCK: Did she call him Henry?

JEAN: I think so – but she'd never say it in front of us. She was too bright for that. How long will this go on?

BROCK: Can't say, at the moment. She is so moody. Her stomach muscles are rigid, like cardboard. She is straining inside her, she has to break herself of it.

JEAN: She shivers as if she's cold. Does that mean anything? She won't be violent again, will she?

BROCK: Might. I can't tell with these – they try to bring it out themselves. Unconsciously. They can't hold it inside.

JEAN: Bring her down here – I don't like her on her own.

BROCK [*going off*]: It won't harm her. I don't think she feels lonely.

[BROCK *at Cairy's door*]

JEAN [*down*]: He's bringing Cairy down again.

JIM [*lounging*]: How is she?

JEAN: He's got her talking.

JIM: Don't you think he's a young fellow?

JEAN: He hasn't started long.

BROCK [*upstairs*]: Cairy, put your things on and come downstairs. We can talk better.

CAIRY: Where are we going?

BROCK: Your Mother and Father are down there – [*Hesitant*]

CAIRY: How far – ?

BROCK: O.K.? What about your slippers? They're over there. I'll put them on for you. [*He gets them, then kneels in front of her.*]

CAIRY: Don't touch my feet. They're ticklish.

BROCK: I've got to put them on you.

CAIRY: I like you kneeling down in front of me. It's awfully pleasant . . . I am about to chop off your head . . . or, you've laid a cloak at my feet – to step over – [*She lays her small hand lightly on his hair.*] Johnson . . .

BROCK [*looking up*]: Haven't I got another name?

CAIRY: What?

BROCK: Christian name –

CAIRY [*hesitant again*]: Yes. Henry –

BROCK: That's better. Let's go [*He pushes her in front of him.*]

CAIRY: You are very tall. Does that – you must feel it up there.

BROCK: What?

CAIRY: Feel the cold!

BROCK [*really embarrassed by the mood she creates*]: I touched you before, didn't I? I put your slippers on – and – held hands – you remember?

CAIRY: I remember.

BROCK [*faltering*]: . . . Cairy, did I ever touch you – there – did I? [*He presses his hand against her breast lightly.*] . . . like that?

CAIRY: . . . I can't –

BROCK: No, not ever – ?

CAIRY [*frigid*]: No.

BROCK: Let's go down. We can talk.

CAIRY: What would we do without it?

BROCK: Talk?

CAIRY: I think I'd scratch – to tell people . . .
    [*Both off descending.*]

JIM: What are you going to cook? [*To Jean*]

JEAN: I didn't say I was.

JIM: What is there?

JEAN: I don't think there's enough . . .
    [*The two come on stage.*]

BROCK: There they are –

CAIRY: Who?

BROCK [*to Jean*]: . . . I think she'll talk now.
    [CAIRY *walks strangely to the kitchen door, her arms hold the posts, and looks through the door.*]

JEAN: Cairy, are you talking to us?

CAIRY [*turning to Brock*]: Please let's go out.

BROCK: Where to?

JIM: That's what I asked.

CAIRY [*almost herself*]: . . . Mr Johnson.

BROCK: What's out there?

JIM: A tree.

JEAN: That's their little secret – the flower tree.

BROCK: What would you do if I took you out there?

CAIRY [*vaguely*]: Yes . . .

BROCK: What would you do?

CAIRY: . . . Just laugh. I'd want to laugh out loud until I cry – under it, there is shelter. You'd like it, may I take you – [*She faces round to Brock.*] – your hands. [*Holding out her hands*] Come on.

BROCK: What is there in just sitting underneath it?

CAIRY: It shelters you. If you say it to yourself – it will. Say you are cold then it will be a bed, or are you an old man? You can be young out there . . .

JEAN: I want to be sick.

BROCK: Perhaps it doesn't want you to go out there.

CAIRY [*startled*]: You're playing with me.

BROCK: Why that tree? Cairy?

CAIRY [*squats*]: Nothing is so natural as that.

BROCK [*softly*]: There are others.

CAIRY: There are not. They are made of people or flesh and wood.

BROCK: Isn't that made of wood?

CAIRY: It's not made of anything. You know? You should know. It's your tree, isn't it?

BROCK: There's more to it than that.

CAIRY [*loud*]: I want the window opened!

BROCK [*holding her*]: Now quiet!

JEAN [*to Jim*]: Can't he do more than that?

BROCK: Now are you steady, now? No more, Cairy.

CAIRY: Well, it's all over.

BROCK: You're not fit to go out. [*Kneels*]

CAIRY [*sinking on to floor*]: Don't make me disbelieve you. I can't see without you, I want to wear glasses, and walk with a stick. I was running backwards, with you, I daren't stop. You wouldn't make me stop until I tripped. I don't need my eyes. You can tell me. I don't need ears or tongue, you can tell me, if you say you know everything I need, you do – you do –

[*Pause.*]

JIM: Tell me what to do and I'll do it.

BROCK: I don't know. [*Rises.*]

JEAN: Up now. Get up. Can you hear me? . . . [*To Brock.*] I'm afraid to touch her in case –

JIM: If Bob was here, he'd probably burst out laughing.

BROCK: Let me count up to ten.

JIM: Have you got any medicine for her?

BROCK: I'm afraid to. Whatever I give her. It might break into her nervous system, and that's what I don't want. It might harm her. I don't know – you need a psychoanalyst, not a doctor.

JIM [*to Brock*]: Shouldn't you know all the answers?

BROCK: I'll write out a note for barbitone tablets. You can get them tomorrow. And [*writing*] sprinkle it in milk . . . for her. By then I don't think she'll need them. Shock goes as quickly as it comes. But she might get a slight fever. Hence the tablets.

JIM: Leave her down here?

BROCK: I'm pretty sure she'll need a hot-water bottle. If there is one ready . . .

JEAN [*crossing*]: There's some water left in the kettle . . . yes. She only needs it half full.

JIM: She could bath . . .

BROCK [*sitting her on sofa*]: You feel her hands. They're freezing.

JIM: I'll take her up. [*Crossing to her*] Up you get. I did this sort of thing when you were half this age. Taking you to bed.

JEAN: It'll be ready in a minute.

JIM [*sits by Cairy on sofa*]: No more shouting. There's nothing to make too much fuss about. Now you stop it.

BROCK: I believe there should be as many people around her – as soon as she can get them. This isn't a doctor's job at all. Not at the present. I can't prescribe anything. It's up to her –

JIM: You talking to me?

BROCK: Well, either of you, it's just how soon she can break it. [*Sitting*] I suppose the police are on to him already?

JIM: I've got some of my own boys working on it. There's some down at Brixton as well – giving a hand. That's my brother-in-law, Bob. Before the week's out, the whole local force will be out looking for him.

BROCK: If he's not caught by then, I suppose you'll both want a full report –

JEAN: Well. Of some kind.

JIM [to Brock]: What about this afternoon? Are you coming over? Or leave it till tomorrow –

BROCK: I don't think it will be that necessary.

JEAN: Tomorrow then.

BROCK: I'll come in the morning. She'll be all right by then. I'm sure. She's not too young to fight it. Any child of thirteen or fourteen can react subconsciously.

JIM: How soon will you know – if it's bad or not?

BROCK: You don't. Nobody can tell you how soon her nervous system is or is not going to climb back.

JEAN: It might last weeks.

BROCK: Not with a girl like that. She's too young to keep it tight inside her. Children heal quicker, they forget and they grow.

JIM: Now if I was a kid of thirteen or so, and some bloody old man attacked me, I just couldn't get myself tied up like that. And have her crazy fits. I'd take it quite different. You know – I wouldn't mope over it.

JEAN: If you were thirteen, you wouldn't have the sense to think things – like that. She's not lived as long as you have – has she?

JIM: As I said –

BROCK: I follow you. But it would not be likely that you, personally, would ever get into that position. That's not important. What is – the fact that Cairy has that indisposition. When you were that age were you liable to be raped by the lodger?

JIM: I very much doubt it.

BROCK: So do I. I can't imagine you having much sex-appeal at that age. I bet you were a little tyke – shouting down streets, and tying cats to dustbin lids.

JIM: About Cairy, I'm worried. Suppose – I don't want to bother her with it. But where does she go from here? When it's all over and she settles down . . .

BROCK: Yes –

JIM: . . . at school amongst the other kids what will happen? Suppose she gets a kink against men, she might change completely –

BROCK: If I know children, there's nothing to worry over.

JIM: . . . I can't see it like that. She was always nervous, before he came. She's easily frightened. She's the type of child you can imagine reading poems to herself, and daydreaming –

BROCK: Never! Children appear to be hurt deeply. They can cry their heads off. It's nothing. It's an exuberance.

JIM: She won't forget him – not that quick.

BROCK: She will.

JIM: The man intoxicated the girl! Every little word he said, she noted it down in her head. [*To Jean*] You can tell him that, can't you? . . . She doted on him.

BROCK: Maybe.

JIM: You see you don't know as much as I do even!

BROCK: Obviously. But whoever knows the most – either side, that's unimportant. This is a matter of chance – and I back her to pull through.

JEAN: He must have hypnotized her, I think.

BROCK: By my reckoning he must have hypnotized you two too.

JIM: What is your Christian name?

BROCK: Owen.

JEAN: Doctor Owen Brock.

BROCK: It's Welsh. I know you both quite well, in a way, but we've never had a real chance to get together.

JIM: Right! The farther we are from you the better.

BROCK: I don't think anybody really likes a doctor in the house.

JIM: I don't believe in shouting for one as soon as someone's got a cold – the smallest thing.

BROCK: . . . if you knew how many pensioners bother me with the most trivial complaints. They're the only type that really need me. I think they're lonely. They live in small rooms, one foot in the grave and one half out – it terrifies you that there are so many.

JEAN: Poor things.

BROCK: A doctor's a one-man band. Everything – everybody.

JIM: You're quite a youngster for this job. It's a lot to take on.

BROCK: Honestly, I think it's too big. I'm depended on for far too many things. People rely on you, and it's life or death often. They put so much faith into you – you let them down, and you're nothing. They never bring that faith back again.

JEAN: How old are you?

BROCK: Twenty-seven. That's nine years' training.

JIM: After I'd been nine years in the Force all I'd made was a sergeant. I tell you, the locals had less faith in me than in a stray cat!

BROCK [up]: Well, this is where I came in . . .

JEAN: There's no hurry to go.

BROCK: You've got more people coming – I think I'll get out of your way.

JEAN: Really.

BROCK: No. I'll push along.

JIM: You don't have to.

BROCK: Oh yes. In any case, I'll be here tomorrow. [Moving away to put on his coat] I don't want to impose upon you – the more you keep me out of work, the happier you will be.

JIM: No. We were only kidding.

BROCK [turning round]: I'll disappear then – thanks for everything, you know? – ring me if you want –

JEAN [up]: But we'd love you to stay. There are too many lonely bachelors as it is. Are you lonely?

BROCK: With all those patients of mine?

JEAN: They're not the real thing –

VOICE [off]: Jim! Jim!

JIM: Did you hear? [Listening]

JEAN: Where?

JIM: In the garden?

JEAN: No.

JIM [looking through the back window curtain]: I heard something . . .

JACK [off – a broad coarse voice]: Hi – Jim?

JIM: It's those two young fellows from over the flats.

JEAN: Which two?

JIM: Jack and his mate – what's his name.

JEAN: Oh – they're not coming in here –

JIM: What?

JEAN: They're the last couple I want to meet now.

BROCK: Who are they?

JIM: A couple of teds who talk of joining the Force.

BROCK: Why?

JEAN: Because – there's only one reason why they come in here and that's to get a free drink off Jim.

BROCK: I only asked as I thought they might help Cairy. Are they friends of hers?

JEAN [*firmly*]: No!

JIM: That's the kind of conversation women make nowadays! [*Winking*]

JEAN [*around*]: They think Jim's a hero.

BROCK: Are they friends of Mr Johnson?

JIM: Never! They're nice kids – I helped them once when they were in a spot of bother.

BROCK: Tell me – how normal was this man?

JIM: He was normal.

JEAN: He was not.

JIM [*to Jean*]: You're not listening to the trend of the conversation!

JEAN: Everything about him was abnormal, everything about him was –

JIM: What I mean is – he was normal in an abnormal sort of way.

JEAN [*to Jim*]: What?

JIM: I mean he wasn't normally abnormal. If you see what I mean.

JEAN: No. I don't!

BROCK [*to Jim*]: Why do you like those lads out there?

JIM: Well, they're nothing to do with you, are they? I have a little bit in common with them –

JEAN [*sneering*]: What have you got in common?

JIM: They said they wanted to join the police, didn't they?

JEAN [*stamping her feet*]: Oh for God's sake! You're more like a child than Cairy.

JIM: Why am I?

JEAN [*to Brock*]: They're just a pair of juvenile delinquents, Jim once tried to straighten out. He'd made a promise to their father.

JACK [*off*]: Jim . . .

JIM: Aw – let them in, girl!

BROCK: Shall I go?

JEAN: If you don't I will! I don't like rough types.

JERRY [*off*]: Hey – Cairy!

JEAN: They sometimes used to play with Cairy – but they're too old now for that sort of thing. It's all girls now –

JACK [*sharply – off*]: Cairy!

JEAN: They want to come around to tell us how sad they are because Jim rang their Dad and told him what had happened. He was too desperate to think of anyone else to tell.

JIM: He and I play billiards regular like up Coldharbour Lane.

JEAN: I notice how he never invites me along.

JIM: You can't play billiards.

JEAN: I can try.

JIM: It's men only.

JACK [*off*]: Can we come in?

CAIRY [*sitting up*]: Who is that? [*Not loudly*]

JACK [*pushing open the kitchen door*]: Hallo – Jim.

CAIRY: Listen – to the tree, talking, oh we can all hear it if we try hard enough . . . listen.

JEAN: You see! You see what happens. She's getting excited.

BROCK: No, don't do that.

JEAN [*she glares round*]: Whose side are you on?

JACK: Hallo, Cairy love, not so well today?

JEAN [*turning away bitterly*]: Who listens to me anyway?

CAIRY: . . . Isn't this our little secret . . .

[*JERRY and JACK edge inside the door staring at Cairy in absolute fascination.*]

JIM: Well – don't just stand there!

JEAN [*reluctantly*]: Hallo Jack – Hallo Jerry.

CAIRY: This would be our tree, you see, and this is – and this is . . .

JIM [*to Brock*]: Speak to her then.

BROCK: She doesn't need me to, she makes up her own answers.

JEAN: You're not very helpful.

BROCK: I have better things to do than to play games with Cairy here; I'd like to find out how to get to the bottom of it.

JERRY: Are we in the way?

JEAN: Yes.

JIM: No.

CAIRY: I love the tree, Mr Johnson.

JACK: Can we talk to her?

CAIRY [sitting up]: Oh yes.

JEAN [to Brock]: Now what do you do?

BROCK: Listen to her.

JEAN: Is that all?

BROCK: You'll learn more by listening to her and watching what she does than by talking.

CAIRY: Please – what is the tree saying to me now . . . the tree says – Ouch! My finger! The bark splintered into my finger-nail.

JERRY: Cor . . . ain't she weird. Ain't she?

JACK: Jim? What has happened?

JIM: Shut up for a minute –

JEAN: Do you know, sometimes there is a moment when you feel nobody quite knows what to do anywhere, all over the world, there is a small space of time, very rarely, but it happens. I am sure this is it now . . .

JIM: Jean.

JEAN: Say something happy, Jim? Don't joke like those two do; don't pretend to me like Cairy is doing to them. I can't act back any more. I want to prove to Marie when she comes that I'm still a good entertainer. I want to forget about Cairy altogether.

[JIM holds her shoulder.]

. . . Nobody can pretend for long, because somebody knows what you are doing; you can never lie about a thing that nobody else in the world knows of, you have to share a lie somehow.

JIM: What's come over you? This isn't the time to crack up.

JEAN [stepping forward and away from Jim]: There you are, you don't know what comes next, do you? [*Sits.*] It's difficult to imagine what will be said three sentences away. I'm the only one talking, aren't I? Yes, I'm the only one. I'm exhausted – not her.

JIM [*to Brock*]: What can you do for her too?

JERRY: Well, we do look some proper Charlies, standing around asking what next to do . . . I must say, like.

CAIRY: But you are the tree, and I'm always trying to share it with you.

BROCK: I'm still trying to listen to her.

JERRY: Then come and see the tree with us, Cairy? [*To Jim*] . . . What tree?

CAIRY [*loud*]: Who is it then if you're not the tree! Mr Johnson. Who is in the garden besides you?

JACK: It's not me – straight – I can tell you.

BROCK: Ssshh.

CAIRY [*loud and clear*]: Who is out in the garden!

JACK: That was us, see – your pals from over the flats.

JERRY: Here, Cairy, what about them games we used to have?

CAIRY [*running to the window and leaning out shouting*]: Will you come out of that garden! Whoever you are!

[*JACK and JERRY smirk dim-wittedly, thinking she is playing with them.*]

JERRY [*nudging Jack*]: You wouldn't catch me under any tree with old Henry there! The things they say about him . . . the creep.

[*JACK giggles.*]

CAIRY: Go along! Please leave, get away from the tree. . . . Whoever said they could go out there? Nobody should be out here because nobody is coming back!

JEAN: I'm very tired of it all.

CAIRY [*throwing open a second window in the kitchen*]: They're out there by . . . they were pulling the branches. They like breaking things. They want to smash it down because it can't do anything for them. It's the only tree . . . he said, it's ours, and he said it was so much older than me, how old did he say . . . ?

BROCK: Cairy, come back and talk to me. [*He leads her to the settee.*] . . . Now I must go. But before I do, I want you to go back to bed upstairs, and I'll come back in a day or two and we'll see you well and healthy. Will you do that?

[CAIRY *goes silently upstairs.*]

JEAN: We'll look after her, I promise you.

JIM: We'd like you to stay –

BROCK: No thanks.

[CAIRY *is wandering slowly up the stairs.*]

JEAN [*to open door*]: You will come soon?

BROCK: I'll be back before Tuesday.

JEAN: Thank you.

BROCK: Goodbye. [*Exit.*]

[*Pause.*]

JEAN [*folding her arms*]: . . . Well?

JACK: What about it then, Jim?

JIM: Well . . . let's sit down and jaw a bit first.

JEAN: Jim!

JIM [*to Jean*]: Let's try to have a laugh once, eh?

[JACK *and* JERRY *settle down.*]

JACK [*to Jean*]: . . . Are you worried, Mrs Mount?

JERRY: Proper turn up for the books – eh?

[JEAN *turns away.*]

JIM: Tell us a joke, Jerry.

JERRY: My Dad sends you his regards.

JIM [*uninterestedly*]: Yes . . .

JERRY: Do you know he's not forgot that day yet – when you found that stolen cashbox for him.

JIM: That's right – that was quite a day, wasn't it?

JERRY [*to Jean*]: Did Jim ever tell you about my old man's money, Mrs Mount?

JEAN: I don't know – I suppose so.

JERRY: He's a dark horse is old Jim. I bet he never told you nothing.

JEAN: Why aren't you both at work today? You ought not to be at home.

JACK: I work for Jerry's dad – same as him.

JERRY: My old man's a street bookie – a corner-tout; we're his runners.

JEAN [*to Jim*]: Did you know that?

JIM: Yes.

JERRY: That's what I meant when I said Jim did my old man a favour – that's what I was saying. You see my dad keeps all his money in an old rabbit-hutch underneath a floorboard under the cocktail cabinet –

JEAN: A rabbit-hutch!

JERRY: My old man fitted his rabbit-hutch inside the floorboards – and this is where he always had all his money.

JEAN: But why doesn't he use a bank, like everybody else!

JERRY: Ah – that's a good question. My old man's a canny nut, he don't believe in banks, if you see what I mean.

JEAN: No, I don't.

JERRY: He says to me he says – never give your money into a bank, they'll have it off you in no time – using your money for Building Armaments and Implements of War, my Dad says – he's a pacifist.

JIM: That's how he avoided the last war.

JERRY: As I say, my old man's canny –

JIM: He avoided the First World War too –

JERRY: That's right; they put him in the fields plucking potatoes; and that was like putting a silver spoon in his mouth. He soon had them all betting on his own Horse-Syndicate, a guaranteed fool-proof system it was. He made a pile, I reckon.

JEAN: I'm sorry, I really can't follow you – if you don't mind, I don't see what –

JERRY: I'm coming to it now: because he wouldn't trust banks –

JIM: He wouldn't trust banks because he made no mistake about hiding his takings, that's the truth.

JACK: I bet your old man hasn't paid income tax for forty years.

JEAN [*to Jim*]: And you've been fraternizing with him all these years –

JIM: I've been playing billiards with him all these years, if that's what you mean.

JEAN: It doesn't sound right to me.

JERRY: I've passed a fair tip to you and all now and then, haven't I? Buckshee and all.

JIM: To cut a long story short, when their flat was burgled I happened to know of two coloured brothers who had just come out from lock and key for a similar offence – me and Jerry called on them in Arlington Fields – and we caught them barefaced with the loot.

JACK: Fifteen thousand quid there was.

JERRY: How about that for fancy work – and you never told your missus neither!

JEAN: So we're all good pals together, are we?

JERRY: Summat like that.

JEAN: Well – now if you'll excuse me, I've got –

JERRY [*standing*]: I understand – still, we called on the off-chance, see, that we might be able to help. I'm not on call for 'placings' until lunch-time.

JACK: Don't forget – tell us if there's something. We was always pally with old Cairy.

JIM: I won't.

JERRY: Well then – ta ta.

JIM: Ta ta.

JACK: Ta ta.

JIM: Ta ta.

[JERRY *and* JACK *exeunt.*]
[JIM *returns from the door.*]

JEAN: Did you know that boy was illegally 'running' bets for his father – all this time!

JIM: He's often handed a good tip to one of the boys on the beat beside their flats.

JEAN: Why do you encourage them here?

JIM: That boy Jerry's a bright one.

JEAN: But he's a hooligan.

JIM: He was.

JEAN: It wasn't that long ago when he was up in the juvenile courts.

JIM: That's right. I straightened him out – introduced him to a probation-fellow I knew. He's turned out quite bright.

JEAN: When I first laid eyes on him, I thought he's certainly not the type for my Cairy. Too damn' rough. I sent him packing last year when they tried to persuade her to join them in their pranks.

JIM: I know – you preferred nice quiet Mr Johnson, didn't you?

CAIRY [*shouting out through her window at the boys outside in the garden*]: . . . Go away . . . go away.

[JACK'S *voice replies* 'It's only us: Don't you remember us?']

. . . Go along! Please leave . . . [*She gets up and runs across the landing, pulling her dressing-gown with her. She enters again down on the stage making for the back door.*] . . . Whoever said they could go out there. [*Running and talking all in the same breath*] . . . Nobody should be out there. Because nobody is coming. Suppose they break pieces off it. They've done that before.

JEAN: Jim?

CAIRY [*on stage*]: . . . They're out there by the – [*Opens the door and stands there stiffly.*] – they've gone. . . . He shouted to me they were pulling the branches off and I had to do something. He said – I know it was the same last week – they like breaking things. He warned you before to put up a wall instead of that fence. They jump over and seem to want to . . . Because it can't do anything for them, so they must do something back instead . . . at least, not that one, and he said – it's ours.

JEAN: Bring her back. If she should catch a cold, that would cap everything.

JIM [*to Cairy*]: You hear? . . . If you expect your Aunt to see you then you've got to act natural.

CAIRY: . . . Where is he? [*Looking round*] He promised to be back. As soon as anything. Goodness . . . they wanted to know about the tree, just then. I told them they'd have to buy a life-interest in it before I told them. If they do, what he said was . . .

JIM: Leave her alone for a while. She'll be more natural if we act as if we are –

JEAN: Can't we imagine something prettier in the middle of it all like she does. She can create something out of nothing –

JIM: A flower tree!

JEAN: Yes. Anything.

JIM: Where did you learn this from? Mr Johnson?

JEAN: Maybe I did, what of it?

JIM: The same to you with knobs on, silver bells, and forget-me-nots and Christmas boxes on every branch! I think I'm the only sane one in the house –

JEAN: We are all out of step, you aren't! . . . Jim. There's nothing more real than pain. This is it. Reality. She believes in that tree because it's quite natural –

JIM: Aren't we? Skin and bone is enough, isn't it?

JEAN: That tree and the green and things – they're what we aren't. Somehow.

JIM: Baloney!

[*Door-bell rings.*]

JEAN: I suppose so. But doesn't it make you wonder just which is the reality?

JIM: Cairy – Take her upstairs to wash herself . . . they're about outside now.

JEAN: She's old enough to take herself up . . . I think I will though. I'll change these shoes . . . [*To Cairy*] Coming? . . . Come on . . . it's like talking to a deaf mute. For all she notices. Cairy [*catching her arm*], we'd better hurry – or Auntie Marie will find me in carpet slippers.

JIM [*crossing and opening the door*]: Well – if it isn't my beautiful sister-in-law . . . [*Hugging her like a bear*] You look all right. How is everything?

MARIE [*who is quite slim and wears a small-grey-pinhead suiting, and flat ugly shoes*]: Jimmy . . . Oh I'm fine. You're getting a little fat down there, aren't you?

JIM: Where's the rest of them – ?

MARIE: Oh, they're out there . . . [*Calling outside.*] Terry – come on in . . . [*To Jim*] I don't know what he's doing out there. [*Forward.*] . . . Isn't it quiet. Where are the others?

[TERRY *enters. He is about fourteen.*]

JIM: By Christ! When does he stop growing! Look at him now!

MARIE: He'll end up taller than Bob. Bob wasn't – how tall are you now?

TERRY: About five foot seven. Or so –

MARIE: He's much bigger than I am.

JIM: You're no giant!

MARIE: Yes. I know but –

JIM: What's Bob doing out there? I guessed he was coming as you had the car.

MARIE: He's doing something to the handle. We left the car keys behind us.

JIM: Take your things off then. Here, Terry, I'll take yours.

BOB [*in doorway*]: Sergeant Robert O'Neil reporting! . . . Hallo lad! [*To Jim*]

JIM: Hallo. . . . Is that old car of yours losing its wheels or something –

BOB: No. We were all at sea this morning. She got into a flap as usual. Cairy and all that – so we charged out half naked. Where is she – young Cairy?

JIM: They'll be down. She's with Jean. . . . I'll take your coat, Bob. . . . [*To Jean*] Come on. Come on. We've got guests!

MARIE: Terry – you sit over there . . .

[JEAN *crosses to go off downstairs.*]

Sit down, Bob . . .

JIM: Make yourselves at home. I haven't seen you for months.

BOB: You sound happier than I expected.

JIM: I'm not kidding. You're like a breath of summer in here. It was like a graveyard yesterday. I didn't expect you to come. You usually play sports on Sunday –

BOB: We could have played tennis. But Marie wasn't going. They rang up the last minute – they couldn't open the groundsman's hut. So, no game – it suited me.

MARIE: Thank God someone else has lost keys today.

JEAN [*coming on stage*]: Well now . . . what a large family.

MARIE: Hallo, darling. [*They clasp hands.*]

JEAN: Sit down. Sit down . . . Bob. I thought you couldn't come. We didn't drag you from your –

BOB: More than glad to come, lovey.

JEAN [*looking at Terry*]: I can't say – young Terry any more. He might clout me. He looks like a young bull! . . . It's good to see you. This place is like a graveyard!

[MARIE *and* BOB *laugh.*]

. . . What's funny?

MARIE: Darling. That's just what Jimmy said – it's a graveyard! You are a perfect pair of glums.

JEAN: I'm not surprised. It's a nightmare in here. I wish we could get out of it.

MARIE: Is it that bad?

JEAN: It's all over now. But it was like watching the world explode before your eyes last night.

BOB: Sounds as if you need the doctor. As well as Cairy.

MARIE: Oh, Bob. Where's that suitcase? We didn't forget that as well? I hope not. [*To Jean*] That's his clothes.

BOB: I don't know.

MARIE: I reminded you about it before –

BOB: You never said a word.

MARIE: It was in the boot – I think.

BOB: I'll look. I can't remember putting it there . . .

MARIE: Scatterbrain you are.

BOB [*off front door*]: Excuse me.

MARIE: Bob. Bob!

BOB [*back*]: Yes?

MARIE: In the boot – remember?

BOB: . . . Where do you think I'm going to look – in the oil-tank!

MARIE: No – I know. Have you – have you got the keys to the boot?

BOB [*off*]: Ain't it real! . . .

MARIE: Nobody knows with that man what he has got and hasn't. He'd lose an elephant if he had one.

JIM: What's the case for?

JEAN: Terry?

MARIE: Yes.

JEAN: We've got plenty of things here. He could borrow some of Jim's things. He only wants pyjamas and things.

JIM: Can you imagine him walking round in my trousers?

JEAN: I said pyjamas.

MARIE: He'd still look like a mouse in a sheepskin!

BOB [*back*]: . . . One suitcase . . . [*Carrying it*] *Well!* You going to enjoy yourself here, Terry.

TERRY: Mmm.

JEAN: Oh, leave him alone. You embarrass him.

BOB: Not him. Nothing can. Eh? [*To Terry*]

JIM [*to Jean*]: ... A bit different from Cairy?

JEAN: Nobody asked you to say that.

JIM: Oh, cut your long hair off. I was only cracking –

JEAN: Well I didn't hear it crack! Sorry and all that!

JIM: Never mind ...

MARIE: Aren't you two edgy!

JEAN [*tired*]: I don't know what we sound like. I couldn't care.

JIM [*to Bob*]: You haven't got any beer in that boot as well, have you?

MARIE: Where is Cairy? I thought she was with you –

JEAN: She's upstairs. She wouldn't come down.

JIM: If she keeps looking at that flower tree – she'll wear it away!

JEAN: She's crazy for that tree.

MARIE: Perhaps its because of what's-his-name –

JEAN: It must be – they – that's our handicap, they did so many things together, and we can't know half of them. I think she wants to bring them all back –

BOB: Take her to see a specialist.

JIM: That's no damn good. Dr Brock said it would take a couple of days to clear up. If it doesn't – then – I tell you – I'll willingly beat it out of her myself. What I think is, she's worrying about him. Being caught or not. She doesn't want to tell us.

MARIE: Jean, did he examine her physically?

JEAN: Nothing – at least he hasn't harmed her. It was so spontaneous – well – there was nothing –

BOB: Only mental shock.

JEAN: Yes.

JIM: Say that as much as you like. Believe me, that wasn't spontaneous. From the minute he came here, he'd worked it all out. I said to Jean he was an old hand at it.

JEAN: She looked so lovely, like a spray of flowers ... there was blood on her lips ... she could have been a jewel box – suddenly broken open and they all fell out ...

MARIE: Jean –

JIM: Poetry! There's always blinking poetry when someone is ill!

JEAN [*coming forward to Marie*]: . . . Have you ever felt that there's a voice inside your head screaming itself hoarse at you – and the pain; I feel dreadful – all I want –

MARIE [*holding Jean tightly as if she might fall down*]: Now, you shouldn't have asked us round – there was no need. You're not fit –

JEAN: Hold me like that . . . you're a fine sister you know – you don't grow old, do you, like me? You are very clear-skinned – how do you do it? [*Her voice is a whisper.*]

MARIE: We never get a chance to see each other –

JEAN: That's all wrong, isn't it? We should be next to each other – Oh God, I wish something would happen terribly quick.

MARIE: Never mind, darling.

BOB [*stretching*]: What a sickly sounding bunch we are . . .

MARIE: You do come out with some sane remarks, don't you!

BOB: Oh, I've got millions of them! . . . You know what I mean? . . . There's an air about the house –

JEAN: Don't worry, Bob. We are dead.

JIM: What's up with you?

MARIE: Leave her alone –
  [CAIRY *walks on slowly.*]

BOB [*seeing Cairy*]: There she is!

MARIE [*up*]: Hallo, dear.

JEAN [*moving to Cairy*]: . . . Darling, come and sit down –

JIM: Leave her alone. Let her find her own way here – she's not blind –

JEAN: I was only getting up –

JIM: She doesn't have to have you –

MARIE: Come over here, Cairy. By me. You look a little – isn't she pale? She's quite white compared to Terry.

BOB: Terry. [*Looking at him*] You haven't said a word since we got in.

TERRY: I'm all right –

BOB: I wish you'd say something. Your old man's sitting here holding the fort – talking his head off – and you don't back him up!

TERRY: What shall I say?

BOB: You think of something.

JIM [*to Terry*]: He's kidding you!

JEAN [*to Cairy*]: . . . You know Aunt Marie and Uncle Bob? . . . And Terry?

MARIE [*holding Cairy's shoulders*]: You haven't seen Terry for a long time.

JEAN: Say you know them, Cairy – you're not dumb . . .

MARIE: Well? . . . Are you pleased to see us?

JEAN [*waiting*]: Ssshh.

JIM: Oopsie-boopsie-boo! You whine like school kids! Can't you talk properly to the girl? She's not two years old! You'd think this was her christening!

MARIE: . . . Never mind. Look, this is Terry – [*Exhibiting him to Cairy*] He's staying with you for a few days . . . you don't mind that?

BOB: How would you like a bit of company, Cairy? Terry's a good playmate! Go on, Terry – you're not shy!

MARIE [*laughing*]: They're both a little tongue-tied! Don't you want to say anything, Terry?

JEAN: She's staring . . .

CAIRY [*turning round to the kitchen door*]: . . . Quiet . . . [*Looking round*]

JIM [*following her eyes*]: Eh?

CAIRY [*to herself*]: Isn't it? . . . [*As if listening*] You see you were right after all . . . I can see them . . .

JEAN [*tentatively*]: . . . There's no one out there now, they went – please don't go out there – we've got friends, Cairy.

CAIRY: . . . I said if they were quiet, I could hear them . . .

MARIE: What is it?

JIM: That blinking tree!

MARIE: Sssh! She's listening to something . . .

JIM: She'll listen to me in a minute!

CAIRY: Every time they talk, he says something, and I miss it. He wanted to say it then. Even if your skirt rustles, or – and it's lost.

MARIE: Let her take Terry outside then. They can't come to much harm, can they?

JEAN: If I could get some peace and quiet –

MARIE: Well then.

JEAN: Jim. Send them out.

JIM: She's spent the whole morning trying to get out there. I might as well.

BOB: Go on, Terry, then – with Cairy.

JIM [to Cairy]: And you – [Taking her hand]

MARIE: All right, Terry?

JIM [moving to door]: He's fine.

TERRY: Where to?

JIM: Blimey! That's the first word he's said to her! [Opening door]

BOB: Out in the garden. Cairy will look after you. Now you do whatever she says. And – well you've got to help her to get better; you know that?

TERRY: Yes.

BOB: You don't know, do you? Never mind.

JEAN: And don't move away from each other. You stay together.

JIM: How far do you think they're going – Brighton?

JEAN: I don't want those children from the flats – interfering –

JIM: They won't touch her. [Holding door wide]

TERRY [beside Cairy]: . . . What's out there? . . .

    [The stage blacks out.]

SCENE TWO

This time it is the evening of the same day, Sunday. Upstairs there are no lights except on Cairy's face and Terry's. They are in bed. Downstairs the hall and kitchen and to the left are shaded in half light.

    The two single lights pick up Cairy's face more strongly. Terry is turned the other way, you can see the back of his head. Downstairs the large clock's ticking is magnified. The rhythmic beating comes quite clear and loud all the time during this scene.

CAIRY: Terry . . . Terry . . . Terry . . . Now you remember the fair at Tooting? There was the Whip. And the cars swung round in a huge circle. It was loose, on one of its wheels. In that one next to us. Didn't he swing round – that fast, that much. Then snap and the

whole carriage shot right through the barrier. He, there was – how
many were in it? Two? An old man and a boy. He was about – he
was younger than me, Terry. Are you awake – ? He was the same
age as you. Did you hear? Terry . . . Like you. It was just as if you –
he shouted as loud as he could. And it hit the barrier. And – and
you were dead. One minute you are looking at – it comes charging
towards you, hits you, and you don't see any more. You haven't
got any eyes. Or heart. That clock downstairs – it's beating like a
heart. I can hear it quite plain. That's what tells our time – our
hearts – ticking away. [*Joking*] My heart's on my wrist! . . . You
were dead. The car had twisted over, and rammed your head against
the wall . . .

[TERRY *turns over and gapes at her dully.*]

The old man cried. I had never seen a man cry. It seems unnecessary
– because he's too old . . . His face was wet, he wanted to die instead
of you – they wouldn't let him. It wasn't his mistake – and – it
was – all – over. He shouted out, 'I can't live, and him die! I can't
live –' Why don't you ask him? . . . Ask him . . . [*No answer.*] Are
you frightened to? It's only old Mr Johnson! [*Giggling*] . . . He's
listening . . . [*Gets out of bed*] Look – come over here –

[TERRY *folds the blankets over his head in amazement.*]

It's all right. It's safe, Terry! Terry! I'll bring him to you – now
stay there – everything will be correct and in orderly fashion. [*She
moves along landing, with the light on her face.*] Now, now where are
we – ? . . . We are not alone . . . You know – there's Terry to think
about! . . . He is awfully talkative! . . . He might tell anybody – I
can't see in the dark. Don't move . . . and I'll touch you.

TERRY: You are sleepwalking, Cairy – there'll be trouble! You –
CAIRY: Ssssh, I've got him. He's terribly shy with new – you are his
friend? Yes? You are – aren't you? Here he – say – say you are his
friend . . . say . . . No. He won't! You remember the Whip at the
fair? When the car swung round and lost a wheel, the carriage shot
through the barrier at an old man and a boy – your age. The old
man started to run but it caught you and rammed your head against
the wall. You saw it. I needn't tell you! And that clanging the
ambulance made! You did see it. Yes. I was with you. And the

most beautiful moment. You said it. That it was the loveliest second in your life. We were up there, right on the top of the switchback! You couldn't be any higher. In the back of the car. As it dipped, and we stood up for a moment. There was everything beneath us. Nothing was missed out. The lights, and far out to the end of London. You could see it stop. There were cows, and streets, and tall buildings and things, then a park and gas-works. Quiet sort of colour, and the roads were less sharp. Didn't we stand up and shout out! What did you say after that? . . . You only learn to love something by seeing enough of it. We saw enough! We saw so much then, there were millions of people, you were in love with the whole world. Go on – listen Terry – I saw it then more than ever before. I'd never been up in a plane. When I looked at all that ground. People I had never spoken to, millions, they'd never heard of me. I couldn't shout loud enough, up there, to tell even one of them who I was. And that I loved them! I'm so small . . . If they could hear my name, once. I did once; I wrote to the personal column in an evening paper; I was willing to pay double – I told them. All I wanted was a simple line – like 'I'm Henry Johnson'. But they refused! They said it didn't mean anything! It wasn't a trick-advertisement, or a message home, it didn't do anybody any good. That was the worst thing to say. It would have helped me. Wouldn't it? . . . Does everything in this world have to be of use to somebody, can't the smallest thing just stand there, and people take notice of it, just because it is being there? Terry doesn't. [*To Terry*] Do you? You don't?

TERRY: You're crazy! It's – it's – I'll shout for somebody!

CAIRY: I do. Out of everybody. Even the tree. I know some people are like electric bulb-sockets. You fit them – and the lights go on.

TERRY: Aren't you cold? Go back in to bed.

CAIRY: No.

TERRY: Why?

CAIRY: Come on. [*She pulls the blankets partly off him.*]

TERRY: Don't do that; it's too late to mess about –

CAIRY [*softly but urgently*]: You must. Because he's going soon, he's going out.

TERRY [*scrambling out from under the coverlet; Cairy nearly pushes him out*]: Who is?

CAIRY: He is –

TERRY: I don't care –

CAIRY: You can stop him – you can try –

TERRY [*bewildered*]: Look at me – you can't look at me straight; your eyes are blank. Aren't you mad? You must be mad.

CAIRY: I've got no time –

TERRY [*making for the door*]: Nor have I –

CAIRY: You can't go without me –

TERRY: I can. Because I'm going; to tell them.

CAIRY: You mustn't go out! I didn't say –

TERRY: Please don't stop me. I'm going. [*He pushes her aside.*]

[TERRY *runs out of the door, but* CAIRY *slams herself down on his heels, grappling at his legs; she can't quite hold him. She screams at the top of her voice.*]

CAIRY: ... Oh no! Not to them – they wouldn't believe you. Nobody would. It's a complete pack of lies. He never even existed! ... But it doesn't matter, because I was there. Because, in the fair, when it happened, and the wall hit you – I screamed!

[TERRY *runs away from her, leaving her on the floor yelling.*]

... No one can scream louder! I screamed right out loud because I thought you were dead!

TERRY: I wasn't there – it was a mistake ... Hey! [*He hammers on Jim's door at the end of the landing.*]

JIM [*appearing*]: For Christ's sake, Terry! [CAIRY *lies still on the floor, breathing heavily.*] ... Ssssh, your Aunt's asleep.

CAIRY: Each time they say anything they are not the same person; whenever I look – the face isn't the same ... I'm dizzy with it.

JIM [*hissing*]: Will you shut up!

TERRY: What shall I do?

JIM: What has she been doing?

TERRY: What?

JIM: Look; you go in my room. You can sit on the bed for the moment. Cover yourself up. [*To Cairy*] Now you; I wish you could see yourself, right now – you wouldn't like what you saw.

JEAN [off]: Jim? . . . What is it?

JIM: I don't know; you stay there.

[CAIRY is coughing.]

JEAN: What are you doing? Is that Cairy?

JIM: Yes.

JEAN: Put a light on.

JIM: I will.

JEAN: Where is she?

JIM: She's here.

JEAN: I'm getting up.

JIM [beside Cairy]: You can stay there.

JEAN [on landing]: Put the light on – I can hardly see.

JIM [kneeling beside Cairy]: Come over here and look.

JEAN [to Terry]: Now stay there. [Over to Cairy] Is she out?

JIM: No. She's awake. Put your hand there, by her mouth.

JEAN: It's blood!

JIM: It's spit. She's salivering all over the place.

JEAN [away to left to switch light on]: Ugh! I don't want to be sick.
[Lights on] Is that better.

JIM: I'll take her back to her room.

JEAN: I'll call Brock.

JIM: You'll do no such thing! [Lifting Cairy]

JEAN: I won't have her left on her own. Jim!

JIM: I'll stay with her then. Now go back to bed. You can look after
Terry. He was shivering out there.

JEAN: Where are you going to sleep?

JIM: We'll be all right. Turn the light off. [He carries Cairy back to her
bed.] Go on. Hop it. And close your door. [He shuts his.]

JEAN [turns the light off. And stands by her door looking at Terry]: . . . We
shouldn't have brought you here, Terry, so soon, I'm sorry we did
that – [Her voice fades as she shuts her door.]

[The stage blacks out.]

CURTAIN

[Only when the curtain has fallen does the loud ticking of the clock stop.]

ACT TWO

SCENE ONE

The next morning.

[JEAN *shouts upstairs.*]

JEAN: Terry . . . Cooooeeee . . .?

TERRY [*poking his head out from the bathroom*]: . . . Yes?

JEAN: You're not still in bed – ?

TERRY: I'm up.

JEAN: Are you ready then? The food is down here ready –

TERRY: Mm.

JEAN: Two minutes then – and come down. [*She hums to herself.*]

TERRY [*whining from off in the bathroom*]: . . . Where are they – ?

JEAN: Yes?

TERRY: They're not here!

JEAN: What's missing?

TERRY: Auntie, have you got them?

JEAN: Oh yes! I keep everything in this house in my pocket!

TERRY [*standing on landing in a long white shirt, but no trousers*]: Where – where have they gone – ?

JEAN: Bring yourself down here and tell me.

TERRY [*off a moment, descending, on again*]: . . . Look at me!

JEAN: What's this!

TERRY: I've lost my trousers!

JEAN: That I can see! Well now – there are ladies in this house, you know! You can't toddle about like that.

TERRY: I came in a pair, didn't I?

JEAN: I hope you did!

TERRY: I think they are in – her room –

JEAN: I thought you changed in the bathroom last night?

TERRY: No.

JEAN: Go up and see if Cairy's got them. On your bed.

TERRY: No. I don't think – they . . .

JEAN: Now, you're not frightened?

TERRY: I can't go.

JEAN: I'll go with you.

TERRY: You go up.

JEAN: We'll both go together.

TERRY: Let's not go up there at all. She doesn't want us, does she?

JEAN: You'll catch cold otherwise. I suppose I must. There's no – really I asked you over, Terry, to stay with her; you're not filling that job very well, are you? . . . [*Going off*] You're fourteen now . . . isn't that – Oh, Terry – [*Off.*] How much pocket-money did Marie give you?

TERRY: I never had any – she never –

JEAN [*on landing*]: She? Who is She?

TERRY: Mother –

JEAN: So you want a bit of money too – I'll be broke by tonight.

TERRY [*playing about with the furniture; to himself*]: . . . She doesn't want anybody . . . and that – what does she imagine? . . . That tree – [*Balancing himself on the chair arm*] If I had that tree – I'd cut it down – You can't see the kids out there playing – it blocks up the view! . . . Auntie? . . .

JEAN [*in Cairy's room*]: . . . Cairy? Awake? You'd best get up. It's late enough. Cairy? I'll take that blanket off you today. You don't need it now. Isn't it stuffy in here! [*Opening window*] That's better. How's that?

TERRY: I'm standing here naked! Auntie – [*He is playing about with the breakfast food.*]

JEAN [*bustling*]: Yes. They're here, Terry.

TERRY: I'm waiting.

JEAN: Come up then.

TERRY: Bring them down.

JEAN: Oh, you children! Do parents ever stop doing things for you! Even after you are married and gone – you still come back. And ask for something! . . . Now, you be up. Cairy, there's some food left on the table – if you feel you want it. I suppose you're hungry too, are you, Terry? [*Off, descending. Then, on stage again, to Terry.*] Now jump in them.

[TERRY *sits and puts them on; upstairs* CAIRY *goes into the bathroom, carrying her morning clothes.*]

You look quite odd putting long trousers on – do all boys your age wear long pants? . . . Now what shall we do? [*Looking round*]

TERRY: Can I eat?

JEAN: You've been scratching about at the table already –

TERRY: I was hungry.

JEAN: You should ask if you want anything. Find a seat – then you can dive in. You want milk, don't you? Or, now you wear long trousers, is it coffee?

TERRY: Please –

JEAN [*with it*]: There is milk in it . . . [*Puts the cup in front of him.*] Oh my gosh! What a wonderful week-end! Everything that could happen, has happened! Do you agree? *You're* too young, aren't you? You don't understand what's been happening.

TERRY [*eating*]: Yes.

JEAN: Do you know whether there's anything worth living for – more than your own child? . . . When you're grown up I hope you don't have the same trouble – with yours!

TERRY: With what?

JEAN: Your children, dear! You're going to have plenty of them. I can see that – by the way you look.

TERRY: Yes.

JEAN: Are you brainy?

TERRY: No – well yes – and no.

JEAN: Make up your mind whether – what's it like to be fourteen or fifteen? I've completely forgotten. It was a long time ago. What is it like?

TERRY [*timidly*]: Oh, I'd like to be older.

JEAN: You would?

TERRY: As old as you.

JEAN: Thank you very much – am I a good age to be?

TERRY: How old are you?

JEAN: Ah now! That's an improper question. Don't ask me that. You are punching below the belt there.

TERRY: If I was your age I could go on my own – anywhere.

JEAN: Do you believe that I can? If I leave this house for half an hour – my daughter is – well – anything, in fact everything happens that shouldn't when I'm gone. But I know. It's all so safe and clean, at your age. Is that daft?

TERRY [*vaguely*]: Yes . . .

JEAN: Aren't you useless to talk to. You're merely discouraging. Well? Have you finished grubbing yourself? I can't see that there's much left on the table. Now suppose Cairy is hungry?

TERRY [*up*]: I don't mind what she does – but I'm not doing it with her.

JEAN: You know best. I won't force you to play with her. What will his lordship do? Have a rest?

TERRY [*lightly*]: I've just got up.

JEAN [*playing up*]: Oh yes, of course! Well, there's – or take a walk. You haven't seen the local surroundings for a long time. Scan your notes for the day!

TERRY: Can I go out?

JEAN: In the garden only. With respects to your royal person, you must be watched over. But only the garden. Until Cairy has come down. I hope she doesn't want to eat as well. The doctor gave her a bit of food,

[CAIRY *crosses back to her room, fully dressed.*]

when he was here. This morning. Oh blimey these meals are as irregular as a dog to a lamp-post! Aren't they? . . . Go outside for a while.

TERRY: Yes. But – will she be down, Auntie?

JEAN: That certainly won't bother you.

TERRY: Don't send her out.

JEAN: Nothing to worry about. Now off . . . [*She opens the back door for him. He exits.*] Cairy – do you want breakfast? . . . You've had something already . . . [*To herself*] I'm at sixes and sevens here – hardly anything to eat . . . [*Calling*] Cairy?

CAIRY [*calling out of her window, off*]: . . . What are you doing out there? Come away!

TERRY [*off, loud*]: No! I'm not touching . . .

CAIRY [*agitated*]: Yes! Yes! Yes!

TERRY [*more timid*]: Not because of you –

CAIRY: You're not to be . . . you're not allowed!

TERRY: Hen –

CAIRY: What?

TERRY: Hen. Hen. You are a hen!

CAIRY [*taking off her slipper and banging it violently against the window frame*]: No right! No right!

TERRY: Hen-Henney! Hen-Henney!

CAIRY: He said no one must go near it – without him! And you have! It will change colour. Or break. It can snap in two if you touch it. It can vanish, and they'll all go if it –

TERRY: If it what? Cairy?

CAIRY: When it does. It's so wrong. Because because nobody nobody said you – stop that! You are lousy! You – [*Her voice rises.*]

JEAN [*shouting*]: Cairy! You can stop that noise now! Making that row! Do you hear?

TERRY [*off*]: Henney . . . Henney. Henney . . . Henney. Henry Johnson! . . . Henney – Henry – Johnson! [*His voice fades. He is retreating up the garden.*]

CAIRY [*quieter, more pleading*]: . . . Oh please! [*As if it really hurt*] . . . Don't do that! It hurts – like – [*very softly*] a knife into –

TERRY [*still distantly*]: Henry Johnson . . . Henry Johnson . . .

JEAN [*hurrying off and up, then across landing to Cairy*]: . . . I'll have no more . . . and shut the window . . . [*Off.*] Get yourself dressed properly . . . there are flats opposite. What do you think they are saying? . . . [*On landing*] Cairy, this isn't right to anybody here. [*By her door*] Making up – that's all you are doing. You're playing a game. Now finish – please.

> [CAIRY *slowly shuts the window, and turns round; she chucks herself down disconsolately on the bed. And* JEAN *stands at the far end of her bed, speaking softly.*]

JEAN: . . . Darling, you are getting better, every hour. Don't slow things down. Until you practically go back to where you started. You are doing – I mean gradually, improving, the whole time. And with Terry – isn't it more right to play the same game as he does?

CAIRY [*burying her head in the pillow*]: Oh, I've heard it all before!

JEAN: Perhaps not enough.

CAIRY [*slowly*]: If I believe in what I think – I can do without you –

JEAN: But nothing you say is right. Now is it? Ask yourself.

CAIRY [*up from her bed*]: I'll go.

JEAN: Ask yourself, is it right? What do you do to me, and the others –

CAIRY: I'm quite as old as anyone else is.

JEAN: And – and we're all children – if that's the case I'm as old as you and vice-versa!

CAIRY [*nearly off*]: Am I talking too much? . . . Yes . . . Am I? Yes?

JEAN: I wish I could show you – it's quite an honour to become a woman when you grow up! But I haven't reached that stage yet. I'm still in the kindergarten. I'm not very good am I? I can't give you that – I'm not old enough! It is – it – what is it? You can tell me! It's terribly funny – I want to cry my eyes out, and nothing will come out. I must be dried up somewhere. You can, you're young. Why don't you cry for me, Cairy? This time it would be a good exchange. You must have all my tears by now. I'm much too old.

CAIRY: I know more than you, and he gave it to me, when it was lost, nobody can find it, you couldn't . . . that's for certain.

JEAN: Life begins at eighty!

TERRY [*off*]: Jean, Jean.

JEAN [*off*]: The name's Auntie!

TERRY [*opening the door, he stands there*]: . . . There's two men out there.

JEAN [*on stage*]: There are two men.

TERRY: Yes.

JEAN: Not there's! Who are they?

TERRY: Just two fellows. Spivs, I think.

JEAN: I know. They come from the flats.

TERRY: Are they spivs?

JEAN: Street touts.

TERRY: What?

JEAN: They're bookie's runners.

TERRY [*uninterested*]: Oh.

JEAN: They're friends of your uncle.

TERRY: He's got some funny friends, hasn't he?

JEAN: They're nice boys though – not as tough as I thought they'd be.

JERRY [*off*]: Hey! Missus!

JACK: Wanna buy a good horse! [*Both laugh.*]

JEAN: Perhaps you'd like to play with them.

TERRY: No thanks.

JEAN: I'll have to let them in.

JERRY [*opening kitchen door*]: Hallo there!

JEAN: Hallo – goodbye!

JACK [*both inside*]: Seriously though – how is she?

JEAN: All right.

JACK: Really, I mean?

JEAN: She's all right!

JACK: Is she?

TERRY: That's what the lady said.

JACK: Who are you?

JERRY: Joker, ain't you?

JEAN: This is my nephew Terry. This is Jack and – ?

JERRY: Jerry's the name – Jerry Maloney.

JEAN: Terry's come to lend a hand with Cairy.

JACK: Been old friends, like?

JEAN: That's right.

JERRY: Older friends than us?

JEAN: Just about.

JACK: See – we was going to offer some assistance like, this afternoon –

JEAN: That's very nice of you, but –

JACK: We thought you and Jim would need a hand-out like.

JEAN [*calling*]: Cairy! Come down will you?

JERRY: Ain't that right?

JACK: Yeah.

JEAN [*to them*]: Are you hungry?

JACK: We just ate.

[CAIRY *walks across above stage.*]

JEAN: Do you want to play with Terry then?

JACK: Nah . . . we're too old for games.

JERRY: We're not kids.

TERRY [*challenging*]: How old are you?

JERRY: How old are you?

TERRY: How old are you?

JACK: How old are you?

[CAIRY *on stage*]

JEAN: Cairy . . .

CAIRY: I only want a cup of coffee.

JEAN: Yes dear – it's over there.

TERRY: Good morning.

[CAIRY *ignores him.*]

JEAN: Say good –

CAIRY: No!

TERRY: Don't you know me?

CAIRY: No.

TERRY: You knew me all right last night.

CAIRY: No! No! No!

JEAN: Leave her be then – let her be.

JACK: What a carry on then! in't it?

JERRY: It's a chuckle.

JEAN: Shush – let her eat.

JACK: Are you going out?

JEAN: No. Why?

JACK: We could stay and look after things – if you was.

JERRY: We ain't back on the beat until the last race.

JEAN: And what time is that?

JERRY: 4.30. Newcastle.

JEAN: I wasn't going to go –

JERRY: Here's your chance.

TERRY [*slumping down, watching Cairy whispering provocatively*]: . . . I know who the Hen is . . . Henney . . .

[CAIRY *jumps nervously.*]

JEAN: Well, I can't ask you two to shop for me.

TERRY: Henney.

JEAN: Can't trust boys to fetch the right things.

CAIRY [*to Terry*]: When I speak to him about you, he'll do something dreadful to you!

TERRY: He's a hen, a rotten mangy hen.

JEAN: Stop that! I heard what you said – clever dick. You can stop that or you'll be outside the door.

JERRY: We do want to stay. When we met Jim on the corner he said it was O.K.

JEAN: Could you handle these two?

JERRY: Jim said we might change old Cairy round to the good. Seeing as how we're a bit different like from her usual friend.

JEAN: Friends, not friend.

JERRY: That's what I meant.

JEAN: All right – I'll go and do my errands. I won't be long.

JERRY: That's right – go on then.

[JEAN *picks up her bag and coat.*]

JEAN: Put that boy in the garden if he's any trouble.

JERRY: Yes.

JEAN: Ta ta, Cairy.

[TERRY *clucks like a hen.*]

TERRY: Curout cut cut! Curout cut cut!

[CAIRY *jumps up and throws a plate at him. He runs playfully out of the kitchen door.*]

CAIRY: Now will you stop that! Oh! he does that – don't you listen to him! What time does the bus come? Just in time for him to hurt you – why won't you leave him alone? – because he is jealous of our companionship . . .

JEAN: Cairy . . . please try not to do that, please – Terry may be playing you up, but please don't scream like that.

CAIRY: He's not hurting me – he's doing it on purpose to him –

JACK: Who is he?

JEAN [*to Cairy*]: You mean Johnson?

CAIRY: I mean what I say. No, don't touch me – I mean what I say.

JEAN: You must let Terry play with you, darling.

JACK: Run along then, lovie . . .

JEAN: Open the door for her . . .

JACK [does so]: There you are.

CAIRY [hesitating, crosses to the door, and looks out]: Why doesn't he come back? and the flower tree would be different. It's begun to wilt . . . as if it is going away too . . . usually it brightens the whole garden this time of year. He takes his time as if it doesn't matter to him.

JEAN: You see – you terrify Terry, that's why he acts up.

CAIRY [TERRY whistles off key]: I'll play a game with him. Shall I play that if I come out and wish something touching the tree – and he has to guess what I'm wishing – but he doesn't know, I'm wishing him dead all the time.

TERRY [off; stops whistling]: Hey Cairy – don't just stand there – I'm pulling at the branches – see!

CAIRY: I'm coming. [She exits.]

JEAN: I'm in a terrible dither. [She changes into a pair of high heels.] . . . I wish I could mark everything fragile; that's how I feel, tucked in here. Listening to her; I feel like a bull in a china-shop . . . these shoes of mine are tight somewhere – I'll leave the rest of the dishes. I want to get some money. [She opens a side drawer and takes out her purse.] . . . Bag? gloves? and handkerchief? . . . Now I won't say anything else: only keep them out of trouble. I suppose you know what you are doing?

[She exits.]

JACK [looking around]: . . . ain't it silent?

JERRY: Ain't it.

JACK: Yeah.

JERRY: I'm bloody hungry.

JACK: Open up shop then.

JERRY: Shall I? [Opens a cupboard.] . . . cheese, mouldy cheese!

JACK: Cook yourself something if it's that bad then.

JERRY: Here – you wouldn't believe it wouldja –?

JACK: What?

JERRY: Cairy and that . . .

JACK: Queer, in't it?

JERRY: I spoke to that fellow once – Johnson. Right customer! I said 'Here, you lives around these parts, don't you?' He says 'Do I?' – like that! Some nut he was. He says 'Do I?' to me, he does on my life!

JACK: Weird.

JERRY: And I said 'Do you like a bit of a gamble?' and he looks up at the sky goofy as golf balls – then he looks at me –

JACK: Stuff it will you!

JERRY: What?

JACK: Pack it in.

JERRY: What for?

JACK: You get me down you do – always reminiscing and that –

JERRY: Me?

JACK: Can't you take it serious?

JERRY: For Christ's sake!

JACK: Don't it ever strike you something serious has happened?

JERRY: Aw – don't be so stupid.

JACK: Aw – don't be so stupid.

JERRY: Don't be then.

JACK: Drop!

[*Suddenly* CAIRY *scrambles through the door from the garden – breathless. She pulls Terry after her. They are chuckling together.*]

CAIRY: I've got a dog at my heels! . . . I've got a dog at my heels!

[CAIRY *drags him too quickly. She seems to panic at Terry's laughter.*]

TERRY: Hey!

CAIRY: Leave go! will you? [*She pulls too hard, releases herself, but Terry slips and falls.*]

TERRY [*scrambling up*]: . . . You're mad! she's mad!

CAIRY: As much as you are.

TERRY: Oh, but you see things – that aren't.

CAIRY [*heatedly*]: And you're stupider; you see things that are!

TERRY: Perhaps if you knew more about the truth – you might understand.

CAIRY [*to herself*]: You'd say to him something sharp – and he'd regret it. Tell him you know more about the truth than he does.

TERRY: You need watching you do – you're a proper case!

JACK: Shut up, will you! We're in charge – no mucking about like.

JERRY: We're in charge! Who are you?

CAIRY: Who am I? I'm Henry Johnson.

TERRY: Nuts.

CAIRY: You play a game like that – that's right, aren't you hiding from me? No, you are forever hiding from people.

JACK: You see – she's talking to him. Ain't she?

TERRY: Nuts.

JACK: See – she is.

CAIRY: Listen! that tune – he wanted that played at the Reunion Dance. You remember that they hadn't got the music sheets to it. The man tried to play it on the piano ... The strangest moment when you're so close to somebody. Your breath mixes, you've eaten fruit – smells sweet.

JERRY: In't she queer, in't she, eh?

TERRY: Ssh. She's mad.

JACK: You see – he's in here. He's in the room.

JERRY: Get out of it!

CAIRY: Now I remember what you were talking about. You said you are the thief. Now why do I say that? Oh, I don't know, that's what you said. I say a word you said and my face answers back. That's when I steal. You said, I'm stealing your eyes from other people. When I look at you they belong to you. Please don't ever stop giving me something. I want to be a great thief of you ... Why? Where did you come from? Lancashire. From a village? Yes? But you never talk of parents: I hated them. They embarrassed me. They were so stupid, they died before they knew they were dead. And you never ever married? No. But you won't talk about it? No. Have you ever loved somebody? Oh, I had an aunt who had a pony and trap who hid me under her shawl when she caught me out walking in the rain. That was years ago. Yes. [*She carries the chair to the front stage, and sets it down ceremoniously in front of her and she addresses it.*] ... I mean really love? Yes, I love someone. Now? Yes. Who? That's my secret. Oh, I'm sorry. Won't you tell me? No.

TERRY [*bored*]: What a lot of stuff, Hen .... Hen – Don't you talk like a hen? [*He squats on the floor studying her closely.*]

JERRY: What is she doing?

JACK: Like I said – she's bringing all them things back . . .

JERRY: Like hell.

JACK: She's talking to him, see –

JERRY: I reckon winning at Doncaster on Saturday went to your head.

JACK: Get out of it.

JERRY: How much did you make for my old man – and how much did you keep for yourself?

JACK: Good night.

TERRY: Do you back horses?

JACK: Do we? Do we!

JERRY: They're our bread and butter, kid . . .

TERRY: I'm not 'kid'.

JACK: What are you then?

TERRY: I'm about a year younger than you . . .

JACK: So?

TERRY: So.

JACK: So?

TERRY: You're all right, you've only got to stay here a couple of minutes, I'm booked in for the week. Some school holiday this is . . .

CAIRY [*moving away from them*]: Now – the big experiment; can you do it? Everything or nothing this time . . . Are the doors shut? And the windows? Oh, no . . . I left the window, oh, golly . . .

JERRY: Come on ducks – here what about us, eh?

CAIRY: There . . . everything is shut tight. Yes – what is still happenin? I don't know . . . Yes I do. We are moving, aren't we? So stop us. Now – you are moving! Be still –

JACK [*to Jerry*]: Stand up straight then – do as she says.

JERRY: What?

CAIRY: Don't breathe . . . hold your breath . . . And you too? Yes. It's hard. Stand still!

JERRY [*doing so*]: If the lads could see me now!

JACK: Be humorous like – join in her game.

[CAIRY *holds her breath. She lets herself fall down slowly. She lies down – then jumps up giggling.*]

CAIRY: I'm going giddy ... I'm going ... I'm gone ... I've stopped everything. I've stopped the sun. I've stopped myself. What do you think about that? Oh – so so. Nothing more? Well – so so so. Huh! You don't know how to enjoy yourself.

JERRY: Oh – is it over now?

JACK: You're a bit dim, aren't you?

TERRY [*to Cairy*]: Why can't you act normally [*gripping her arm, swinging her round*] – do the things everybody else does? Stupid I call it.

CAIRY [*away*]: ... But I forgot my own heart; I didn't stop that, did I? Oh, you silly little girl – how do you make me laugh so much? Me? Kind sir? You ... you ...

JACK: I couldn't act like that – I couldn't do all that; shows what a state he must have left her in.

JERRY: Shows – hell! You soppy old thing. What a custard pie you are and no mistake.

JACK: Bloody higorant type you are – I'm helping her.

TERRY [*chasing after her*]: Hey – do something else instead! Perform, be different!

CAIRY: ... What is it you most wish? I've thought of that. I suppose you want me to say – be terribly generous or good-natured. Not at all. But to break something – oh, yes. That's what I'd do. That's more my style. I could walk into the highest domed cathedral, and inside it would be cool, and the silence could be a fragile glass ball. I'd kick it, my feet would shatter it, and the cool stone would burn up before my eyes.

TERRY: Don't you ever put the radio on in this house? Why can't she go for a long walk – and forget all about it?

CAIRY: ... Could I put my hands on the jewelled cloth and drag it down, candlesticks, alterpieces, and saucers crashing about – the noise? I'd walk back – leaving it behind me ... or I'd stand up on top of it, and looking at the grey slab of stone beneath me – now look about, the lectern is broken, and let me shout at the top of my voice above them all. Gallery seats and pews and tall windows – the echo hums away. Tremendously far, like an audience of leaves, swinging like tiny cradles, whispering down, green fingers prattling and tinkling behind choir boxes. It would be a music of silences . . .

TERRY [*from the kitchen, clashing pan tops together*]: . . . Music! Music! Music! . . . Crazy old Cairy!

JACK: Shut up!

TERRY: Oh hell!

JACK: You're hurting her . . .

TERRY: Oh hell!

CAIRY: He says shut up, shut up, shut up! He says shut up!

JACK: Go on, Terry – go and play in the garden.

TERRY: Why should I play?

JACK: Go on.

TERRY: Who are you, anyway?

JACK [*chasing him half-heartedly*]: I'll give you what for in a second! . . .

[TERRY *runs out slamming the door behind him.*]

JERRY: . . . Nervous, aren't you?

JACK: What time is it?

JERRY: Races don't start until three.

JACK: I don't know what to do now.

JERRY: Play with her – Genius!

JACK [*to Cairy*]: Come and sit down over here. Cairy – you've about said your lot.

[CAIRY *sits beside him.*]

JERRY: That's right, you sit beside this dirty old man here!

JACK: Got any more of them funny games of yours? Course not – they're all going now, aren't they?

JERRY: Isn't it agony!

JACK: Try for yourself then, if you can do better.

JERRY: Not me matey – I'll, eh – make some tea . . .

JACK: No, no, think of something – think of anything.

JERRY: You're the psychiatrist, cock.

JACK: But what for example?

JERRY: Pretend you're this fellow then – that's what the quack was doing.

JACK: Will you talk to me then, love? Perhaps it ain't so easy like to have it out with your old man, he's a bit rough like, isn't he? Tell old Jack here what else there is to tell?

[CAIRY *remains silent.*]

... now imagine I was Henry Johnson, see, now what would you say?

[*No reply.*]

... Would I say, why haven't you been out with me lately? Would I?

[*No reply.*]

JERRY: Don't ask her, just say it.

JACK: Why haven't you been out with me, playing our old games and that, Cairy?

CAIRY: Is it a game then ...

JACK: Games can be serious.

JERRY: You see – what did I say!

JACK: I'm on your side Cairy – I'm not laughing.

JERRY: See – what did I tell you?

CAIRY: I suppose you really do these things for my sake. You don't? Oh, I think you do. You don't take me very seriously.

JACK: Course I take you seriously – see, course I do. Hey! Wakey! wakey!

CAIRY [*suddenly understanding*]: You do?

JACK: Yes.

CAIRY: Really?

JACK: That's right, see – I'm your mate.

CAIRY: But you must admit you're a bit too old to play games?

JACK: Oh I don't know – you're never too old and something something.

CAIRY: I'm exactly a third your age. You've had three times my life – are there three of me inside you?

[JACK *looks blank.*]

JERRY: Answer her then ...

JACK: Look – let's change the subject; what did we do on Saturday? Did we do something special like?

CAIRY: You were going to take me in the evening to see – oh, I forget if you did or not. And you said in the afternoon – but I don't quite remember . . .

JACK: Think hard then.

CAIRY: Why didn't we go then? Isn't it so? You often make promises but when the time comes –

JACK: Well, I suppose I did promise you, but something came up sudden see, I must have changed my mind.

CAIRY: Yes?

[JEAN *opens the back door and listens.*]

JACK: But you were getting dressed, weren't you? And your Mother was out, wasn't she?

CAIRY [*vaguely*]: What time was that?

JACK: About half past three.

CAIRY: It all goes black somehow –

JACK: But try . . .

CAIRY: I can't, I really can't . . .

JACK: Did we talk?

CAIRY: You are always getting up to things. It doesn't really matter what – as long as it is you. You must always be ten feet tall imagining yourself doing this or doing that. You're rather frightened of everybody, aren't you? Admit it to me?

JACK [*lost*]: What?

CAIRY: That you aren't quite as big as you think sometimes?

JACK: Oh, I don't know . . .

JERRY: Big head!

CAIRY [*fervently*]: Are you? Tell me – are you? Tell me – are you? What? What? What?

[*While* JACK *looks surprised and bewildered the boiling kettle Jerry put on begins to whistle.*]

JACK [*to Jerry*]: Turn it up!

[JEAN *enters from the back door with* TERRY.]

JEAN: I found him in the garden. Is anything wrong?

JERRY [*pointing to Cairy*]: Sssh . . .

TERRY [*mimicking*]: Sssh!

JEAN: I'm back, has anybody noticed! Oh I'm sorry – I didn't quite remember my place properly – [*sarcastic*] Cairy is it?

[*She takes off her coat and hangs it up. She is very worried and tense.*]

JERRY: Old Jack here has been doing wonders with her . . .

JEAN: But what were you doing out there on the lawn, Terry?

JACK: I put him out there, see – I thought –

JEAN: But he's meant to be in here helping her, isn't he?

JACK: I thought –

JEAN: Please don't!

[*Embarrassed silence.*]

JERRY: What is it?

JEAN: . . . I'm sorry – I'm a bag of nerves, I'm sorry.

JACK: That's all right.

JEAN: How is she?

JACK [*putting his arm round Cairy's shoulders*]: She's fine.

JEAN: How can she be? Fine?

JACK: I've been talking to her . . .

JEAN: You know the people in the shops look at me – they look at me . . .

JERRY: Doesn't she look all right?

JEAN: How should I know!

JACK: Ask her then . . .

JEAN: Why? Why? I'm terrified of her!

JACK: Try.

JEAN: I get nothing from her. I've already tried. I heard what she was saying to you. I get no more than that out of her.

JACK: This was all about Saturday?

JEAN: I was getting ready to go out. She knows – oh, she knows. She's like a tape-recorder bringing it all back.

JERRY: Tell the quack then . . .

JEAN: He knows.

JERRY: He doesn't know it's Saturday and Friday she's talking about.

JEAN [*exhausted voice*]: He knows.

JACK: Well, we ain't done badly, have we? Eh?

JEAN: You've done very well.

JERRY: See – my idea.

JACK: Who asked you!

JERRY: It *was* my idea.

JEAN: . . . Cairy? . . .

[CAIRY *wanders off slowly. She reappears on the upper landing.*]

JACK: She's all right.

JEAN: What do you mean 'she's all right'! She's not all right.

JACK: She's all right.

JEAN: She's not! She's my daughter, and she's not all right.

JACK: Just as you say, just as you say.

JEAN: I know my daughter. I know what those faces out in the street mean when they study me. They watch my face and I know my daughter isn't all right. Don't worry about them – but I know.

JACK: . . . I wonder why she's gone upstairs?

JERRY: Would you like some tea? I've boiled the kettle.

JEAN: No – yes.

JERRY: Do you like it weak or strong?

JEAN: Anything, anything.

JACK: I wonder why – eh?

JEAN: What? Oh – do you mind if she goes upstairs for one minute?

JACK: No, I don't mind –

JEAN: Then that's fine, isn't it?

JACK: Yes, yes, I suppose it is.

JEAN: Good.

[*They stand staring at each other limply.*]

JERRY: Sugar?

JEAN: Yes, please.

JERRY: And milk?

JEAN: Oh God!

JACK: Pack it in, will you – can't you see she's not well!

JERRY: Have I said something wrong?

JACK: Here, Terry – why don't you pop upstairs and offer Cairy a drop of tea – see if she's all right.

TERRY: She is all right . . .

JACK: How do you know?

TERRY: I know.

JACK: Go on, be a pal.

TERRY: Knock it off will you, I'm not your servant, am I?

JEAN [*exhausted*]: He doesn't need to go.

JACK [*to Terry*]: I thought you were her friend . . .

TERRY: I play with her – sometimes.

JACK: Do her a favour then?

TERRY: I don't want to. She's dead odd . . .

JEAN [*to Terry*]: Darling, you're upset too . . . because of last night. But you mustn't be afraid of her.

TERRY: I can't help myself.

JERRY: Is he kidding!

JEAN: What did you all do, Terry – while I was out?

TERRY: We mucked about . . .

JEAN: Is that all?

TERRY: Oh, I don't know – ask them.

JEAN: Look, I'll ring up your Mother tonight, and ask for her to take you back. I think that will be better for all of us. You don't want to hear any more of this shouting and things . . .

[CAIRY *is walking about on the landing above.*]

JACK: Sssh – do you hear?

JERRY: What?

CAIRY: . . . And who did you say? Crikey, and Mrs . . .

JACK: She's off again.

JEAN: Is she? Do you hear that, Terry? Can you hear your cousin? Cairy's talking to herself, what do you make of that now?

JERRY: Don't it all seem weird, don't it?

CAIRY [*moving about*]: . . . I've never seen you angry. Do you ever lose your temper? There's nothing to lose it on. Children must make you mad at times. Nothing does. They don't really enter into my world. I do though . . . Yes. Every time? Wherever I go, whatever I look at. I always include you. Cairy . . . Cairy . . . Cairy . . . Children never bothered to talk to me when I was a child – called me the odd one out.

JEAN: Did you hear that?

JACK: Yes.

JEAN: Did you hear that? That was on Saturday – after lunch. The exact words. I was just going out and I heard her say 'I've never seen you angry. Do you ever lose your temper?'

CAIRY: . . . We do that. I know. But it's too much like starting a treasure hunt. But I've been given a lead. I'll catch you up then.

JEAN: Isn't that queer . . .

CAIRY: . . . I could miss all this house. But not you. I want you near by, you can make me look for things. To see them in an entirely different light. Then again, say I went away from you, what would you do? I'd become my own age again. But you're always you're own age. No – not when I'm with you. With you, when your Mother goes out and leaves us alone, I'm as old as you are.

[*They wait downstairs for more, but Cairy is silent.*]

JACK: She's not saying any more.

JEAN: No?

JACK: She's stopped.

JEAN: Oh . . .

JACK: Here – has Jim heard any more about catching the fellow?

JEAN: I don't think so.

JERRY: He told my old man this morning that there was a big search on.

JEAN: All I know is they'll phone when they've got him.

JACK: There's not much else we can do now, is there?

JERRY: No, that's right.

JACK: Don't you think we ought to toddle along?

JERRY: I got these slips to place for the 4.30 –

JEAN: Never mind your slips, they can wait. You've been very kind staying with me.

JACK: It was nothing.

JEAN: I mean you're not the sort of fellows one thinks one ought to rely on. You're a couple of spivs really – aren't you?

JACK: Oh, I wouldn't say that.

TERRY: I would!

JEAN: You're not exactly a pair of church wardens are you?

JERRY: No . . . no . . . I'd admit you're right there.

JACK: I don't look like a spiv, do I?

JERRY: Course you look like a spiv, in fact you look right common, if you got down to thinking about it.

JACK: And what about you?

JERRY: But I admit it, see – quite right, I'm a bit of a spiv. If you look at it that way – like.

JEAN: What I mean is – you look like the types who throw bottles through windows and fetch out razors ...

JACK: Really? I really look like that?

JEAN: You've got narrow trousers and long hair – what else is any self-respecting person expected to think?

JACK: Proper carry on, isn't it?

JEAN: But don't go –

JACK: Eh?

JEAN: But please don't think I want you to go. I need you.

JACK: Well, it don't exactly sound like it, does it ...

JEAN: Go over there, anywhere ... I want to talk about Henry Johnson. I want to describe him. He wasn't very tall. But big and heavy. He used to creep around on brown boots all day. Dirty old brown boots. Never cleaned them. Or pressed his trousers. And the same old tie each day. He had sandy, thinning hair. The type that goes bald quickly. He was ugly and he had a lisp.

JERRY: He sounds like Heaven, doesn't he!

JEAN: He never spoke about women. But he never spoke about his job either, the boys at school. He could only mention Cairy. I don't think he knew anybody else's Christian name but hers. Then if I asked him how many people he knew before he came here, he wouldn't answer me. He'd say he never knew people long enough to become friends. So much mathematics and stuff, you could never really talk to him. He'd calculate his answers. Every time, weigh them up to see if they balanced. And try to talk to him! He acted timid. He told me once, people are like houses. As they grow older they shut some windows, those that they particularly dislike. But the others they leave open, and if they are not wide enough, they break down the bricks around them so as they can have more light just there. But he said children were merely exploring the houses, trying to find out what all the windows looked upon. What I think is – he did everything purposefully. From the moment he set eyes upon her, he worked it out carefully. Games and telling stories. They had little secrets. He must have watched her like an eagle above a sheep; I'd swear even before Saturday morning, he had all his clothes packed. He knew we'd all be out at some time or another, like any Saturday. I suppose he had his ticket and money ready. Reserved. I must have been the fly in the ointment. And the old tricks came out. The stories and paraphernalia. He told me he was restless. That he had to keep on the move. Terry, you're not like that, are you? You don't hold a secret inside you until it's ready to burst out ... children get like that. I suppose he was a child. You won't forget Cairy and Mr Johnson, I can see that. What do you think of them, Terry? They've done something bad, haven't they? What do you think?

TERRY: ... I don't know.

JEAN: Oh, but everybody's told you – but really you are too young – everyone's told you to steer clear of that sort of person?

TERRY [*wildly*]: I said I don't know!

JEAN: But they do tell you, don't they?

TERRY: Yes – anything! Yes!

JEAN: You see, I'm right!

TERRY: Can't I go now – ?

JERRY: Jean, let me talk –

JEAN: I'm talking –

JERRY: You're making a big mistake. These aren't children any more. Cairy is thirteen. You treat her as if she were ten! And Terry – how old is he? Fourteen or so – and you make him out to be half that age! Let them grow up.

JEAN: My house is all tumbling down. Oh God, when you've got four walls surrounding you – you wish to high Heaven, you only wish to Heaven you – that there could be five, to turn round to – and see something new and clean, that wasn't there before. Why can't I hear more and see more than there is now in front of me?

[*They all pause.* JIM *off whistling loudly.*]

JIM [*entering*]: ... Whatcha, girl! Ay! Who do you think I am? The postman?

JEAN: Where did you spring from?

JIM: Don't you want to hear some news?

JEAN: Yes. Of course.

JERRY: About who?

JIM: Aha!

JEAN: Cairy? Is it?

JIM: Not telling.

JEAN: Yes you are. What is it?

JACK: Somebody has found him?

JIM: Where is that girl? Shouldn't she be down here? Hi, tosher! You haven't seen your cousin, have you?

TERRY [*pulling away*]: . . . Tish!

JIM [*calling*]: Cairy! . . .

JEAN: She's upstairs. If you want her. I want to know –

JIM: Yes. Well. It's not very much – they've – ah – seen him.

JACK: Johnson?

JERRY: Wonderful!

JIM: It's not important.

JERRY: I should say it is!

JIM: The night watchman spotted him at the Edward the Seventh Dock. London dry docks. The alarm went off – but there was no one on duty round there – and we weren't told until mid-day.

JERRY: He could be anywhere now.

JIM: No matter, we know he's in London – or thereabouts. Does that make you feel better about it?

JEAN: I'm not worrying in the least. Am I?

JIM: Well, you look edgy –

JEAN: I won't be satisfied though – until he's under locks and bolts.

JIM: They are going to ring me tonight. If they hear anything more. Or that they've got him. But it doesn't matter, believe me – if he has to crawl around in a London dock – last night – he can't have much money.

JACK: Well, I suppose we must go.

JIM: Yes. Well. Thank you very much! Everybody's grateful.

JERRY [*still standing*]: O.K.

JACK: Bye-bye, Terry – Jean. Give our love to Cairy, won't you?

JIM: I wouldn't entertain it!

JERRY: Bye! [*Goes off.*]

JACK: Bye! [*Goes off.*]

JIM: . . . That's that.

JEAN: That's a relief!

JIM: It's strange to find ourselves on our own – nowadays.

JEAN: At least I know nobody dreams nightmares like this –

JIM: Don't worry. There'll be more tonight. If that phone call doesn't come through.

JEAN: Why don't you sit down –

JIM: I ran into young Brock, over here. I told him a few things! . . . He says not to worry. But he might be in here tonight, sometime. She might be violent again – so he's coming over.

JEAN: God! I've been sweating – as if it's a hot summer's day. I'm wet right through me. He said not to worry?

JIM: He did –

JEAN: He should try taking my place then. He'd soon change his mind.

JIM: I'm not worrying about anything.

JEAN: I know that.

JIM: Yes – well?

JEAN: I say everybody should at this time!

JIM: This would be a fine old world then. Everybody shouting at everyone else! Eh?

JEAN: Don't argue with me, Jim. You're right every time. I don't know why you bother to. I don't know a thing, do I?

JIM: You'll do.

JEAN: Oh yes.

JIM: I could cry for you.

JEAN: And tonight and after tonight, and then later on – isn't it our tragedy? Isn't it?

[*No answer.*]

. . . Isn't it? . . . Jim? . . . Jim?

[*The stage blacks out completely.*]

The evening of the same day.

JEAN: There was a young boy walking in the middle of the road today. He was absolutely cocksure of himself. And all the cars were streaming past him. He had on those sandals with no backs in them. He stubbed his toe somehow – and the sandal came off his foot. He stopped and turned round to pick it up. Then he saw the cars behind him – like that, without his shoe on, on one foot. His whole face changed. He was terrified. Just at that moment when he realized he shouldn't be there. And what might really happen to him. . . . Where all the cars . . . that's what I mean – it's terribly bad when people don't see what's happening to them – until it hits them and it's too late. . . . What's the time?

JIM [*reading*]: There's a clock up there.

JEAN: It's slow.

JIM: Blimey! You only put it right a minute ago!

JEAN: You don't have to snap!

JIM: I was not.

JEAN: Well then . . .

JIM: Let's not both upset each other again – tonight. Eh?

JEAN: I'm not going out of my way to try exactly. Am I? You do act as if you're quite useless at times – and I get agitated.

JIM: I get the blame every time, don't I?

JEAN: . . . They won't ring later than twelve, will they?

JIM: What?

JEAN: I said they won't ring later –

JIM: I'll be in bed by then.

JEAN: I'm staying up. In case –

JIM: You can –

JEAN: I might as well. Because that phone won't wake you – upstairs – will it?

JIM: I can hear it all right.

JEAN: It might be urgent –

JIM: Someone might blow up Scotland Yard! What does it matter?

JEAN: Now that's what I mean! This don't-care attitude of everybody!

JIM: Never mind. Forget I said it.

JEAN: ... There's nothing much to do in the evenings, is there? ... Now if we had a television set – it would be different ... isn't it boring? ... I don't believe the town is made for anything else but to work in ...

JIM: Ssshhh –

JEAN: Why should I?

JIM: I'm concentrating –

JEAN: I'm going outside. The atmosphere seems sticky in here ... it looks clean and fresh out there ... [*Opening door, and standing staring out*] Jim? Come out and look at the tree ... The lights from those flats is all caught in the branches. It's quite pretty. It does look different at night time ... Jim? ...

JIM: No, I'll stay in –

JEAN [*off*]: There's a cat out here – Jim?

JIM [*more to himself*]: You're as restless as I don't know what.

JEAN: ... I can't imagine ... it must be a stray ... nobody's got a cat anywhere near us ... Jim? ...

JIM [*over to door*]: ... Don't bother. I won't come out –

JEAN [*farther away now*]: It's cool out here.

JIM: Yes ... I know.

   [CAIRY *has got up out of bed, hearing Jean outside, and she is watching her out of the window.*]

CAIRY: ... That's not for you to touch ... leave it ...

JEAN: Cairy – go back to bed.

CAIRY: I said that's not for you to ... you didn't hear me –

JEAN: Keep quiet! Terry's asleep!

JIM: That reminds me – wasn't he going home tonight?

CAIRY [*soft*]: I don't care ...

JEAN: Does it bother you, Cairy? I'll go in ...

CAIRY [*runs back to her bed, and sits on it. She is taut again*]: You were shaking the tree ... because of a cat! ...

JEAN [*calling softly*]: ... Cairy? ... Go to sleep. You'll wake Terry up! ...

JIM: I'll go up to look at her.

CAIRY: ... Can you hear her? ... No. I think she's gone. She does that at times – uses the back way. You were saying about a game. Has she gone? And I said yes. Well, let's start. What? The game then. You tell me? ... It's got a long – story ... Yes? When you are asked to remember someone's face, what do you do? I think. Yes? Right down deep inside. That's if it is difficult to – somebody's inside. That's if it is difficult to – somebody's face, or go right back as far as you can remember. That sort. I can think like that – it gets ...

[JIM *on stage above watches Cairy by her door.*]

Don't look at me like that, I'm not an ogre, am I? You don't want to put them there, put your hands there – like that. [*She topples slowly to her knees as if pushed there. She holds her hands up limply.*] ... No, this is wrong. It's perfectly correct. It's what everybody has to face at one time or another – and this is our moment. It never was this way. Oh yes. But like this? Oh yes. But never with as much care and attention, never with so much love you see – please, please, please. Not throwing it away, I want to try to understand so much more. But please ... please ... please ... Don't. Don't hurt. But please ... [*Her knees give way and she lies gently on the ground. Downstairs the telephone has started to ring.* CAIRY *sits up silently. After a pause,* JEAN *swiftly runs down to the phone.*]

JEAN: Jim? Jim! Do you hear it?

JIM: What do you think?

JEAN [*dazed*]: I'll answer it ...

CAIRY [*looking up at Jim*]: Hallo ... Hallo, stranger. [*Smiling at him*]

JEAN [*lifting the receiver*]: Hallo. Yes, that's right.

JIM: Now you stay quiet. Don't say another word. It's all over now. Don't say another word.

JEAN: Yes ... yes. This is she speaking.

CURTAIN

MORE ABOUT PENGUINS
AND PELICANS

Penguinews, which appears every month, contains details of all the new books issued by Penguins as they are published. From time to time it is supplemented by *Penguins in Print*, which is our complete list of almost 5,000 titles.

A specimen copy of *Penguinews* will be sent to you free on request. Please write to Dept EP, Penguin Books Ltd, Harmondsworth, Middlesex, for your copy.

In the U.S.A.: For a complete list of books available from Penguins in the United States, write to Dept CS, Penguin Books, 625 Madison Avenue, New York, New York 10022.

In Canada: For a complete list of books available from Penguins in Canada write to Penguin Books Canada Ltd 2801 John Street, Markham, Ontario L3R 1B4.